FIRES OF HATRED

FIRES OF HATRED

ETHNIC CLEANSING
IN TWENTIETH-CENTURY EUROPE

NORMAN M. NAIMARK

HARVARD UNIVERSITY PRESS

Cambridge, Massachusetts

London, England

First Harvard University Press paperback edition, 2002

Designed by Gwen Nefsky Frankfeldt

Library of Congress Cataloging-in-Publication Data

Naimark, Norman M.
Fires of hatred : ethnic cleansing in twentieth-century Europe / Norman M. Naimark.
p.   cm.
Includes bibliographical references and index.
Contents: The Armenians and Greeks of Anatolia—
The Nazi attacks on the Jews—
Soviet deportation of the Chechens-Ingush and the Crimean Tatars—
The expulsion of Germans from Poland and Czechoslovakia—
The wars of Yugoslav succession.
ISBN 0-674-00313-6 (cloth)
ISBN 0-674-00994-0 (pbk.)
1. Europe—Ethnic relations.   2. Racism—Europe—History—20th century.
3. Population transfers.   4. Political atrocities—Europe.   I. Title.
GN575 N15 2001
305.8′0094–dc21
00–057500

To Anna and Sarah

Contents

See how efficient it still is

how it keeps itself in shape—

our century's hatred.

From "Hatred" by Wislawa Szymborska

Introduction

The history of Europe in the twentieth century ended badly. In the southeastern quadrant of the continent, former Yugoslavia has been overwhelmed by war, ethnic cleansing, and civil strife. The worst fighting in Europe since World War II has displaced millions of people and produced hundreds of thousands of casualties. Where Serbs, Croats, Bosnians, and Kosovar Albanians lived in relative peace and prosperity, there is now hatred, devastation, and fearsome poverty. The tenuous multinational culture of Yugoslavia has been obliterated. Anger and resentment divide ethnic communities and imperil attempts by NATO and the European Union to rebuild multinational institutions and societies. Civil and ethnic strife threaten Montenegro, Macedonia, and Albania. As a result, the stability of the European continent remains a source of great concern to the world community.

In Eastern Europe as a whole, the great hopes of 1989 have not materialized, in part because the optimism was unwarranted in the first place and in part because the transition from communism to democracy and from centrally run economies to market-style capitalism has been fraught with structural impediments, some anticipated, some not. For forty-five years, Germans longed for an end to the division of their country, but unification proved much more problematic than expected. A few success stories can be found in former communist Europe—Poland most notably—but the much longer line of failures, not the least of which is Russia itself, causes serious uneasiness about the new century. Yet nowhere has the descent into a dark cloud of pessimism been as steep as in former Yugoslavia. No country in formerly communist

Eastern Europe has fallen apart with such violence and wanton destruction.

How could it happen that the hopes and dreams associated with the fall of communism in 1989 and the collapse of the Soviet Union in 1991 were shattered by nearly a decade of war, brutality, and ethnic cleansing in former Yugoslavia? Once again, war on the European continent had disgorged tens of thousands of haggard refugees, telling horrific stories of rape, torture, and death. Once again, innocent civilians were executed by firing squads and buried in mass graves. Once again, villages were set aflame, animals killed, and houses of worship blown up. Once again, whole ethnic populations were crowded into railway cars and deported from their homelands. And once again, the "world community" looked on in horror, seemingly incapable of preventing or ending these acts of forced deportation and mass murder. Was the twentieth century's sordid history of genocide simply repeating itself in this last decade? Or was there something new in these wars of "ethnic cleansing" about which the media spoke and wrote so often?

To try to answer these and related questions, I have chosen cases from twentieth-century European history that help illuminate the process of ethnic cleansing, its causes and effects. Comparative history is Clio's own modest form of social science, allowing the observer to ask what is structurally the same and what is different in these cases and to think about what has changed and what has remained consistent over time. Most importantly, comparison provides the potential for better understanding the causes of ethnic cleansing in our era. Bound up in the comparative method of historical analysis are a number of conceptual problems, however—problems that are compounded by the geographical and chronological limitations I have placed on this work. To explore these limitations, the following discussion focuses on the three components of the book's title itself: ethnic cleansing, twentieth century, and Europe.

Ethnic Cleansing

This term exploded into our consciousness in May 1992 during the first stage of the war in Bosnia.[1] At that time it referred to Serb attacks on Bosnian Muslims aimed at driving the Muslims from their home territories. But the term had been initially devised by Serbs themselves to describe what was happening to their own people in neighboring Kosovo, at the hands of Kosovar Albanians in the early 1980s.[2] "Ethnic cleansing" quickly became part of the international lexicon of crimes associated with Serb aggression in former Yugoslavia, though it was later used to describe similar attacks by Croats on Muslims, Serbs on Croats, and, most recently, Serbs on Kosovar Albanians. What all of these cases had in common was the intent of driving victims from territory claimed by the perpetrators. Journalists, NATO spokesmen, European jurists, and American politicians invoked the concept with amazing consistency.[3] Yet almost from the beginning, some commentators criticized the term as being at best imprecise and at worst a euphemism for genocide. More academic voices objected to use of a term that derived from contemporary journalism rather than from scholarly or juridical sources.[4]

In this book I will argue that "ethnic cleansing" is a useful and viable term for understanding not just the war in former Yugoslavia but other similar cataclysmic events in the course of the twentieth century. New concepts are consistently being invented to describe, classify, and arrange events of the past in order to understand them in the present. In this sense, "ethnic cleansing," which was used with increasing frequency after May 1992, is little different from the term "genocide," which derived its meaning from Raphael Lemkin's writings during World War II to describe what was happening to the victims of Nazism. Moreover, ethnic cleansing is presently taking on a juridical meaning through the war crimes courts in the Hague, just as genocide was defined by Article II of the United Nations Convention on the Prevention and Punishment of the Crime of Genocide of December 9, 1948.[5]

A new term was needed because ethnic cleansing and genocide are two different activities, and the differences between them are important. As in the case of determining first-degree murder, intentionality is the critical distinction. Genocide is the intentional killing off of part or all of an ethnic, religious, or national group; the murder of a people or peoples (in German, *Völkermord*) is the objective. The intention of ethnic cleansing is to remove a people and often all traces of them from a concrete territory. The goal, in other words, is to get rid of the "alien" nationality, ethnic, or religious group and to seize control of the territory they had formerly inhabited. At one extreme of its spectrum, ethnic cleansing is closer to forced deportation or what has been called "population transfer"; the idea is to get people to move, and the means are meant to be legal and semi-legal. At the other extreme, however, ethnic cleansing and genocide are distinguishable only by the ultimate intent. Here, both literally and figuratively, ethnic cleansing bleeds into genocide, as mass murder is committed in order to rid the land of a people.

Further complicating the distinctions between ethnic cleansing and genocide is the fact that forced deportation seldom takes place without violence, often murderous violence. People do not leave their homes on their own. They hold on to their land and their culture, which are interconnected. They resist deportation orders; they cling to their domiciles and their possessions; they find every possible way to avoid abandoning the place where their families have roots and their ancestors are buried. The result is that forced deportation often becomes genocidal, as people are violently ripped from their native towns and villages and killed when they try to stay.

Even when forced deportation is not genocidal in its intent, it is often genocidal in its effects. Millions of people in this century have been marched in hungry columns across huge expanses of land and crowded into freight cars, buses, or holds of ships for journeys in which thousands, even tens of thousands, become sick, starve, and die. Even those refugees who survive forced deportation and transportation out of their homelands must deal with hunger, disease, and the sheer sorrow of living in refugee camps, begging for food, and seeking shelter in new lands out of reach of their persecutors. Many give up on life and commit suicide.

In addition to making a useful distinction from genocide, the term "ethnic cleansing" is also valuable because of its associated meanings. In its Slavic forms *chishchenie* in Russian and *ciscenja* in Serbo-Croatian, cleansing often refers to political elimination or the purging of enemies. The purges in the Soviet Union, for example, were called *chistki*. The German word for cleansing, *Säuberung,* has the same kind of meaning, especially in the history of communism, but is also tied to the development of racial "science" in Germany at the turn of the century.[6] As it came to maturity at the beginning of the twentieth century, eugenics itself was about racial cleansing, *Säuberung,* though its implications were not necessarily genocidal.[7] Although the phrase ethnic cleansing itself was not used in the German or Slavic context, as far as I know, at the beginning of the century,[8] German racial thinking did create the term *völkische Flurbereinigung,* which uses a metaphor from agriculture to indicate the cleansing, in this case of alien ethnic elements from the soil. Himmler, for example, favored this concept in describing the Aryanization of German territory.[9] In both Slavic and German usages, "cleansing" has a dual meaning; one purges the native community of foreign bodies, and one purges one's own people of alien elements. This latter association, which emphasizes self-purging, accounts in some measure for the fearsome up-close killing and barbarous mutilation of neighbors and acquaintances that characterizes a number of cases of ethnic cleansing.

"Ethnic" refers to what we call today an ethnic group, deriving from the Greek "ethnos" or nation. Some uses of the term tend to be pejorative, meaning that the group involved is something less than a nation or nationality. No such meaning is intended here. At the same time, "ethnic group" and "ethnicity" are extremely hard to define, and often their contours are delineated by dominant groups that wish to create and characterize the "other." The borders of ethnicity are constantly shifting; who is included and excluded has little to do with "objective" categories, since any categories we might use—race, religion, skin color, and so on—are themselves socially constructed and reified by their repeated application.

The definition of ethnicity I find most compelling is that of Geoff Eley and Ronald Suny, who note: "Ethnicity arises in the interaction of groups. It exists in the boundaries constructed between them." Equally important, these constructions change over time and are mutable, depending on circumstances even within the same societies. Ethnicity, in other words, is specific to time, place, and culture, and even to the individuals shaping its meaning. "It is *in* history, the flow of past events, that the emergence and variation appear, and only *through* history can we understand them."[10] This book makes a similar argument about ethnic cleansing: its definition can be understood only through the ebb and flow of its history in this century.

The Twentieth Century

From the beginning of recorded history, dominant nations have attacked and chased off their lands less powerful nations and groups they deemed subordinate and alien. Homer's Iliad is full of brutal and shocking examples of what one might call ethnic cleansing, as is the Bible. The first and still most important scholarly book on ethnic cleansing by the Boston sociologist Andrew Bell-Fialkoff begins its historical overview with the Assyrians and Babylonians.[11] From this point of view, events as widely dispersed in time and place as the destruction of Carthage (146 BC), the murder of the Albigensians (1209 and following), the expulsion of Jews from Spain (1492), the Spanish conquest of the Incas and Aztecs (sixteenth century), the German massacres of the Herreros in southwest Africa (1904–1905), and the driving out of Indians from their North American homelands (nineteenth century) all belong to the phenomenon of ethnic cleansing. One problem with such a broad understanding of the concept, however, is that it encompasses too much chronological territory and too many variations on a similar theme. The realm of explanation is reduced to finding essential characteristics of humankind or tracing modern behavior to mythological origins and biblical tropes.[12] My understanding of ethnic cleansing in the twentieth century is that its occurrences are highly dependent on the particular characteristics of the state, society, and ideology during the period itself. Bell-Fialkoff calls the twentieth century the third "contemporary" phase of ethnic cleansing.[13] I think of it as so distinct in critical ways from earlier events that it belongs to a separate historical category.

Ethnic cleansing as experienced in former Yugoslavia, from this perspective, is a profoundly modern experience, related to previous instances in the twentieth century but not a product of "ancient hatreds," as so often suggested by politicians and journalists, who repeatedly cite Ivo Andric's *The Bridge on the Drina* to prove that the Balkans are endlessly violent. That Andric's Nobel-prize-winning work belongs very much to the struggles of World War II rather than to Ottoman Bosnia seldom seems to influence its use. From this perspective as well, the episodic pogroms of late nineteenth-century Russia, which cost remarkably few Jewish lives given their bad press in the West, constituted a very different kind of attack than Stalin's reputed plans in 1952–53 to deport Russian Jews to Siberia. These plans, which still remain mostly unresearched because of inaccessible Russian archives, might well have resulted in a second Shoah. The Turkish attacks on Armenians in 1894–95 under Abdul Hamid II (the "Red"), though terrible in their scale and brutality, belong to a different social and historical phenomenon than the Armenian genocide of 1915, which constituted a concerted attack on the Armenian nation as a whole. The Nazi mass murder of the Jews was not simply an advanced stage in the development of German anti-Semitism from medieval times to the present, Daniel Goldhagen's analysis notwithstanding.[14] There were essential differences that tied the Holocaust to the century in which it actually occurred.

One of those differences was the increasing popularity of modern, racialist nationalism as it developed throughout Europe and the West during the late nineteenth and early twentieth centuries. Post-positivist and post-Darwinian, this new extreme form of nationalism represented an essentialist view of nations, a view which excluded the "other" and forswore assimilation. Not only were races exclusive to themselves, but the mixing of others into the national corpus would compromise the people's native strength. German anti-Semitism took on a much more virulent character than it had assumed in previous times; even those Jews who had fully assimilated were threatened by anti-Semitic laws. Johann Gottfried von Herder's nationalism of the early nineteenth-century romantic era encouraged all nations to develop their languages and culture on a more or less equal basis.[15] The late nineteenth-century nationalism of Roman Dmowski in Poland or Francis Galton in England or Ernst Haeckel in Germany was fundamentally different. Ostensibly "scientific" in character, it measured the size of skulls, the shape of torsos, and the width of crania to understand race and diagnose its supposed defects. In the form of social Darwinism, the new race thinking postulated a world of nations engaged in a life-and-death struggle with one another for survival. The strong and determined—the fittest—would succeed, while lesser nations, like lesser species, would fall by the wayside. When such notions of integral nationalism became mixed with imperialism's harsh suppression of native populations and their aspirations around the turn of the century, the genocidal potential among dominant nations increased exponentially. Mass murder on the basis of race was already part of European colonial history at the dawn of the new century; nationalism became the fuse that would ignite an explosion of genocide.[16]

Modern racialist nationalism was necessary for ethnic cleansing in the twentieth century but not sufficient. The modern state was a critical part of the story as it organized itself by ethnic criteria, especially after the Balkan Wars and World War I. According to Zygmunt Baumann, this marriage of modern nationalism and the post-World War I state was fatal in particular for the Jews: "Racism is unthinkable without the advancement of modern science, modern technology and modern forms of state power. As such, racism is strictly a modern product. Modernity made racism possible. It also created a demand for racism; an era that declared achievement to be the only measure of human worth needed a theory of ascription to redeem boundary-drawing and boundary-guarding concerns under new conditions which made boundary-crossing easier than ever before. Racism, in short, is a thoroughly modern weapon used in the conduct of pre-modern, or at least not exclusively modern struggles."[17] Religious difference in this schema is not the salient issue in ethnic cleansing, as it often was for mass murder in centuries past. Even in Bosnia and Kosovo, religion serves as a marker of ethnic identity, not primarily as an indicator of faith.[18]

Ethnic cleansing in the twentieth century is a product of the most "advanced" stage in the development of the modern state. This is the era of what James Scott calls "high modernism," a state ideology which seeks to transform society into the regularized and "healthy" organism that reflects the state leaderships' own needs for order, transparency, and responsiveness.[19] The modern state takes the census, organizes cadastral surveys, counts, measures, weighs, categorizes, and homogenizes. It reifies geographical boundaries and enforces zoning regulations. It also subjects its population to surveillance and manipulation.[20] It interferes in family life and establishes natalist policies. The media inculcate the values of the state's governing elite. High modernism has little use for minority rights, language differences, asymmetrical development, and primitive agriculture or artisanry. But, as Baumann points out, it insists on identifying ethnic groups and concretizing difference and otherness with the goal of banishing it. Of course, the state and its bureaucracies engaged in these activities long before the twentieth century. The origins of the modern state go back certainly into the eighteenth-century Enlightenment and even beyond, to the Scientific Revolution and the Age of Discovery.[21] But the twentieth-century state, prompted in good measure by its mobilization of society around World War I, has engaged in the control and ordering of its population to a level previously unimaginable.

The modern sovereign state's inability to tolerate large minorities within its borders leads sometimes to programs of assimilation and sometimes to ethnic cleansing, depending on the political circumstances and the historical context. But the impetus to homogenize is inherent to the twentieth-century state. Of course, the twentieth-century state has also provided an unheard-of level of welfare, medical care, and educational benefits to the populations it manages. In some cases, it has also brought to fruition many of the Enlightenment principles of human dignity and the rights of citizens. In the most fortunate societies, these rights allow individuals and groups to use the power of the state and the political system to check some of their own worst instincts. In the least fortunate societies, tyrants use the state to enforce their own nightmarish racialist fantasies.[22]

The achievements of modern science and technology are unimaginable without the direct support of the state and its institutions. Yet these achievements are a double-edged sword when nations turn to ethnic cleansing. The messages to deport are sent by telegraph, teletype, telephone, and now by computers and email. Members of a particular minority can be tracked down by passport lists, village censuses, and tax rolls, where their ethnicity and religion are dutifully recorded by state employees. The justification for deportation is published and broadcast by modern mass media: newspapers, radios, and newsreels originally, then by television, video, and internet. Propaganda—used both to bolster the image of the state and to demean that of the internal enemy—coevolved with the modern media. The infrastructure of the modern state supports not only mass communication but also the mass transportation that ethnic cleansing requires; people are forcibly moved by railways in particular, but also buses and trucks, often built by the state. Technology has also given us the Uzis and AK-47s that are the preferred weapon of today's ethnic cleansers; in both cases these are weapons initially mass-produced by state arms manufacturers. Even the machetes used by Hutus against Tutsis in Rwanda were imported from China, where they had been mass-produced in modern factories. The drive toward ethnic cleansing comes in part from the modern state's compulsion to complete policies and finish with problems but also in part from its technological abilities to do so.

As many scholars have pointed out (Omer Bartov and Elisabeth Domansky among them), World War I was a crucible for the development of the modern nation-state and its willingness and ability to engage in mass population policies.[23] Both in the Balkan Wars and in World War I, forced deportation and population exchange became a regular part of peacemaking as well as warmaking. In mobilizing their populations for total war, the European state bureaucracies inserted themselves increasingly into the individual lives of their citizens, whether in reproductive policy, housing issues, or work norms. But particularly in post-World War I Germany and the Soviet Union, state intervention in and regularization of citizens' lives reached a new height. Even in relatively backward countries, like the newly constituted Turkish Republic of Mustafa Kemal (Atatürk), the state assumed a modernizing posture, intervening in the lives of its citizens in areas that had earlier been left to the Ottoman religious communities, the millets. The Great War also introduced "industrial killing" into the consciousness and reality of the European state system. Killing was routinized and perfected; the use of gas and airplanes brought more and more scientists and "scientific principles" into the prosecution of war.

Although the modern state and integral nationalism have been critical to ethnic cleansing in this century, political elites nevertheless bear the major responsibility for its manifestations. In competing for political power, they have exploited the appeal of nationalism to large groups of resentful citizens in the dominant ethnic population. Using the power of the state, the media, and their political parties, national leaders have manipulated distrust of the "other" and purposefully revived and distorted ethnic tensions, sometimes long-buried, sometimes closer to the surface. They have initiated campaigns of ethnic cleansing by their orders and intimations; they have held the power to stop them if they wished, and they did not. Ethnic cleansing could not have taken place in the twentieth century without the direct involvement and connivance of political leaders. It is not an unpremeditated outburst of hatred, though it feeds on the potential for interethnic violence in society. As a witness to atrocities carried out by both Turks and Greeks during the Greco-Turkish War of 1921–22, Arnold Toynbee noted that political leaders have ignited the fires of ethnic hatred and resentment. "This is an ugly possibility in all of us; but happily, even when the stimuli are present, atrocities are seldom committed spontaneously by large bodies of human beings . . . More commonly the rabies seizes a few individuals, and is communicated by them to the mass, while in other cases the bloodlust of the pack is excited by cold-blooded huntsmen who desire the death of the quarry without being carried away themselves by the excitement of the chase."[24]

Political elites do not act alone in pursuing the goals of ethnic cleansing, however. They are backed up by state and party apparatuses, police forces, militaries, and paramilitaries. They also are supported by professionals—lawyers, doctors, professors, engineers—who more often than not are both the architects and the beneficiaries of the modern state. The Young Turk revolution and its eventual assault on the Armenians owed a great deal to the active involvement of military doctors.[25] Robert J. Lifton, among others, has demonstrated the important role played by Nazi doctors in the development of German racial ideology and Nazi practices of elimination, some of which they supervised and even carried out themselves.[26] Well-educated and well-trained technocrats oversaw the ghettoization and eventual murder of the Jews, the transport of Chechens-Ingush from their home territories in the Soviet Union, and the deportation of the Armenians from Anatolia. Radovan Karadzic, the leader of the Bosnian Serbs and an indicted war criminal, is a trained psychiatrist. Slobodan Milosevic, another indicted war criminal, earned his law degree and worked in banking in Serbia. Both men studied abroad and enjoyed a cosmopolitan lifestyle. One can only conclude from these and other twentieth-century examples that modern professional codes of ethics do not deter some people from participation in ethnic cleansing and mass murder.

Europe

The cases examined in this book are taken from European history, including the history of the Soviet Union and the Ottoman Empire and Turkey. The reasons for this are two-fold. First, I do not feel competent to investigate and write about ethnic cleansing in regions whose cultures, history, and historiography I have not engaged in any depth. I am not able to explore the histories of Africa, Latin America, Asia, South Asia, and North America in the same way I can in the case of Europe. Although I am not familiar with the languages of some of the areas in Europe I discuss, I have studied their past, been involved in their present, and traveled extensively in their lands. The comparative method is hard on historians, who generally insist on knowing the languages and cultures of the lands they write about. My choice for the topic of ethnic cleansing was to stretch far enough to encompass some European groups whose histories I had studied through secondary works but had not been able to research in original-language sources. I did not think I could stretch so far as to make up for my ignorance of the histories and cultures of, for example, Cambodia, Rwanda, or India and Pakistan.

I have an intellectual as well as a practical reason for both confining my work to Europe and then attempting to cover its major episodes of ethnic cleansing. The cases I examine are nested in the history of twentieth-century Europe as a whole—not just in local circumstance. Officers from the Imperial German Army, for example, were deeply involved in the Armenian genocide in Anatolia. But Russian and French actions also influenced the course of events there. British politics and politicians were essential to the outcome of the Greco-Turkish war and the Treaty of Lausanne which concluded it. Young Turks fled to Germany to escape prosecution for their crimes; one of the most prominent, Talat Pasha, was assassinated on the streets of Berlin by an Armenian nationalist. Hitler and the Nazis were intimately aware of the Armenian catastrophe and referred to it in their discussions of mass murder. There is a clear and apparent relationship between, on the one hand, the rise to power of Nazism and its domination of the continent and, on the other, the ascendancy of Stalin and Stalinism in the Soviet Union. When the Czechs and Poles deported Germans from their territories at the end of the war and beginning of the peace, they quite consciously reversed the tables on their former persecutors. The ethnic cleansing in Bosnia and Kosovo is closely linked to the wartime policies of the Nazis and the peacetime influences of Moscow. The Treaty of Dayton (1995), which concluded the war in Bosnia, is tied to the treaties of Potsdam (1945) and Lausanne (1923). The point is that ethnic cleansing in Europe has its own history. The cases I explore are interconnected and embedded in the European twentieth century. They need to be historicized, as well as compared.

The Cases

Each chapter deals with the history of one case or set of cases involving ethnic cleansing. In some instances I have done some archival work in order to bolster the otherwise weak historiography or incomplete documentary sources. In other cases—the Holocaust is the most notable—the published material is so extensive and well-researched that archival work was unnecessary. In all the cases, I owe a great debt to fellow historians, who have labored long and hard to establish the fundamental contours of ethnic cleansing in each location. At the same time, where possible, I have sought out documentary sources as a way to break through the layers of controversy on difficult issues involving national pride and collective memory.

The first case I examine is the Armenian genocide of 1915. In many ways, this is the most contentious of all the cases I consider in this book. Turkish and Armenian historians have yet to reach the kind of consensus on fundamental issues that would allow for deeper investigation of discrete episodes. Passions are high when the events of 1915 are discussed, and an "objective" history of the events has not yet been written. Reputable historians on both sides still have wildly different estimates of the number of Armenians killed. Ronald G. Suny cites figures between "a few hundred thousand," the lowest estimate, and 1.5 million, sometimes claimed in Armenian accounts.[27] The essential question of intentionality also remains highly debatable: did the Young Turk leadership plan to kill off a part of the Armenian nation, or were the deaths an unintended byproduct of the deportation plans? Armenian and Turkish historians differ radically in their answers to this question. In association with the Armenian case, in Chapter 1 I also review the expulsion of the Greek population from Anatolia, some 1.4 million people, as a consequence of the Greco-Turkish War of 1921–22. This forced deportation took place under the auspices of the new Turkish government of Mustafa Kemal and was legitimized by the Treaty of Lausanne in 1923. Because Lausanne is seen later in the century as a model for the peaceful exchange of populations under international humanitarian supervision, it is important to look at the background and circumstances of the exchange.

In Chapter 2 I examine the Nazi attack on the Jews. The scholarly literature in this case is enormous, detailed, and, for the most part, scrupulously fair-minded. I can contribute very little indeed to our factual knowledge of "the road to genocide." My task, as I see it, is to focus on the question of whether the "Final Solution" can be seen as a case of ethnic cleansing, and if so, at what point did ethnic cleansing stop and genocide begin? In exploring this question, I concentrate on the period between the Nazi attack on Poland in September 1939 and the invasion of the Soviet Union in June 1941. In the late summer and early fall of 1941, the Nazis entered a new and terrifying stage in their assault on the Jews. Behind the advance of the Wehrmacht, the SS Einsatzgruppen, sometimes with Wehrmacht cooperation and participation, massacred large numbers of Jews. At some point in the early fall of 1941, according to Christopher Browning and Philippe Burrin, the decision was reached to exterminate all of the Jews.[28] The Wannsee conference in January 1942, which designed the system of death camps, was the conclusion of a process of planning the mass destruction of the Jews. Certainly from that point on, if not earlier in the fall, ethnic cleansing or forced deportation were no longer options under discussion; the Nazis had taken the final steps toward the Holocaust, the Shoah, the mass destruction of an entire nation.

The third case—or, better, pair of cases—are the Soviets' forced deportation of the Chechens-Ingush from the northern Caucasus in February 1944 and their forced deportation of the Crimean Tatars from the Crimea to Central Asia in May 1944. The Chechen-Ingush and Tatar cases have their own peculiarities which relate to the unique characteristics of the Soviet system. The peoples were not deported abroad, nor were they displaced by a single nationality. But large numbers died in the process of deportation and resettlement, some 35–45 percent of the total deportees, and the thoroughness of the process of ethnic cleansing was remarkable. Every single Chechen-Ingush, some 489,000 people, and Crimean Tatar, some 185,000, was forced to go. No one was allowed to stay behind; no traces of the nations were permitted to remain. Even the names of their territories were changed or eliminated. No one talked about what had happened. It was as if these nations had disappeared into thin air.

The expulsion of the Germans from Poland and Czechoslovakia at the end of World War II and beginning of the peace constitute the set of cases I examine in Chapter 4. Roughly 11.5 million Germans were expelled from these territories; as many as 2.5 million died in the process, many from hunger and disease.[29] Gerhard Weinberg calls this "the largest single migration of people in a short period of which we know."[30] The Polish and Czech cases are interesting because they reverse the moral lenses through which we view ethnic cleansing. The destruction the Germans perpetrated in Czechoslovakia and especially in Poland meant that few outsiders sympathized with their plight. Moral categories are also complicated by the brutal way in which both the Poles and Czechs expelled their respective German populations. In the Polish case, one can understand the brutality; after all, the Germans had killed some 6 million Polish citizens, half of them Polish Catholics, half Jews. The Nazis systematically drove the Poles into the ground, with the goal of turning the Polish nation into helots who would provide menial labor for the Reich's industry and agriculture. The Czechs were treated much differently. Relatively few died during the war; Czech industry prospered, as did its workers; and direct attacks on Czech nationals were sporadic and rare. Yet the Czechs were as brutal as the Poles, if not more so, in taking revenge on the Germans.

The Polish and Czech cases are also instructive in the sense that ethnic cleansing was conceived and carried out by democratic regimes. Located in London, both the wartime Czechoslovak and Polish governments-in-exile called for the expulsion of the Germans.[31] There was little difference in either country between the policies of the liberal and conservative politicians in London and the communists in the underground or in Moscow. Almost everyone agreed the Germans had to go, whether they were fascists or antifascists, resistance fighters or not, men, women, or children. In Czechoslovakia, these policies were implemented by the government of Edvard Benes, otherwise well-respected as a democratic politician. The communists provided plenty of help. In Poland, where the government was controlled primarily by communists and the ethnic cleansing supervised by communist leaders, the major noncommunist politician, Stanislaw Mikolajczyk of the Agrarian Party, consistently called for the expulsion of all the Germans. Neither Benes nor Mikolajczyk showed any concern for the violence and brutality these expulsions engendered. For them, like the communists, the issue was reconstructing their countries on an ethnically homogeneous basis.

The final cases I examine are associated with the war in former Yugoslavia. Initially, I intended to focus Chapter 5 on Serb attacks on Muslims in Bosnia-Herzegovina, which earned ethnic cleansing worldwide condemnation. Though in no way diminishing the Serbs' responsibility for the depredations in Bosnia, I thought it was important to include Croat ethnic cleansing of Muslims and Serbs in Bosnia and Krajina, respectively, as well as the sporadic Muslim-initiated attacks. Alas, the history of ethnic cleansing in former Yugoslavia did not conclude with Bosnia and the Dayton Treaty of November 1995, which ended the war. The Serbian ethnic cleansing of Kosovo in the winter and early spring of 1998–99 prompted NATO's bombing of Serbia and the occupation of Kosovo. After NATO took control of Kosovo, the Kosovar Albanians also engaged in ethnic cleansing of the Serbs, a process which continues into the new century. In the former multiethnic republics of Yugoslavia, political elites seem to be doing everything they can to complete, one way or another, "the unmixing of peoples."[32]

In comparing these cases of ethnic cleansing, I hope to elucidate the causes and consequences of this devastating process and to underline the fact that ethnic cleansing has terrifying potential for genocide. For this reason it demands the attention of the world community and those institutions that have some hope of preventing its initiation or stopping its progress. The cases I examine make clear that this is no easy matter. Shared principles of state sovereignty make intervention by multinational institutions difficult. Furthermore, the national interests of great powers are rarely defined in humanitarian terms; nations believe that they have few incentives, and many disincentives, to become involved. No forceful actions were taken to prevent the Armenian genocide, the expulsion of the Greeks, or the Holocaust, events that were well known to the public and political leaders at the time. The deportation of the Chechens-Ingush and Crimean Tatars was not known in the West, but that fact had little relevance to the outcome; no more action would have been taken against the Soviets than is now being taken against the Russians who are pummeling Chechen civilians and leveling Chechen cities and towns. By August 1945 when the Potsdam Agreement called for the humane transfer of Germans from Poland and Czechoslovakia, the worst of the ethnic cleansing had already taken place. In this sense Potsdam resembled both Lausanne and Dayton, where international treaties tended to confirm the worst cases of ethnic cleansing rather than prevent them.

A comparative study of these cases of ethnic cleansing also sheds light on their political and social bases. Commentators on the Balkans too often and too assuredly attribute ethnic cleansing to the cultural and historical peculiarities of the South Slav peoples, the Serbs in particular. In my view, the issue is not so much culture—Western or Eastern, Orthodox or Muslim—as it is historical contingency, the confluence of events, political leadership, and intercommunal hostility within the modern state. Neither the Turkish genocidal attacks on the Armenians nor the German elimination of the Jews were inevitable. They were based on concrete circumstances that emerged from the world wars, and they were ignited by the warped ambitions of modern politicians. This does not lessen in any way the responsibility of individual citizens for the atrocities perpetrated against minorities within their communities. Nor does it relieve international institutions of their responsibilities for not having intervened when they might have prevented or alleviated these dire consequences.

Comparative reflection on the problems of ethnic cleansing also leads to the conclusion that each case must be understood in its full complexity, in its own immediate context, rather than merely as part of a long-term historical conflict between nations.[33] Ethnic cleansing is not the product of the cultural peculiarities of Turks, Germans, Serbs, or other peoples. Unfortunately, its traces can be seen in every society, and its potentiality is part of us all. Only by looking at ethnic cleansing in this fashion can we understand how it happens elsewhere and how to prevent it happening again, there or here.

The Armenians and Greeks of Anatolia

The collapse of the Ottoman Empire at the onset of the twentieth century provided the backdrop for a hundred years of genocide and ethnic cleansing in southeastern Europe and Anatolia. One need not romanticize the Pax Ottomanica to understand that the Turkish empire's passing released forces of extreme nationalism and errant state-building whose aftershocks remain with us even today in Bosnia and Kosovo. Ottoman weakness, Western (including Russian) interventionism, and powerful national movements among the empire's subject peoples created pressures at the faultline which led to the Balkan Wars of 1912–1913. The 1913 Carnegie Report's description of the killing, atrocities, and ethnic cleansing in this region could well apply to the terrifying events of the recent wars of Yugoslav succession—only a few dates, names, places would have to change.[1] As a result of the Balkan Wars, massive population transfers and ethnic separatism first became part of modern European conflict and made their way into the vocabulary of peacemaking. Bulgarians, Serbs, and Greeks sought to create nation-states in new borders by expelling minority populations and fostering the exclusive interests of their own kin.[2] In the years before the slaughter of World War I permanently altered the European landscape, demands for new state boundaries and ethnically homogeneous territories in southeastern Europe undermined the stability of the old European order.

The assassination of Austrian Archduke Franz Ferdinand in June 1914 by terrorists from the group Young Bosnia brought the great powers directly into the Balkan conflict, internationalizing and militarizing it in ways unexpected by any of the combatants. In the turbulent aftermath of the Great War, not just the Ottoman Empire but like houses of cards, one after the other—Imperial Russia, the Habsburg monarchy, and the German empire—came tumbling down. The collapse of multinational empires and the emergence of nation-states founded on the principles of self-determination left ethnic and racial minorities vulnerable to the state-building ideologies of the dominant nationalities. The minority-protection treaties attached to the Versailles Settlement did little to alter the fundamental weakness of the Wilsonian notion of self-determination: the question *whose* right to self-determination would dictate the policies of the new states? Political elites representing the majority nations tried to answer that question by diminishing the rights and influence of the minorities. Given the powerful influence of racial theories on the nationalist ideologies of both dominant and subordinate peoples, ethnic conflict, if not war or civil war, seemed the inevitable consequence.

The Swiss anthropologist and ethnographer George Montandon was one of the first to recognize the dangers inherent in the situation and to propose a solution. As early as 1915 he wrote that "natural" borders should be established according to ethnic criteria and that those nations which neither wished to nor could be absorbed into the majority population should be subjected to "massive resettlement" beyond the borders of the new states, ostensibly to join their own national groups abroad.[3] In Montandon's scheme, the minority nations would lose all rights to own property or to live as citizens in the new nation-state. After the Balkan Wars and the nationality struggles of World War I, academics and politicians of various stripes who looked at the problems of minority populations sometimes came to the same conclusion as Montandon: that population transfer was the only way to defuse antagonistic minority issues.

The Ottomans and the Armenians

Historians of the Ottoman Empire tend to paint a rosy picture of the minority peoples within its borders.[4] By contrast, historians of the subject peoples—Serbs or Bulgarians, Greeks or Armenians—tend to do the opposite, emphasizing the brutality of the Ottoman yoke and the inevitable victories of their respective national movements or, in the case of the Armenians, the inevitable tragedy that engulfed the nation.[5] The disagreement centers on different evaluations of the millet system, by which the major Ottoman religious groups enjoyed freedom of conscience and relative autonomy within their religious communities. Compared with what came before (the Byzantine Empire) or after (modern Turkey), unquestionably the minorities lived relatively well under the Ottomans, enjoying greater religious tolerance and communal autonomy in the early modern period than minorities in contemporaneous Western and Central European societies. It would be anachronistic to suggest that the Ottomans demonstrated racial and ethnic tolerance, because they did not think at all in those terms. Without exception, Islamic faith and Ottoman loyalty were the essential requirements for membership in the empire's elites. But converts to Islam among Serbs, Albanians, and Greeks were prominent in the Ottoman government and army. During the rise of the Ottoman Empire between 1453 and 1623, only five of the Grand Vezirs were of Turkish extraction. Even among those groups that did not convert to Islam in large numbers—such as the substantial Sephardic Jewish community which had fled from Spain for the Ottoman lands, or the indigenous Armenian community of the ancient Gregorian Christian faith—opportunities to gain prominence, wealth, and status were not lacking in the Ottoman system. Indeed, the Armenians were known as the most loyal millet, *millet i-sadika,* because of their deference to official authority and their remarkable accomplishments under the Ottomans in trade, commerce, and artisanry.[6]

This picture of the relative tolerance of Ottoman society needs to be balanced by the fact that Islamic ideology unambiguously proclaimed the inferiority of non-Muslim peoples.[7] Benjamin Braude and Bernard Lewis write that "persecution was rare and atypical" but that "discrimination was permanent and indeed necessary, inherent in the system and maintained by both Holy Law and common practice."[8] Ottoman law and custom relegated infidels *(gaour)* to second-class status in the empire. Christians did not enjoy equal standing with Muslims in the judicial system; the tax system openly discriminated against them; they were not allowed to serve in the higher ranks of the government or the military; and they were forced to pay a hefty tax for their exemptions from military service. But as long as Christians and Jews accepted these strictures, they were able to prosper and develop in their communities. Because Islamic law discouraged Muslims from participating in commerce and banking, Armenians, Jews, and Greeks increasingly dominated the developing economic and industrial life of the country. In the nineteenth century, Greeks from the Peloponnese and islands migrated in large numbers to the coastal towns of Aegean Anatolia, where Greek communities had already achieved high standards of economic development and civic culture. The Sephardic Jewish community of Salonika, in Ottoman Macedonia, dominated the local economy and helped to create a vibrant commercial entrepot. The Armenians in Constantinople and in the coastal Mediterranean cities of Cilicia increasingly took on the visage of a modern European bourgeoisie, heavily involved in the medical, engineering, and law professions, in textile manufacturing, and in agriculture.

Over the course of the nineteenth century, this delicate balance between official inequality and relative tolerance was upset by the inability of the Ottoman state to keep pace as an economic and military power with its European rivals. Labeled at mid-century "the sick man of Europe" by Nicholas I—whose own Russian Empire wasn't exactly healthy at that point—the Ottoman Empire commenced a profound decline from which it never recovered. Many factors underlay the weakness of the Ottomans, not the least of which was the overwhelming sense of superiority and permanence accorded them by their Islamic faith. The last phase of the reform movement (Tanzimat) of the 1860s came too late and offered too little, in large part because of a general lack of enthusiasm for its possibilities among the Ottoman elite. The Islamic ethos of imperial pride, aloofness from European problems, and imperviousness to domestic shortcomings made military pressures on the Ottomans from the Russians above all, but also from the Serbs, the Greeks, and the Austrians, even more nettlesome.[9] The Ottomans would have to modernize the army; that much was clear from the increasing interest, as well, of the French, the British, and eventually the new German Empire in the potential imperial spoils of the Middle East. The "Eastern Question" fundamentally centered on control of the Straits but also included a wide variety of issues confronting the Ottomans, from the fate of Egypt to the struggle for independence of the Balkan peoples.

The heightened interest of the European powers in the future of the Ottoman Empire led increasingly to their interference in the affairs of the Ottoman government, the Sublime Porte. As early as the seventeenth century, the Ottomans granted trade privileges to European countries and city-states through special concessions—the so-called Capitulations. In the late eighteenth century, the Capitulations spread to include European rights to intercede on behalf of Christian minorities in the empire. Meanwhile, the Christian communities, predominantly the Armenians and Greeks, sought to use European influence at the Porte to achieve minority rights, both formal and real, within the empire. They found allies among a small, Westernized segment of Ottoman elite liberals, who, as part of their struggle for a constitution, promoted the ideal of "Ottomanism": equal citizenship in the empire for Muslims and non-Muslims alike. Great hopes were attached to the promulgation of the constitution of Midhat Pasha in 1876, which sought to shift the balance of power in the Ottoman system from the theocratic sultan and his council of imams to the government and its secular ministries. But Ottoman Muslims in and out of government were little interested in constitutional reform. In the midst of the government crisis provoked by the Russo-Turkish War of 1877–78, Abdul Hamid II was proclaimed sultan and the constitution was abrogated. The Ottoman Empire would be ruled by the despotic and traditionalist sultan for more than thirty years.

Despite this return to traditional centers of authority in the empire, the Armenians took heart from potential allies at home and abroad and exerted even more resolute pressure on the government for reforms. In the Treaty of Berlin (1878), for the first time Armenian pleas for protection against the periodic attacks of Kurds and Circassians were recognized by the great powers. Article 61 of the treaty read: "The Sublime Porte undertakes to carry out, without further delay, the improvement and reforms demanded by local requirements in the provinces inhabited by the Armenians and to guarantee their security . . . It will periodically make known the steps taken to this effect with the powers, who will superintend their application."[10] The Armenian Catholicus, patriarch of the Gregorian Church, went to Berlin to intercede for this measure. But groups of young, educated Armenians wanted more. After a decade of socialist agitation, often of the Russian *narodnik* variety, in 1890 they formed the Armenian Revolutionary Federation, Dashnaktsutian, in Tiflis (Tbilisi).[11] From the Dashnaks' perspective, equality under the law, the slogan of the Young Ottomans, would lead to the abrogation of the Armenians' national aspirations and rights, which could be guaranteed only by autonomy within the Armenians' traditional lands. The Hnchak (Bell) party, founded in Geneva in 1887, was even more radical in its approach. Though Marxists, the Hunchaks advocated the use of terrorism to foster the independence of the six vilayets of eastern Anatolia, traditionally known as the homeland of Armenia.[12]

The Dashnaks and Hunchaks were tiny political formations, and the vast majority of Armenians knew little or nothing of the protections afforded by the Treaty of Berlin. Still, both conservative and liberal Ottomans looked upon these Armenian initiatives with considerable suspicion. The empire's "most loyal millet" had become in their eyes the most treacherous. To Sultan Abdul Hamid II (1876–1909), known as "the Red" for his blood-thirsty disposition, the Armenians represented everything that was wrong in the Ottoman realm. They supported reform and constitutional change. They sought protection from the European powers and were closely aligned with the enemy Russians. Their business and professional elites were secular, Western, and wealthy; in Abdul Hamid's view, the Armenians had gotten rich from the sweat of simple and devout Muslim laborers and the naive support of government procurement officials. "Trouble arose," write Braude and Lewis, "when Jews or Christians were seen to be getting too much wealth or too much power and enjoying them visibly."[13] The wealthy Armenian elite, gathered in the Galata section of Constantinople, began to attract the attention of the Turkish public and resentful Ottoman officials. Most important, the Armenians had broken the informal social contract of the Ottoman realm by crossing the boundaries of the millet system, and as a result they had given up their rights to protection from the Islamic state. From the Sultan's viewpoint, punishment was the only legitimate answer to the Armenians' transgressions.[14]

In the summer of 1894 the Armenian highlanders in the Sassoun region refused to pay the double taxation imposed by the Ottoman government and the local Kurdish chieftains. Hunchak agitators sought to turn the tax revolt into a national Armenian uprising. While armed resistance sporadically appeared, no serious rebellion took place. Nevertheless, Abdul Hamid unleashed his irregular troops, the so-called Hamidians, on the Sassoun Armenians, and a terrible slaughter ensued.[15] The Armenians turned for protection to the European powers, insisting that the provisions of the Treaty of Berlin be guaranteed by granting limited autonomy to the six Armenian vilayets. The temerity of the Armenians was too much for the irate Sultan, who instigated a campaign of terror against the Armenian population. Violent massacres took place in Trabzon on the Pontic coast in October 1895 and quickly spread to the highlands.

These bloody pogroms of 1894–1896 were far more deadly and destructive than the pogroms against Jews in Imperial Russia. But they shared several important characteristics with their tsarist counterparts. First, these urban riots and ethnic clashes were fed by intercommunal tensions but also by class resentments, religious antagonisms, and economic frustration. Equally important, the signals for the attacks in both cases came from their respective governments, and the police let the violence continue until ordered by the government to end the mayhem. The perpetrators were sometimes arrested but then later let go or only lightly punished. In the end, some 200,000 Armenians were killed or wounded.

Despite the terrible death toll of the Armenian massacres of 1894–1896 and the role of government in provoking them, they do not qualify as genocide, as the events of 1915 later would. The goal was severe punishment, not extermination. Nor do the events of 1894–96 share the general characteristics of ethnic cleansing; no attempt was made to remove the Armenians from their homes or to deport them. Richard Hovannisian notes that the massacres of 1894–1896 were intended to keep the Armenians "in their place," whereas in 1915 the Young Turk triumvirate looked "to create a frame of reference that did not include the Armenians at all."[16] In his work on the German wars of colonial pacification in southwest and east Africa at the turn of the century, Trutz von Trotha distinguishes between a "limited war of pacification" and a "genocidal war of pacification."[17] The massacres of 1894–1896 clearly belong to the former category. The violence could be compared to the actions of "punishment expeditions," whose intention was to reinvigorate domination and ensure control, while punishing for ostensible disloyalty. Unlike genocidal schemes, the victims who were able could escape and return; the violence reached a peak and then ebbed, leaving large portions of the victim community unscathed.

Von Trotha makes the relevant point in the case of the Armenians that massacres often entail the dehumanization of victims rather than the other way around, as is usually propounded in theories of genocide. "The massacre is a form of collective dehumanization," he writes.[18] In other words, that the Armenians were "slaughtered like sheep" in 1894–1896, as so often mentioned by observers, fostered the Ottoman indifference to their suffering and death in later massacres and, eventually, in the ultimate dehumanization and mass murder of the Armenian genocide of 1915.

Periodic massacres of Armenians continued until the outbreak of World War I in the region. The 1909 massacre in the province of Adana was by far the worst: 15,000–20,000 Armenians were slaughtered.[19] A mutiny of Islamic fundamentalists in the capital—"The *Seriat* is in danger, we want the *Seriat!*" was their battle cry—was supported by Hamidian officials in the provinces.[20] The situation in Adana was complicated by thousands of hungry and homeless migrant workers, some of whom were Armenians but most of whom were Muslim Turks and Kurds. The Adana tragedy started with tales of Armenian "atrocities"; a young Armenian man had shot and killed two Turkish ne'er-do-wells who had reportedly sexually molested both him and his wife. When Armenians defended themselves with weapons, as in this case, rumors abounded among Muslims that the takeover of Adana by armed and vengeful Armenian bandits was at hand. The first killing of Armenians started in the Adana marketplace on April 14, and word quickly spread to the migrant communities outside of town, where the Armenians had fewer places to hide. With the police standing aside, the Armenians had no chance. Even worse, the units of the Turkish army that arrived to restore order participated in the killing and plundering before the fury was spent.[21]

The Young Turk Movement

The Ottoman attacks on the Armenians occurred within an empire that teetered on the edge of extinction. If it had simply collapsed under its own weight, as had the Habsburg monarchy or the Russian Empire (with a considerable nudge from the Bolsheviks), the Armenians might well have escaped the finality of genocide. Ironically, it was the Young Turks' efforts to reform and reinvigorate the empire that tragically ended Armenian existence in Anatolia. The Young Turks at the forefront of national revival came primarily from the ranks of progressive junior officers in the army and medical corps in European Salonika and Monastyr; they were educated professionals dedicated to modernization and constitutional government. Their political base, the Committee of Union and Progress (Ittihad ve Terakki) was founded at Constantinople's Military Medical School in 1889 as a secret society dedicated to democratic principles. Before coming to power, the party focused primarily on restoring the constitution and replacing the theocratic and reactionary government of Abdul Hamid II.

The Ittihadists sought and found allies among their Armenian counterparts, especially among the Dashnaks. The Armenian radicals supported the Young Turks when they seized power in 1908 and came to their defense against counterrevolutionary movements in 1909. The Young Turks even armed the Armenians so that they could participate in the struggle against the Islamic conservatives for a new Ottoman constitution. Both groups rejoiced when the counterrevolution was defeated and Abdul Hamid was deposed in April 1909 and replaced by his more pliable brother, Mehmed Reshad. But once the sultan was overthrown and the constitution restored, the Ittihad leadership concentrated on the problem of maintaining its power and mobilizing the resources of the state. At no time were the Young Turks interested in the autonomy, much less independence, of the Armenian vilayets. From their point of view, there was no "Armenian question" in the Ottoman Empire; "general reforms in Turkey" would settle all nationality issues.[22]

Most importantly, the Young Turks were influenced by a new generation of Turkish nationalists, who, like other modern nationalists across Europe at the end of the nineteenth and beginning of the twentieth century, extolled the inherent virtues of their own folk, in this case the sturdy Turkish peasant. Ziya Gökalp, the movement's leading ideologist and member of the party's Central Committee from 1908 to 1918, denounced the precepts of Ottomanism—equal attention to the needs of all Ottoman citizens—and substituted a version of Pan-Turanism that called for the union of all Turks, from Anatolia through Central Asia, in an empire recalling Ghengis Khan and Tamerlane. "The lands of the enemy shall be devastated," declares one of his most famous poems at the beginning of World War I. "Turkey shall become Turan."[23] Gökalp's vision had little to do with Islam, for the nation had become his religion.[24] Ismail Gasprinskii and Yusuf Akcura, Turkic intellectuals from the Crimea, supported Gökalp's call for the development of a pan-Turkish movement, as did other so-called Outside Turks from the Russian Empire.[25] Before the Young Turks, few members of the Ottoman elite even thought of themselves as Turks. Now, Gökalp and his Ittihad comrades increasingly talked about the great "Turkish race," whose military prowess had conquered and ruled over vast territories in Asia and Europe.

Despite the critical influence of Turkish nationalism on their thinking, the Young Turks' ideology remained eclectic and fluid. It combined justifications for the maintenance of the traditional multinational empire ruled by an Islamic elite with a new dedication to Turkish nationalism.[26] It meshed Ottomanism with Pan-Islamism and Pan-Turanism.[27] Each of the members of the ruling Young Turk triumvirate—Djemal (Cemal) Pasha, Enver Pasha, and Talat Pasha—expressed somewhat different perspectives on their ideas. Djemal Pasha wrote in his memoirs of his ongoing dedication to Ottomanism: "Speaking for myself, I am primarily an Ottoman, but I do not forget that I am a

Turk, and nothing can shake my belief that the Turkish race is the foundation stone of the Ottoman Empire."[28] Enver Pasha was more attuned to the needs of the Outside Turks and never lost his dedication to Pan-Turanism. Talat was much more pragmatic and interested in secular modernization. He best fits Caglar Keyder's characterization of the Ittihadists as committed to turning the empire into "a 'Japan of the Near East,' secular and with universal legal norms and citizenship."[29] The final step in the growth of Turkish nationalism—which entailed the rejection of Pan-Turanism, Pan-Islamism, and Ottomanism, and the glorification of the Anatolian homeland and its Turkish inhabitants— came only with the ascension to power of Mustafa Kemal (Atatürk) in 1923.

Turkish nationalism—when combined with concessions to the still powerful Islamic elites—could be used by the Ittihad to isolate enemies on both the left and right. The ongoing challenges to the Ottoman domination of the Balkans, most notably the Austro-Hungarian occupation of Bosnia-Herzegovina in 1908, the Albanian rebellion of 1911–12, and the Balkan Wars of 1912–13, only fed the nationalism of the Ittihadists and their followers. Faced with these challenges to the integrity of the Ottoman lands, the Young Turk triumvirate quickly buried the liberal Ottoman tenet of equal rights for all citizens of any nationality and insisted on the domination of Turks in the Ottoman state and society. In the period between 1908 and the outbreak of World War I, this meant the mandatory teaching of Ottoman Turkish in all schools and the promotion of Ottoman Turkish values, including Islam and its institutions.[30] Especially after the coup of 1913, which returned the ultranationalist wing of the Ittihad to power, the Young Turks' nationalism and Pan-Turanism led them to promote active ties with Turkic allies in the east for the ongoing struggle with the Russians and their Christian allies, including the Armenians.[31]

Like the Bolsheviks in Russia and the Nazis in Germany, the Ittihadists not only were interested in achieving power and articulating an ideology to mobilize society but also were eager to build and maintain their control over the party and the state. As a result, they paid great attention to organizational questions, expanding the Ittihad's branches throughout the empire and to all the major cities and towns in Anatolia proper, where they initially had been weakest. The triumvirate wielded power through a twelve-man Central Committee, which was responsible for the eventual decision to deport the Armenians.[32] By the outbreak of World War I, the Ittihadists also controlled the most important positions in the state. Enver Pasha was Minister of War and primarily responsible for government's pro-German stance. He married an Ottoman princess, linking the Ittihad to the ruling Ottoman dynasty. Talat Pasha, as Minister of Interior, controlled the gendarmerie and police operations throughout the empire. A clever and dangerous man, he, more than any other single Ottoman official, was responsible for the Armenian genocide. Djemal Pasha, Minister of the Marine, served as a trouble-shooter for the leadership; his contributions included ruthlessly suppressing the 1909 counterrevolution, serving as governor of Constantinople, and, after the war, dealing with problems in the south as governor of Syria.

The Armenian Catastrophe

The immediate background of the genocide can be traced to Turkish and Armenian reactions to the loss of Ottoman lands in the Balkan Wars of 1912–13. Virtually the entire Christian population of the Balkans had opposed Ottoman rule, and this fact aggravated the nationalist inclinations of the Ittihadists and thoroughly discredited in their minds the ideas of multinational Ottomanism. The wars in the Balkans and the expulsion of hundreds of thousands of Muslims to the Ottoman Empire produced deep bitterness and anger among the Young Turks. The largest Christian peoples of Anatolia—the Greeks and the Armenians—were looked upon as potential traitors and deserters. The Anatolian Greeks were seen as supporting the anti-Muslim activities of the Greek government, while the Armenians were suspected of collusion with the Russians.[33] By the beginning of 1914, Ittihadist leaders developed plans for cleansing western Anatolia of the strategically located Greek population. The Armenian population, located mostly on the eastern boundary near the Turks' potential enemy, the Russian Empire, also attracted the Ittihadists' attention.

Using the Ministry of War as their base, the Ittihadists created the so-called Secret Organization (Teskilat-i Mahsusa) for the purpose of dealing with special security problems in the empire. Taking its orders from the party leadership but absorbed in the government structure, the Secret Organization was charged with carrying out the forced deportation of the Greeks from the Aegean littoral and Thrace on the eve of the First World War. With brutal efficiency, the Turks deported some 150,000 Greeks from the coast to Greece and the islands and, at the very least, another 50,000 to the interior of Anatolia, a process which continued into 1915 and 1916, and, by the end, took many thousands of Greek lives.[34] But the deportations of the Greeks on the eve of the war was merely prologue to the fate of the Armenians. With its headquarters in Erzurum in eastern Anatolia, the Secret Organization, headed by Dr. Bahaeddin Sakir, was charged with building Turkish networks in the Caucasus beyond the empire's eastern borders even before the Ottomans' official entry into World War I. Taking cadres primarily from the ranks of prison inmates and bandits amnestied for the purpose, Sakir formed hundreds of small armed bands, roughly 12,000 men altogether, which attacked Armenian villages in the Caucasus and secured Turkish strongholds on both sides of the eastern border.[35]

The Armenians were also active in this period. Backed by the Russians, they looked to secure the minority rights guaranteed them by the Treaty of Berlin. As a result, the great powers forced "The Armenian Reform Agreement" of February 8, 1914, on the Ottoman government. Its articles compelled the Turks to accept the presence of international inspectors in Ottoman territory, whose job was to guarantee fair treatment for the Armenians.[36] The Ittihadists were furious about the arrangement. They considered the Armenian initiative an act of betrayal, the presence of foreign inspectors a blight on their personal honor, and the successful pressure of the great powers just another example of the pernicious effects of the Capitulations on Ottoman sovereignty. They were worried that great power protection of Armenian reforms might well mean the creation of an autonomous Armenian region in the six vilayets, a sure step, they feared, to the dismemberment of their Anatolian lands.[37] One of the first acts of the Ittihadist government after joining the Central Powers in World War I in November 1914 was to renounce the February 8 agreement. On September 5, 1916, the Ottoman government also formally abrogated the Capitulations, bringing to an end any internationally sanctioned outside interference in its internal affairs.

The genocide was planned within this dangerous vortex of Ittihadist nationalism, resentment against the Armenians, and mobilization for war. No single order, or single meeting, or single action initiated the events. Much as in the case of the Holocaust, orders from the top are hard to find and substantiate; precise dates for the beginning of the genocide and unambiguous initiatives that prompted it are difficult to document. The initial successful Turkish campaign in the east against the Russians was accompanied by Secret Organization attacks on Armenians. But the victorious Russian counterattack in the winter of 1914–

15 drove the Turks out of Kars and Ardahan and punctured the Pan-Turkic dreams of the Ittihad leadership. Although Armenians had fought loyally in the Ottoman Army, the Ittihadists focused on the fact that Armenian volunteers also fought with the Russians and that many Armenians in Anatolia sympathized with their cause. Anatolia was the last bastion of Ottoman power; and in March 1915 the Ittihadists decided to deport the Armenians.[38] As Talat later explained to an Ittihad party congress, "It was deemed necessary, in order to avoid the possibility of our army being caught between two fires, to remove the Armenians [from] all scenes of the war and the neighborhood of the railways."[39] In the month before, Enver Pasha had ordered that Armenians be removed from their units, disarmed, and placed in labor battalions. In March the gendarmes and units of the Secret Organization received orders to disarm the Armenian population as a whole. Christopher Walker describes the situation succinctly: "The war provided a thick black velvet arras, behind which the Young Turks could act with impunity."[40]

The extreme cruelty and brutality of the Armenian disarmament was a harbinger of worse to come. Policemen went door to door, harassing the Armenians, arresting them if they did not turn over weapons, threatening them in order to get names of neighbors who concealed firearms. "The whip and the club are in constant use by the police," wrote William S. Dodd, an American doctor in Konya, to the American Ambassador Henry Morgenthau, "and that upon women and children too." The poor as well as the "cultivated and refined" are "driven around in this way like dogs by brutes. I have seen women black and blue from the beating they have received."[41] Sometimes, the men were led off to prison, where they were tortured. Some were beaten to death. Armenians frantically tried to buy weapons in order to have something to turn over to the authorities. The deportations and killings began in some places even before the Ittihad-dominated cabinet hurriedly passed the formal order to deport the Armenians on May 27.

When the sizable Armenian population of the eastern Anatolian city of Van received orders in mid-April 1915 to turn over their weapons to the authorities, the community leaders had heard enough from the surrounding region to know that compliance almost guaranteed a massacre. They organized their own defenses, isolated the Turkish garrison, and hoped for a renewed Russian offensive that would save them from Ittihadist reprisals. The heroic uprising in Van quickly became known all over Europe and Anatolia. Citing Armenian perfidy, the Ottoman officials arrested and deported 235 of the leading Armenian citizens of Constantinople on April 24, the day now used by the Armenians to commemorate the genocide. The number of deportees from the capital eventually reached ten times that many, most of whom later died in exile.[42] The uprising in Van was subsequently crushed by artillery barrages from German-led Turkish units, but by that time the Ittihadist fury knew no limits. In May 1915 the general order to deport the Armenians from their homes to the deserts of Mesopotamia beyond the Euphrates was telegraphed or conveyed by word of mouth to government officials throughout eastern Anatolia. In the early and midsummer, similar orders were communicated to central and western Anatolian vilayets, as well as to Thrace. The Ottoman Empire had traditionally employed the mandatory transfer of both Christian and Muslim peoples, the practice of *sürgün,* to populate strategic areas of the country as well as to punish selected communities.[43] But this had occurred neither on the scale of the 1915 deportations nor with the genocidal results.

The specifics of the deportations varied from region to region, city to city, village to village. However, the general pattern suggested a centrally directed plan. First came the campaign to disarm the population; then the arrests and imprisonment of the leading citizens of the community—the church prelates, the leading businessmen, the doctors and merchants. Few escaped the violence; large numbers of men were beaten and tortured in the process of imprisonment. Every sort of cruelty was inflicted on the hapless internees; one that is often mentioned by observers was the "shoeing" of the victims with horseshoes. Another was the bastinado, the relentless beating of the soles of the feet, a torture commonly associated with the Spanish Inquisition.[44] After weeks of torture and persecution, the desperate prisoners, hungry and exhausted, were bound together, sometimes in pairs, sometimes in fours and fives, and driven off into exile, guarded by gendarmes and Secret Organization bands. They seldom got very far before they were shot or hacked to death.[45] Sometimes it was the gendarmes who murdered them in a series of mass executions. Kurdish tribes were also invited to do the deed in exchange for the victims' clothes and remaining valuables. Units from the Secret Organization took over when the gendarmes did not have the stomach to finish the job.

With most of the men under arrest, in prison, or already on a march to their deaths, the remaining Armenian women, children, and old folks lived, in the words of the Reverend Henry H. Riggs, a American missionary in Kharput (Marmuret-ul-Aziz), in a "pitiable state of terror."[46]

The orders for their deportation came with little warning, and they were given from a few hours to four or five days to ready themselves, sell their worldly goods, gather up food and animals, and get on their way. Those who knew nothing about the fate of the deportees worked feverishly to sell what was necessary in order to outfit themselves properly for the trek. They were mercilessly exploited by the local Muslim populations, but they had no choice except to sell everything they could for next to nothing. Toward the end, according to Dr. Dodd, buying "degenerated into robbing, right and left."[47] Wealthier families procured drivers and carriages and hired pack animals and drovers. But these hirelings, having received their wages, often left the Armenians after a few days on the road. Many Armenian families already knew a lot about the deportations and suspected the worst. They had seen the plight of exiles from the north and east as they trudged through their towns and villages. The Armenians did everything they could to save themselves and their children through bribery and escape, usually with little success. A few of the younger women and girls offered themselves as wives or concubines to local Muslims. But other girls, in order to avoid being forced into the harems, marked and charcoaled their faces, cut their hair, and covered themselves as Muslim women.[48] As conditions worsened on the road, however, larger numbers of girls and women sought this avenue of escape. The Reverend Riggs wrote that "some of the girls who thus entered Turkish families were treated fairly kindly and seemed to adapt themselves to the unnatural life. But others suffered indescribably, and some lost their minds."[49]

For all the differences in the way the Armenians embarked on their forced marches across the Anatolian plateau to the deserts in the south, they endured very similar travails. Some Armenians were initially transported by rail, crowded into boxcars and cattle cars along the Berlin-Baghdad railway and its feeder systems. Men and boys sometimes rode on the tops of the cars. A platform was often constructed half way up the freight cars to allow for twice as many riders. The crush of humanity was deadly to many. The cars were rarely opened until they got to the end of the line, where the hungry and thirsty survivors disembarked to a holding camp, before proceeding on foot for the rest of their journey. Each car, noted one observer, seemed like another "Black Hole of Calcutta," full of diseased and starving people.[50] The rail transport was so awful that mothers routinely threw their children from the trains, in the hopes that they could "save them from further misery," to use the words of Dr. Dodd.[51] At Konya, the major transfer point between transportation by rail and the treks to the south, tens of thousands of Armenians camped out in open fields in the most squalid circumstances. Dodd visited the encampment and described hellish scenes of death and dying among nearly 45,000 diseased, ill-clothed, and malnourished men, women, and children: "Around the encampment, I saw men and women lying in ditches half-filled with mud and water gasping out their last breath, some conscious and some unconscious."[52] The Turkish guards surrounding the transit point wore sponges over their noses, to deal with the terrible stench that came from the sick and dying mass of humanity.

Those who went by rail were the lucky ones. Most Armenians were driven across Anatolia like cattle, suffering heat and sunstroke during the day and fierce, cold winds at night. Sometimes, the routes they took were so indirect and roundabout that the purpose seemed to be nothing other than the death of the marchers.[53] Isabel Harley described one pitiable group of Armenians marching through the outskirts of Kharput on their way to the south: "Tired, sick, hungry, beaten, dirty, vermin-infested, frightened, hunted, broken-hearted creatures they were pushed on the next day . . . not knowing where they were going nor when the end would come. It was the plan of the government to keep this up until the last had dropped."[54] The marchers were whipped and prodded like livestock along the way. They were given neither sufficient food nor water, even when it was readily available. One can only conclude that the authorities made no provision for their survival and were not interested in that outcome. Stories of guards selling access to river water are so common that it is hard not to accept their veracity. No tents were provided for the exiles; their only shelter was the lean-tos they could construct themselves from pieces of rugs and aprons. They were not allowed to stay in way stations and were kept isolated from local Muslim populations who might have taken pity on them and provided alms and relief.

The death toll from hunger, exhaustion, and disease spiraled upward, and yet the guards would not allow any rest or time for recuperation. Stragglers too weak to go on were simply shot or left by the side of the road to die. Elisabeth Webb described a group of women staggering along the road outside of Adana: "All were in rags and filthy beyond description. Their skin was burned and dried to the color of a mummy, very many were nearly blind as a result of the hunger, and most seemed dazed or mentally unfit."[55] Reduced to a state of "starving animals," to use the words of the Reverend Riggs, "the Armenians could do nothing else but eat grass, bugs, and weeds." Women and children picked through the manure of their guards' animals to find kernals of barley or grains of wheat.[56] On the occasions when bread was distributed, the exiles fought like demons for every crumb.

Leslie Davis, consul in Kharput, wrote to Morgenthau about the transit of groups of Armenians from Erzurum and Erzincan on June 11, 1915: "A more pitiable sight cannot be imagined. They are almost without exception ragged, filthy, hungry, and sick. This is not surprising in view of the fact that they have been on the road for nearly two months with no change of clothing, no chance to wash, no shelter, and little to eat. I watched them one time when their food was brought. Wild animals could not be worse. They rushed upon the guards carrying the food and the guards beat them back with clubs hitting hard enough to kill sometimes. To watch them one could hardly believe that these people were human beings."[57] Observers repeatedly noted that the Armenians were reduced to an animal state as a result of the terrible hunger. They describe their "claw-like hands" and "gaunt eyes" as they fought "like ravenous dogs" for food.[58] Ruth Parmalee wrote that the Armenians' experiences seemed "to have caused their human feelings to deteriorate."[59]

Just as Goebbels later liked to report on the subhuman state of the Jewish ghetto inhabitants—filthy, disease-ridden, hungry, and crowded upon each other like insects—as a way to justify their extermination, the dehumanization of the Armenian exiles served the triumvirate's purpose of eliminating them from their Turkish Anatolian homeland. No amount of pleading from American, Swedish, or other neutral officials in Constantinople could convince the Ottoman government to allow relief agencies and missionaries to come to the aid of the deportees. The influential German ambassador in Constantinople, Hans von Wangenheim, forbade his country's missionaries from interfering in the Turkish ally's internal affairs. That the Young Turks prevented foreign missions from helping the "exiles" also leads one to the conclusion that the Armenians were slated to die.

Even in their miserable state, the Armenian women were exploited, brutalized, and raped by their guards. They were left prey to Kurdish bandits, who abducted many of the heartiest. They were stripped of their clothes and humiliated in every conceivable way. Some went mad, roaming the desert stark naked, with parched, white tongues and bodies blistered by the sun.[60] Others were butchered by their guards, their naked, mutilated bodies strewn along the road.[61] The entire scene beggared description, as so many eye-witnesses testified. But of all the heartrending suffering endured by the Armenians, perhaps none leaves a stronger impression than the awful choices faced by mothers and children. Some mothers were forced to leave dead and dying infants by the side of the road. Older children had to leave sick mothers behind in the desert. On the rare occasions when they met townspeople or missionaries, mothers desperately tried to give their children away in the hopes of saving them from their horrible fate. Sometimes, older girls—in order to save their mothers and siblings—tried to join the harems of Turkish and Kurdish men they encountered; sometimes they simply gave themselves as concubines or slaves to save themselves. By the time the survivors reached the Euphrates, many mothers were so overcome by hunger and desperation that they tossed their children into the river to drown. Sometimes they jumped in themselves, bound to their children. In other cases, the guards tied their charges together and threw them in.

Local observers estimated that 15 percent survived the marches.[62] But many who managed to cross the Euphrates and make their way to the towns of Aleppo, Dir-al-Zur, and Ras-'ul Ain in the Syrian desert were so emaciated and weak that they died soon after their arrival. Absolutely no provisions had been made for the Armenians who straggled in from the desert. They were forced to camp on town streets, begging for morsels and congregating in unhealthy areas on the edges of town, sometimes in swamps or garbage dumps, designated by the authorities. Many succumbed to diseases like typhus and typhoid despite intermittent assistance from missionaries and charitable Muslims. Outbreaks of malaria occurred frequently among the exiles, and dysentery afflicted almost all of them. Periodically, the refugees were given a new deportation order and forced back on the road to a town further to the south. Some Armenians gradually found their way to Beirut, Jerusalem, Cairo, or Baghdad, where slowly they were able to get back on their feet. Others eventually made it abroad.

Because the Armenians interpreted what had happened to them as another Ottoman "massacre," many—the Armenian patriarchate estimated over 300,000—sought to return to Anatolia once the peak of the violence had subsided.[63] To be safe, they did not return to eastern Anatolia, which in any case was the middle of a war zone. Instead, they congregated in the more accessible cities of Adana, Zeitun, or Aintab (Antep). Protestants and Catholics who had been deported also used the formal exemption order as a way to return to Anatolia. Those who had escaped into the mountains with Kurdish help gradually trickled back to their towns of origin. But often they found Turks and Kurds living in their homes and were forced to find dwellings of their own.[64] The unlucky ones were deported again, or attacked by locals; in some cases, they fled across the Russian lines.

The Question of Genocide

What we now call the Armenian genocide is difficult to write about in the same terms as we use to describe the Holocaust—the paradigmatic genocide of the twentieth century. The fierce and unremitting racial ideology of the Nazis, which impelled them to seek out and destroy every last European Jew they could get their hands on, is absent in the case of the Ittihad's attack on the Armenian nation. The Armenian communities in Constantinople and Smyrna (Izmir) were left for the most part intact, due no doubt to the presence of influential foreign observers in both cities.[65] Thousands—perhaps as many as 20,000—Armenians converted to Islam in order to avoid the fate of their brethren. These were mostly young women and girls who were taken into Turkish and Kurdish harems and converted, sometimes voluntarily, more often than not by force. Sometimes, local Muslim community leaders urged irreplaceable Armenian shopkeepers and artisans to convert—druggists and stonemasons were often considered the most valuable—promising protection from the deportations as a consequence. Similarly, some professionals—particularly engineers and army doctors—were encouraged to convert in order to save their lives.[66] Armenian orphans were sometimes taken into Muslim homes and converted—a nearly unthinkable fate for Jewish children in the Nazi case. In addition, interventions by foreign ambassadors, including German and Austrian officials, put considerable pressure on the Turks to exempt Armenian Catholics and Protestants from the deportations. To be sure, the order for exemption came too late to stay the deportation of thousands in this category. Moreover, some Turkish officials simply ignored the order, and many Armenians who converted did not have the proper documentation to avoid the fate of their co-nationals. Still, the numerous exceptions from deportation for certain groups of Armenians lends this case a character different from that of the Nazi attack on the Jews.

Armenians also fought back, won some encounters, escaped, and survived attacks at rates that were impossible for Jews in Nazi-occupied Europe. Some Armenians were able to buy protection from local Turks or Dersim Kurds, who defended them against government persecution.

In the neighborhood of 250,000 to 300,000 Armenians found their way across Russian lines in the East to Armenian territory, though many eventually died there of starvation, disease, and exposure. Others succumbed to the attacks by Mustafa Kemal's armed forces in 1918. Approximately 250,000 Armenians also survived the genocidal march across the desert. This does not include, of course, the large number of Armenians who escaped to Europe and America, an option also available in limited measure to the Jews before the outbreak of the war.

Yet some of the language of the Young Turks resembled that of Hitler and the Nazis. Hitler's famous promise in the Reichstag speech of January 30, 1939, to annihilate the Jews if they started a war has its parallels in Enver Pasha's threat to the Armenian patriarch that the Young Turks "would be compelled to use extreme measures" if the Armenians supported the Russians in the upcoming war.[67] Ambassador Morgenthau was struck by the fact that the Young Turks spoke about their determination to destroy the Armenian people "as though it were a perfectly justifiable solution."[68] In the end, the Nazi attack on the Jews was much more ferocious and complete. The Nazi ideology of extermination permeated the German state and society in ways that were impossible in the Ottoman lands ruled by the Young Turks. But attitudes at the top about the targets of attack were strikingly similar. No one took pity on the helpless victims.

But if the concept of genocide does not fit the Armenian case perfectly, the concept of ethnic cleansing, as we know it from the wars in former Yugoslavia, does not fit it as well. To be sure, the Ittihadists wanted to remove the Armenians from vast stretches of the Ottoman realm, in particular from regions in eastern Anatolia bordering on and threatened by the Russian Empire. This was the formal justification for the deportations at the time and the official argument proffered by the Turkish government in retrospect. But if the primary goal of the Ittihad was to drive the Armenians out of eastern Anatolia—which, as we shall soon see, was the goal of the Kemalist regime with the Greeks seven years later on the Aegean and Pontic coasts—why persecute, torment, torture, and kill so many hundreds of thousands in such deliberate fashion? Why deport the Armenians from areas that were not at all sensitive to the military situation of the Turks just as ferociously as they were deported from those that were?

Horrified contemporary observers of the events of 1915—foreign diplomats, local missionaries, and Armenian survivors—called the genocide a massacre. Although this made the killing understandable in the context of events going back to the massacres of 1894–1896 and beyond, there was a sense among contemporary observers that this term did not suffice. They all knew they were witnessing something terrifyingly distinct from the earlier events, and they used language such as "a massacre like none other," "a massacre that changes the meaning of the word massacre," "a massacre to end all massacres" in an effort to try to capture that difference. The Reverend Henry Riggs observed that it was not just the extent of the killings that made the "massacre" of 1915 different. This time, he wrote, there was no outbreak of "Muslim fanaticism . . . It was altogether too cold, too calculating and too efficient."[69] Dr. William S. Dodd wrote in similar fashion to Ambassador Morgenthau: "Is there no way of stopping this awful slaughter. The purpose is simply that, the utter destruction of the Armenians. Turks themselves tell us so. It is a massacre, but concealed, and in a more devilish form, more cold-blooded and calculating."[70] Dodd and Riggs were right. The Armenian "massacre" of 1915 was a form of first-degree murder, the result of directives of a ruling party, the Ittihad, and it was carried out as a consequence of the actions of the Ottoman government. The evidence for intentionality, critical in any test of genocide using the 1948 U.N. definition, is, however, not as strong and unchallengeable as the historian would like. The available archival evidence from the period of the killing itself is sparse; the historiography is relatively undeveloped and contentious, certainly when compared with that of the Nazi case;[71] and Turkish and Armenian scholars are still far apart in their evaluation of essential facts and events.[72] That Armenian national organizations on the one hand and the Turkish government on the other have become deeply involved in historiographical questions has not helped to settle disputed issues.[73] At the same time, enough evidence, direct and indirect, exists of Ittihad responsibility for organizing the killing, including the Ottoman records of the judicial investigation of Ittihadist leaders in 1918, that "genocide" seems the appropriate appellation.[74] Despite the absence of memoirs and diaries of Ottoman leaders—the kind that make the Nazi case for genocide that much easier to argue—an overwhelming amount of collateral evidence, including memoirs and diaries of American and German missionaries in the region, not to mention accounts of Armenian survivors, refers to statements of local Turkish governors that the orders for the deportations came from above.[75] There are also numerous references to the fact that Ittihad representatives came to provincial towns and cities of Anatolia to ensure that the orders of the center were followed.[76]

Ambassador Morgenthau was absolutely consistent in his analysis of Turkish intentions. In his diary, he noted that Talat told him that all of the ambassador's pleas on their behalf could not help the Armenians. "They had already disposed of three quarters of them," Talat supposedly informed him, "and the hatred is so intense that they have to finish it."[77] "It is the saddest thing I have ever read about or heard of," Morgenthau wrote to Rabbi Stephen Wise in New York, "instead of contenting themselves with punishing them [the Armenian rebels], they [the Young Turks] think they must annihilate the entire race."[78] The much-quoted conclusion of his published memoirs still strikes at the core of the issue: "When the Turkish authorities gave the orders for these deportations, they were merely giving the death warrant to a whole race; they understood this well, and, in their conversations with me, they made no particular attempt to conceal the fact."[79]

Aftershocks

As a historical event, the Armenian genocide did not have a discrete ending. Many scholars suggest, in fact, that there can be no conclusion until the Turkish government accepts responsibility for the genocide and releases all the documents relevant to its origins and course. This important issue aside, it is also the case that the Armenian genocide subsided in waves rather than at once. Even after the defeat of the Central Powers in 1918 and the flight (or arrest) of the leading Ittihadists in the same year, Armenians were not safe from attack and killing. When French troops took over the occupation of Cilicia from the British in November 1919 as part of the 1916 Sykes-Picot Secret agreement on zones of influence in Anatolia, they brought with them, along with colonial troops from Algeria and Senegal, a substantial Armenian legion. Armenians had already returned in large numbers from Syria to the towns and cities of Cilicia, and the Armenian troops saw to the restoration of Armenian properties and businesses. According to most reports, the Armenians treated the Turks none too gently, exacting revenge when they could.[80] The main problem, however, was the fact that the French were not anxious to expend the resources necessary to establish firm control over the area. Mustafa Kemal and the nationalist movement used the occupation and the restoration of the Armenian presence in the region as a call for resistance and war. With increasing frequency and success, his troops engaged the French legions. When not directly protected by French (and Armenian) troops, the Armenians were once again attacked by the Turks. The widespread massacre that was predicted when the French inevitably lost interest and withdrew in April 1921 did not occur. But many hundreds of Armenian soldiers were killed in the fighting that accompanied the French incursion and withdrawal, and thousands of civilians were massacred in Marash and Mersin during the episode.[81]

Much more dangerous for the survival of the Armenian nation was the fate of the 300,000 or so refugees who had fled beyond the eastern borders of Anatolia to Kars and Ardahan and the Caucasus beyond. After the fall of the Russian Empire in 1917, the Caucasus experienced a series of upheavals and wars that took a terrible toll on the Armenians native to the region, but especially on the refugees, many of whom still lived in transient circumstances. To make matters worse, the entire region experienced a breakdown of transportation and a shortage of food. The establishment of the short-lived independent states of Armenia and Georgia in the spring of 1918 only exacerbated the region's poverty. Armenian forces invaded eastern Anatolia, occupying for a short time Van, Erzurum, and Trabzon. In eastern Anatolia, as in Cilicia, the Armenians showed no mercy to the Turks. Turkish nationalist sources claim that Armenians massacred countless Muslims during their occupation of eastern Anatolia, and unquestionably many of the accounts are accurate.[82] In any case, the nationalist forces of Mustafa Kemal soon turned the tables on the rag-tag army of independent Armenia and in September 1920 invaded Kars and Ardahan, burning Armenian towns and villages on the way and killing as many as 60,000 Armenians, most of them refugees. The Turkish army was stopped short of the Armenian capital of Erevan by the victories of the Red Army in the region and the incorporation of Armenia into the Soviet Union. This averted, in Vahakn Dadrian's words, "the Armenian nation's all-but-certain extinction."[83]

Hunger and disease also stalked the Armenian refugees, especially those living along the border in the former Russian districts of Kars and Ardahan. Armenians suffered life-threatening hunger in Erevan and Tiflis (Tbilisi). American relief missions tried to help, but they could not get nearly enough food to the refugees under the conditions of the day. The Americans who made their way into the area were shocked by the extent of the tragedy. "The condition of all these people is horrible beyond belief," writes Abraham Tulin.[84] "I found the most distressing situation all through this country," reports Howard Heinz, "and what I saw there in the way of starvation and misery actually beggars description."[85] The Americans were stunned that widespread reports of cannibalism among the Armenians were confirmed by many sources. Heinz wrote: "Regarding the reports of cannibalism which have come out of this district [Igdir] from time to time I have been forced against my will to believe these reports to be true. I saw with my own eyes mutilated remains of corpses which had been exhumed from newly made graves and was informed by the Director of one of the Armenian orphanages that he had met a woman carrying a human arm and when asked what she was going to do with it, she replied, 'I have no other food.'"[86] This was hardly surprising given that there was no bread and "not a dog cat horse camel or any living thing in all Igdir Region."[87] The principle food was boiled grass roots, and the death toll was staggering; perhaps a quarter of a million Armenians died in 1918 and 1919 alone.[88]

On August 20, 1920, the Treaty of Sevres which the Allies imposed on the new Ottoman government called for the creation of an independent Armenia centered on the six vilayets of eastern Anatolia. Despite the decimation of the Armenian population in this region, Woodrow Wilson and Lord Curzon gave hope to the Armenians that they would at the very least be given a small independent state, whose borders would include the province of Erzurum and the Black Sea port of Trabzon.[89] But in 1923 the Treaty of Lausanne, which revised Sevres, failed to deal with the territorial aspirations of the Armenians, and the promise of an independent territory in Anatolia faded altogether. Neither Armenia nor the Armenians were even mentioned in the treaty.[90] With their numbers decimated by the genocide, disease, and starvation and their hopes for a piece of Anatolian territory dashed by the Allies, the Armenians understood that they would have to seek their future outside of Turkey.

Establishing firm figures for the number of Armenian deaths during the genocide is very difficult. Attacks on Armenians between 1915 and the conclusion of the Greco-Turkish war of 1921–22 were ongoing, and disease and starvation took a terrible toll in the same period. The issue is further complicated by the fact that no one knows how many Armenians lived in the Ottoman Empire on the eve of the genocide. The Armenian patriarchate's estimate was 2.1 million, while the Ottoman census counted only 1.3 million. Arnold Toynbee put the figure at approximately 1.6 million, 600,000 of whom escaped deportation and 600,000 of whom eventually died in the genocide.[91] The German critic of the deportations, Dr. Johannes Lepsius, estimated that as many as 1.4 million Armenians were deported, most between June 14 and

August 19 of 1915.[92] Recently, a number of Turkish historians have placed the likely number at 800,000, which makes sense if one accepts the number of 1.3 million Armenians living in the empire prior to the genocide.[93]

Reflections

The precise death toll in the Armenian genocide is less important than the fact that the Ittihadists achieved their nefarious goal of eliminating the Armenians as a serious factor in Anatolian politics and society. The Ottoman Empire was ethnically cleansed of the Armenians; the demographic and cultural links between the Armenian people and their Anatolian homeland were permanently severed. The great powers saw no hope for reversing the process. Like other cases of ethnic cleansing and genocide, the Turks sought to destroy even the historical memory of the Armenian people's Anatolian past. Armenian monuments and churches were dynamited, graveyards were plowed under and turned into fields of corn and wheat, and the Armenian quarters of cities were torn down and used for firewood and scrap, or occupied and renamed. The Armenian-American author Peter Balakian writes with some pain that Turkish history texts and guidebooks, as well as tourist information brochures and magazines, seldom mention that Armenia or Armenians ever existed in Turkey. Armenia almost never appears on Turkish historical maps.[94] In short, the Turks not only deny the genocide but obfuscate the important role that Armenians and Armenia played in the Anatolian and Ottoman past, a double white-wash of memory that violates the integrity of both Ottoman and Armenian history.

The Armenian genocide contains many elements of premodern religious persecution, pogroms, and massacres. Islamic Turks and Kurds attacked Christian Armenians because, in their view, the Armenians represented an inferior religious community which had been arrogant and disloyal. They had ostentatiously accumulated wealth and made unjustified appeals to foreign powers. The Turks did not make rigid distinctions between Armenians as a "race" (a biological nation) and Armenians as a religious group. These categories overlapped and mixed, were sometimes separated, but sometimes not. In this sense, the Ittihadists were very different from the Nazis. Race and nationality were porous categories in the Turkish mind; one could—by converting to Islam—even change one's nationality. Protestant and Catholic Armenians could be formally exempted from deportation, even if in practice local authorities made no distinction among the various Christian sects. Thousands of Armenian children were raised as Muslims and Turks, while women and girls were routinely converted, taken into harems, and married to Turkish, Kurdish, and Circassian husbands. In the period 1918–1922, some of these women and children, encouraged by the Western powers and anti-Ittihadist Ottoman officials, reconnected with their Armenian families and communities. But women seventeen and over or those married to Muslims could choose to stay with their new families, and many did. Under the French occupation, many Armenian children were turned over by Turkish families to the Armenian community, but, wrote one American officer, "many of them want to go back."[95]

On the eve of its demise, the Ottoman Empire's development was highly uneven. Though falling far short of being a modern state, the empire and its ruling elite, the Ittihadists, espoused an ideology of what James Scott has called "high modernism," borrowing heavily from German militarist notions and indulging in dreams of a technocratically developed Turkish Anatolia. Building railroads and highways was part of this dream, as was equipping and training a modern army and navy. They believed in modernizing the state apparatus and improving its ability to deliver educational and health services to the people. The modern Turkey of Mustafa Kemal emerged directly from seeds planted by modern Ittihadist professionals: doctors, military leaders, technical specialists, and engineers. Those who directed the attack on the Armenians were a far cry from reactionary Muslim fundamentalists; they considered themselves to be architects of a new, modern, Turkified Ottoman nation, one with no room for people—like the Armenians—who represented pluralism, heterogeneity, disharmony, and therefore treachery.

The Greeks

The situation of the Greeks in the Ottoman Empire was similar to and in some ways different from that of the Armenians. Both peoples had inhabited parts of Anatolia long before the Turks arrived in the eleventh century. Both belonged to eastern Christian religions. The population size of the two groups outside of Constantinople was roughly the same, 1.2 to 1.5 million. (In the Ottoman censuses, Greeks were more numerous because of large populations in Thrace before the Balkan Wars and in Constantinople.) Greek commercial centers on the Aegean and

Pontic coasts rivaled Armenian ports in Cilicia for their vibrancy and contribution to the Ottoman economy. The Greek Orthodox millet was organized much as the Armenian millet was; its ties to the region's rich Byzantine past gave the Greeks a sense of permanence and continuity similar to what the Armenians felt about their traditional homeland in eastern Anatolia.

But the major difference between the Anatolian Greeks and the Armenians was the existence of an independent Greek state in the Peloponnese, which, for all its weaknesses, enjoyed the support and aid of the European powers. The Armenians were something of an afterthought for the Europeans. Even Imperial Russia, the Ottomans' sworn enemy, only very late in its history showed much interest in the Armenians' fate. Consequently, the Ittihadists had to be much more careful in their dealings with the Greeks than with the Armenians, for fear of provoking foreign intervention. But their attitudes toward the two peoples were essentially similar. A new Turkified Ottoman state that sought ties with Turkish and Islamic states to the east had no room for a large, alien, potentially traitorous Christian population, whether Armenian or Greek. On the eve of the First World War, it was the Armenians' sympathies for and ties with the Russians that endangered their people. In the case of the Greeks, their concentration on the Aegean littoral, with its links to expansionist and pro-British Greece, intensified the Ittihadists' determination to deal with the Greek problem. Following upon what Joseph Schechtman calls "the first interstate treaty on the [voluntary] exchange of populations in modern history" between the Ottoman Empire and Bulgaria in November 1913, the Young Turks initiated negotiations with the Greek government to exchange "voluntarily" Greeks from the Aegean coast for Turks under Greek rule.[96] But the outbreak of World War I prevented the implementation of the agreement.

Instead, the Young Turk leadership simply deported hundreds of thousands of Greeks from their homes on the Aegean littoral and in Thrace to the Anatolian plateau, the islands, and Cilicia. There, they were put to work as agricultural laborers and field hands, initially to replace the Turkish peasants inducted into the army and then, after 1915, to fill the severe labor shortage exacerbated by the deportation of the Armenians. Like the Armenians, the Greeks were also inducted into army labor battalions, where they did the back-breaking work of carrying and transporting war materials when other means of transport, including pack animals, were not available. Not all Greeks were deported, and those who were, unlike the Armenians, were not marked for elimination. But the Greek population nevertheless suffered terribly from the forced deportation, resettlement, and harsh conditions of life and labor. Many thousands died in the process. In an interview with the journalist Dr. E. J. Dillon, Talat admitted that "the cleansure" of "the Hellenes from the coast opposite the islands" was deliberately undertaken for the purposes of destroying the Greeks' ability to effect the outcome of a future conflict.[97]

The Greek Occupation

In 1918 the brief incursions of units from the new Armenian state in eastern Anatolia paralleled the decision of the Greek government of Eleutherios Venizelos to establish a zone of occupation in the crumbling Ottoman Empire. In the Greek case, however, the army was strong and unified and backed by the victorious British armed forces. Moreover, Venizelos was considered "the country's greatest political figure in modern times" and had the ability to force the reluctant King Constantine I to support his expansionist aims.[98] At the end of December 1918, the Greek destroyer *Lion* disembarked a detachment of Greek marines in Smyrna.[99] By May 1919 the Greeks had established a formal occupation over the Aegean littoral of Anatolia and its hinterlands. By all accounts, the Greek occupation administration was harsh and difficult for the Turks, arousing the animosity of the local Turkish population and provoking the nationalist movement in central Anatolia to gather strength.[100] Admiral Mark Bristol, the American High Commissioner in Constantinople, wrote to the American Consul in Smyrna: "The Greeks have been better able to stand the Turkish rule than the Turks have been able to stand the Greek rule. From time to time the Turks commit the most horrible crimes against the Greeks, but during most of the time they were pretty easy to get along with. The Hellene is persistent in his oppressions of a petty nature which, in the end, are more effective than the brutal methods of the Turk. The Hellene causes voluntary deportations; whereas the Turk does it violently, forcefully and with massacres."[101]

If matters had rested there, the eventual expulsion of the Greeks from Anatolia might not have been so violent. But Venizelos, the Greek King Constantine, and the Greek army leadership let the relatively easy occupation of Smyrna and its environs go to their heads. They viewed the collapse of the Ottoman Empire as an opportunity to pursue the "Megali Idea," the creation of a Greater Greece by the union of Hellenic with Anatolian Greek lands and the return to Greece of the Byzantine capital of Constantinople. In pursuit of these goals, in early July 1921 the Greek expeditionary force struck eastward and northward from their haven on the Aegean coast, seeking to drive the new nationalist Turkish government under Mustafa Kemal from its new capital of Angora (Ankara). Facing mostly irregular Turkish troops, the Greeks advanced quickly, reaching the Sakarya River, only 40 miles from Angora, by August. There the Greek attack stalled; both sides dug in; and the Greeks proceeded to secure their newly won territories by burning out Turkish villages and visiting upon the Turks some of the ghastly tortures the Anatolian Greeks had endured during their deportation before the First World War.

Many Greeks in the region had been confined in refugee camps on the island of Mytilene (Lesbos). Others had endured terrible conditions in labor battalions in Anatolia. The linkages between episodes of ethnic cleansing are particularly salient in this case, since many of the attacks endured by the Greeks in the region on the eve of World War I were carried out by Turks who had been driven from their homes in the Balkans during the wars of 1912–1913. In a report to the British parliament by a commission investigating Greek occupation policies in the Ismit Peninsula, the center of the terrible earthquake of August 1999, the verdict on Greek behavior during the offensive of 1921 was damning in the extreme. The commissioners wrote of "the burning and looting of Turkish villages" and the explosion of violence of Greeks and Armenians against the Turks. At the same time, the commissioners noted that the depredations seemed to take place by design: "There is a systematic plan of destruction and extinction of the Moslem population. This plan is being carried out by Greek and Armenian hands, which appear to operate under Greek instruction and sometimes even with the assistance of detachments of regular troops."[102]

Arnold Toynbee, who reported extensively on his travels through Greek-occupied Anatolia, was so shocked and dismayed by the atrocities committed by the Greeks against the Turks that he undertook virtually a one-man campaign to bring them to the attention of the world. His observations of the attack in the summer of 1921 are some of the most trenchant in the literature on the violence of ethnic cleansing. With one side armed and the other not, with one side holding all the power over life and death and the other possessing only the terror of complete uncertainty, a vicious and deadly game of cat and mouse was played out, according to Toynbee, in which the victimizer seemed to enjoy the agonies of his prey, delaying the final kill until the full measure of terror had been extracted from the helpless victim. "My strongest impression during this horrible experience," he wrote, "was of something inhuman in the blood instincts of the hunter and in the terror of the hunted."[103]

The Turkish Counterattack

The Greek advance into Anatolia fed the fires of the nationalist movement, which had been gaining momentum since Mustafa Kemal's historic landing at Samsun in May 1919. After setting up the headquarters of the Third Army in Erzurum, Kemal established the so-called National Pact, which served as the basis for the new nationalist movement in Turkey. In Sivas in September 1919, the Kemalists held their first congress, where they outlined their program of Turkism, centralism, and independence. Kemal was a wily politician as well as an able military leader. For the moment he concealed his goals of overthrowing the sultanate and undermining the theocratic principles of the state. As a result, he remained formally subordinate to the Ottoman government and army in Constantinople. But the domination of the capital by foreign powers, the invasion of Cilicia by French and Armenian units, and now the widespread reports of Greek atrocities against Turks in the West provided Kemal with all the ammunition he needed to lead a national resurgence.

In August and September 1921, Kemal initiated a carefully designed counterattack on the Sakarya against the Greek army, which turned the tide of battle and precipitated the full-scale flight of the Greeks back to the Aegean. By all accounts, the Greek retreat was even more devastating for the local population than the occupation. The Greek high command was replaced in the middle of the retreat, causing panic and rebellion among the troops. Both Turkish and Greek villages were set on fire, and atrocities were committed against the remaining Turkish population.[104] Greek refugees fled by the hundreds of thousands for the coast and Smyrna, terrified of Turkish retribution and homeless as a result of Greek incendiarism. An American intelligence officer interviewed some of the thousands of Anatolian Greek refugees camped out at the railway station in Smyrna. "They all had the same story to tell and were even eloquently profane on the subject of the Hellen[ic] Greeks. Each group stated that they were ordered out of their homes by the Metropolitan of the village or by the Greek military commander. That as soon as they were clear of the villages, it was burned . . . They couldn't go back to the Turks after having thrown them over for their Hellen[ic] cousins."[105]

The Greek refugees understood their problem perfectly; the Turks would and did use the opportunity of their advance to the Aegean to rid western Anatolia of the native Greek inhabitants. The Hellenic Greek armies had performed much of the work for them in burning and destroying Greek homes and property. At the same time, Mustafa Kemal's National Pact went one step further than the Ittihad in declaring Anatolia the homeland of the Turkish people, most emphatically not of the Greeks or Armenians. The Turkish counterattack, then, had all the characteristics of ethnic cleansing. The remaining Greeks were driven out or killed. There was a good deal of pillaging and rape, as the armies—and the accompanying Turkish bands of paramilitary chettes—cleaned out the towns and cities of western Anatolia. Some Greek prisoners of war survived the assault, were captured by regular army troops, and were sent to camps in the interior. The rest of the Greek population either fled in terror or were killed by chettes.

The scene after the Turkish takeover was bleak. Lieutenant Perry of the *U.S.S. Edsall* visited the interior and reported back to his superiors: "All cities except Menem practically destroyed by burning. There are many stories of robbing, looting, rapine and pillaging by the retreating Greek army . . . Country absolutely desolate and all shelter and food has been destroyed . . . Mosques were particularly objects of destruction. Harvested crops were destroyed by fire . . . The fields are filled with thousands of people searching for food."[106]

The Smyrna Catastrophe

Greek army units and civilians fled in terror before the Turkish assault. The roads into Smyrna—the great seaport on the Aegean—were crowded with retreating soldiers (often without officers in sight), artillery pieces, camels, women and children, old folks, and two-wheeled carts overloaded with household goods. Between the time the last units of the Greek Army departed Smyrna on September 3, 1922, and the first Turkish cavalry forces arrived on September 9, the city was in a state of panic. Tens of thousands of refugees crowded into public buildings, schools, churches, granaries, and warehouses. Foreign missions overflowed with their own nationals and naturalized citizens. Rumors that the Greek army would burn the city before leaving, as they had burned so much else in western Anatolia, caused throngs of refugees to crowd onto the long quay of the port, hiring boats to leave if they were able but mostly camping out at a safe distance from the buildings along the shore.

Once the Greek authorities left with the army, the town became open territory for robbers, bandits, and brigands of all kinds. Turkish gangs roamed the Armenian quarter, breaking into homes, robbing and killing seemingly at will. The bazaars, wrote one observer, were "a complete wreck and seem to be considered public property."[107] Meanwhile, the substantial foreign community of Smyrna, second only to that of Constantinople in size and influence, made preparations to welcome the Turks. Just outside the harbor, a number of foreign warships pulled within range, in case they were needed to rescue their co-nationals.

When the Turks moved into Smyrna on September 9, the panic and fear among the Greek refugees reached the breaking point. The thousands of refugees packed on the quay, mostly women, children, and old men, feared they would be slaughtered. Many simply jumped into the water to try to swim to the Allied warships anchored near the harbor, or hired small boats and packed them so full that they capsized, drowning the people on board. The scene at the American consulate was typical. One hundred-fifty or so naturalized citizens were crowded inside its confines, guarded by ten sailors in uniform. Outside hundreds of refugees camped out close to the doors, hoping for safety from their very proximity to the premises. A few doors away, the local movie theater still had on its marquee in large letters the title of its last film: "Le Tango de la Mort"![108]

On the whole, the Turkish army was much more restrained and disciplined than the crowds had anticipated, though its officers made little effort to control the killing and robbery that continued in the Armenian quarter and had spread to other parts of the city. Sometimes Turkish soldiers or chettes were involved; mostly they stood aside. The result was that every morning scores of newly dead bodies appeared on the streets and in the doorways of the Armenian and Greek quarters of the city. The primary goal of the Turks in Smyrna was to remove all the Greeks. Men of military age were marched off to the interior or to Cilicia as prisoners of war. Otherwise, none of the refugees were allowed to leave Smyrna to go back to their home villages and towns. When American naval officers suggested to the commander of Smyrna's forces, Nuraddin Pasha, that the best way to relieve the growing panic and sense of doom among Smyrna's 200,000 or so refugees was to let them return to their homes, the Turkish officer's response was firm: "Get them out of Smyrna, bring ships immediately and remove them to some other country." Nuraddin Pasha added that if the Americans "had seen the utter devastation conducted by the retreating Greek army and the atrocities to which they [the Greeks] had submitted the Moslem population," they would realize "that the lives of the refugees would not be safe if returned to their homes in the interior."[109] But this was simply an excuse for ethnic cleansing; Mustafa Kemal and the nationalist movement had determined that all Greeks would be expelled from the country, not just the Greek army and administrators who had come with the Hellenic Greek occupation but also those Anatolian Greeks whose families had resided in the region for centuries.

On September 13, four days after the Turks arrived in Smyrna, the fire that everyone had expected earlier broke out in the city. Some time in the late afternoon, the blaze was set in the Armenian quarter. With the winds blowing toward the harbor and no effort made to contain its spread, the fire quickly threatened to engulf the city. Captain Hepburn, chief of staff of the U.S. Naval Squadron, reported that just after dusk he climbed to the top of the Yantis Tobacco Warehouse, the highest building near the port, and identified three lanes of the fire, two of which came from the Armenian district, the other from an area "somewhat to the left." Most critically, "the first two fires were burning fiercely and sweeping directly toward the waterfront." Captain Hepburn continued: "Returning to the street I found the stampede from the fire just beginning. All of the refugees that had been scattered through the streets or stowed away in churches and other institutions were moving toward the waterfront. Steadily augmenting this flow were those abandoning their homes in the path of the fire . . . It was now dark. The quay was already filled with tens of thousands of terrified refugees moving aimlessly between the custom house and the point, and still the steady stream of new arrivals continued until the entire waterfront seemed one solid congested mass of humanity and baggage of every description."

As night fell, Captain Hepburn worried that the fire might get so intense that the refugees would die from the overwhelming heat. "Still separated from the crowd by a few short unburned blocks, the city was a mass of flame driving directly down upon the waterfront before a stiff breeze. Mingled with the noise of the wind and flames and the crash of falling buildings were the sounds of frequent sharp reports, such as might have been made either by rifle fire or the explosion of small-arms ammunition and bombs in the burning area. High above all other sounds was the continuous wail of terror from the multitude."[110]

Lieutenant Merrill, who had been sent to Constantinople for consultations with Admiral Bristol about how to handle the Smyrna problem, arrived back in Smyrna in the early morning of September 14. His diary aboard ship documented the worsening situation in the city. "All morning the glow and then the flames of burning Smyrna could be seen. We arrived about an hour before dawn and the scene was indescribable. The entire city was ablaze and the harbor was light as day. Thousands of homeless refugees were surging back and forth on the blistering quay—panic stricken to the point of insanity. The heartrending shrieks of women and children were painful to [h]ear. In a frenzy they would throw themselves into the water—and some would reach the ship. To attempt to land a boat would have been disastrous. Several boats tried it and were immediately swamped by the mad rush of a howling mob . . . The crowds along the quay beyond the fire were so thick and tried so desperately to close in abreast the men-of-war anchorage that the masses in the stifling center could not escape except by sea. Fortunately there was a sea breeze and the quay wall never got actually hot enough to roast these unfortunate people alive, but the heat must have been terrific there to have been felt in the ship 200 yards away. To add to the confusion, the packs belonging to these refugees—consisting mostly of carpets and clothing—caught [fire], making a chain of bonfires the length of the street."[111]

To his great credit, Captain Hepburn understood immediately that "nothing short of immediate international action" could deal with the potential catastrophe looming over the Smyrna refugees. With the permission and cooperation of the Turkish authorities and the British admiral in charge of the destroyers in the harbor, Hepburn initiated the evacuation of the Greeks on the quay on the morning of September 24. The operation was far from simple, despite Hepburn's having gotten permission for Greek ships to land under the supervision of the Allied destroyers. British and American sailors tried to maintain a modicum of order on shore as tens of thousands of terrified people pushed and shoved to try to escape the fire and the Turks. On the quay, Turkish soldiers and irregulars periodically robbed their Greek charges, beating some and arresting others who resisted. There are many reports of well-behaved Turkish troops, helping old women with their bundles and trying in good conscience to maintain order among the Greeks desperate to reach the ships, which were loaded one by one on the pier. But these reports are overwhelmed by others that document gratuitous cruelty, incessant thievery, and violence. American and British intervention to protect the Greeks from the Turks did little good. The fire itself also took a terrible toll. Frustrated and terrified, some Greeks took their own lives, jumping into the water with heavy packs on their backs. Young children were trampled in the rush to break through to the ships; the elderly fainted and died.

Not just the Greeks suffered. When the fire broke out, the Turks were convinced—and remain convinced to this day—that it was set by the Armenians, either at their own initiative or at the behest of the Greek occupation authorities before they withdrew. Lieutenant Merrill was told by the Turkish authorities that they had arrested twenty-two Armenians who confessed to having belonged to a conspiracy to burn the city, but he was never able to meet with the alleged culprits.[112] That several young Armenians threw bombs and fired at Turkish soldiers as they marched into Smyrna did not help. In any case, the Armenians suffered terribly as a result of the Turkish occupation. Captain Hepburn got the impression that "every able-bodied Armenian man was hunted down and killed wherever found, even small boys from 12 to 15 years taking part in the hunt."[113]

By September 15 the fire had somewhat died down, but episodic Turkish violence kept pressure on the Allies and Greeks to remove the refugees as quickly as possible. As Lieutenant Merrill noted, Turkish interests in getting the Greeks out of Smyrna were served by keeping them in a state of terror. He even believed—as do Greek historians of the fire—that the Turks set the blaze for that reason. Unlike the Ittihadists' attack on the Armenians, Merrill did not believe the Turks wanted to massacre the Greeks. "If they did, they could have slaughtered the entire lot—hundreds of thousands, in a day. They don't care what the world says, that isn't the reason they don't massacre them, for the ones they have killed have lain for days on prominent streets for all to see. But what they have done they have terrorized the entire Christian population. The Greeks burned their homes in the interior and they took refuge in Smyrna. The Turks have burned their refuge in Smyrna so they must keep going West."[114]

Some evidence supports Merrill's view that the Turks were responsible for setting the blaze. Once the fire was burning, many observers report having seen Turkish soldiers spread kerosene around certain buildings, including the American consulate, to set them on fire. The Turkish authorities responded to these accusations by insisting that they only burned down structures as a way to prevent the fire from spreading.[115] But if this were true, it seems odd that the Turkish quarter did not burn. One is also prompted to ask why no other methods of fire-fighting were used to stop the conflagration. Still, no concrete and substantial evidence that the Turks set the fire has been found, and there are plenty of arguments why it was unnecessary and not in their interests to destroy the city. Moreover, the Greeks or Armenians had their own good reasons to start a fire, given the history of the Greek retreat from the Sakarya and the Armenian attack during the first day of the occupation.

How many Greeks and Armenians died in the fire and during the period of Smyrna's evacuation may never be accurately known. Some Greek scholars maintain that the death toll reached 125,000; more realistic estimates range in the neighborhood of 10,000 to 15,000.[116] First-hand American witnesses think that even fewer died as a direct result of the fire, roughly 2,000 to 5,000.[117]

By September 22, as one Red Cross observer noted, the fire was completely extinguished except "for the tobacco in the ruins of the Gary Tobacco warehouses, which was still smoldering."[118] The thriving entrepot of Smyrna—one of the most exciting and commercially vital cities in the Near East—had been burned to the ground. Some 150,000 to 200,000 Greeks had been evacuated,[119] and roughly 30,000 Greeks and Armenians had been transported to the interior, many of whom died or were executed on the way. The nearly 3,000-year history of the Greek presence on the Aegean coast of Anatolia came to an abrupt conclusion. Dimitri Pentzopoulos writes: "It is no exaggeration to call the year 1922 'the most calamitous in the whole of modern Hellenic history.'"[120] The Smyrna fire brought it to an end.

The Treaty of Lausanne

By driving the Greek expeditionary force out of western Anatolia and seizing Smyrna in September 1922, Mustafa Kemal took a major step toward securing the nationalist movement's domination of Anatolia. In signing the armistice of Mudanya on October 11, 1922, Kemal neutralized further Allied interference. At the beginning of November, the Grand National Assembly abolished the Ottoman sultanate, ensuring, in Kemalist rhetoric, the domination of the Turkish nation in its homeland. "Sovereignty is acquired by force, by power and by violence. It was by violence that the sons of Osman acquired the power to rule over the Turkish nation and to maintain their rule for more than six centuries. It is now the nation that revolts against these usurpers, puts them in their right place and actually carries on their sovereignty."[121] Within a year, Kemal established the new ruling party, which handily won the elections of June 1923, moved the capital to Ankara, and declared a republic. These measures, along with the abolition of the caliphate in May 1924, completed the Turkish revolution first begun by the Ittihadists. A new Turkey—modern, republican, and Turkish national—had been forged; a twentieth-century nation-state had come into being.

Along with consolidating the nationalists' power and control, Kemal's successes sealed the fate of the Greeks in Anatolia. Ethnic cleansing was already part and parcel of the expulsion of the Greek expeditionary force in August and September 1922. Greeks were not only expelled from western Anatolia and Smyrna but were moved out of towns and villages in the interior, out of Cilicia in the south, and out of the heavily Greek Pontic region along the Black Sea coast. The process of forced deportation was violent and bitter. In a familiar pattern, the Greeks were given a few hours to a few days to pack up and leave for ports on the coast, Samsun primarily but also Sinop and Trabzon, where they were to be transported to Constantinople and beyond to Greece and the islands. Underway, they were sometimes harassed and attacked by bandits, robbed, and beaten; women and girls were raped and sometimes carried off. The general lawlessness which was rife in the Pontic mountains was particularly hard on the Greeks.

When they arrived in the major port cities, usually bereft of any goods or means of supporting themselves, they were faced with few facilities for their shelter or upkeep. Missionaries tried frantically to help, but food supplies were short. Refugees camped out in churchyards and school plazas, waiting in anxious desperation for Greek ships to take them to the West. Disease was rife, especially typhus. Even in the large coastal towns, the Greeks were sometimes attacked by Turkish, Laz, and Circassian bandits and were forced to pay exorbitant prices for food and shelter from venal local authorities. As in Smyrna, the Turks did little to relieve the suffering of the refugees precisely because of the policies to evict them as soon as possible. The following observations from Trabzon of Lieutenant Gardner, a medical officer on the *U.S.S. Fox,* is typical of many similar reports on the plight of the Greeks: "The refugee situation is deplorable . . . It is evident that the Turk has no idea of aiding them other than their departure, nor has a single provision been made for their accommodation or comfort . . . That sickness is general, is shown clearly by the fact that the litters of the dead are passing through the streets, many that are ill and unable to walk are being carried on the backs of their relatives, many are huddled in filth and squalor by the roadside with evidence of extreme illness and expressions of pain on their faces and their audible groans add to the din and confusion. Many of the adults and most of the children are undernourished."[122]

Beginning in November 1922, negotiations were initiated in Lausanne to rewrite the Sevres Treaty with Turkey that would include a settlement of the minority issue. From the outset, the Turks refused to entertain proposals to create a homeland in Anatolia for the Armenians. They also insisted that no special minority rights needed to be included in the treaty. All Turkish citizens, including the Armenians, would be treated alike. As for the Greeks, the Kemalist representatives returned to the Ittihadist idea of population exchanges that had been broached on the eve of the First World War. Only this time, the Turks insisted on compulsory, versus voluntary, exchanges. During the winter of 1922–23, the wrangling continued over minority issues; meanwhile, the Greeks suffered terribly, both in the process of deportation and in the refugee camps set up on their arrival in Greece and the islands. Finally, on July 24, 1923, the Treaty of Lausanne was signed, mandating, among other measures, the compulsory population transfer of Greeks from Anatolia and Turks from Greece.

Lausanne authorized the creation of Mixed Commissions to oversee the arrangements for completing the transfer of 1.2 to 1.5 million Greeks who lived in Anatolia and 356,000 Turks, most of whom lived in Aegean Macedonia. Of the Greeks, all but 290,000 had already been driven from their homes and lived in refugee camps and shelters on the islands or in Greece proper.[123] As Greek Prime Minister Venizelos recognized, "The expulsion of the Asia Minor population has not been a consequence of the Exchange Accord, but had been already an accomplished fact—in it I merely received the consent of Turkey to move the Turkish Muslims from Greece in order to reestablish the Greek refugees."[124] Like the November 1995 Dayton Treaty concluding the war in Bosnia, the Treaty of Lausanne can hardly be considered a creative international solution to minority problems; instead, it finished the job of ethnic cleansing and legitimized the Turkish nationalists' desires to homogenize their Anatolian homeland. Lord Curzon, who had led the British delegation at the conference and fought unsuccessfully for a solution that would not uproot whole nations, criticized the obligatory exchange of Turkish and Greek populations as "a thoroughly bad and vicious solution for which the world would pay a heavy penalty for a hundred years to come." He "detested having anything to do with it."[125]

For Greeks and Turks, the "heavy penalty" was paid almost immediately. According to Stephen Ladas, "tens of thousands" of Greeks perished in the process of being driven from their homes and resettling in Greece.[126] Every stage of the transfer was fraught with danger, from the violence of Muslim bandits and the disease-ridden waiting camps on the coast to the crowded and often dangerously underprovisioned ships and boats that transferred them to Greece. The holds of these ships were sometimes so packed with refugees that people died of suffocation, starvation, and thirst before they arrived at their destinations. The Greek government and relief agencies did what they could to deal with the influx of a population almost a fourth as great as that of Greece itself. Refugee camps in Piraeus, Salonika, and on the islands suffered high rates of sickness and death as a result of a shortage of supplies, food, and medicines. Relief workers reported that forty to fifty Greeks died every day in the camps, while hundreds died in makeshift hospitals.[127] Even in mid-1924, one official noted that of the 1,250,000 refugees in Greece, half were destitute and in need of serious help.[128] The complicated provisions of Lausanne for compensation to the refugees remained unfulfilled. Only through the concerted efforts of the International Red Cross, the Greek government, and the American Relief Administration was the situation of Greek refugees stabilized by the end of the 1920s.

Complicating their perilous economic conditions, the Greek refugees from Anatolia often had serious cultural difficulties adjusting to their new homeland. Those who spoke Greek (and many did not) did so in dialects incomprehensible to the locals. Their customs and traditions were so different that serious cultural antagonisms between communities of Anatolian and Hellenic Greeks impeded their integration. Some of these antagonisms continue to this day.[129]

The situation of the Turkish refugees was little better, though it helped that their numbers were absolutely and relatively fewer.[130] Most of them had to find a way to support themselves in the devastated regions of western Anatolia from which the Greeks were driven or had fled. To make matters worse, this region had already been picked over by an earlier generation of Muslim refugees from the Balkan Wars and the First World War. The Anatolian Turks had suffered terrible deprivation during the war and were in no mood to share their meager resources with "aliens" from Macedonia. Many of these new so-called Turks were Greek speakers, knew little if any Turkish, and felt as culturally alienated from Anatolian mores as the so-called Greek refugees felt in the Peloponnese or Macedonia. In the exchange, as in the thinking of the day, religion rather than any other cultural marker served as the primary indicator of nationality. Thus many Muslim Greeks (gypsies, Slavs, and Vlachs) ended up in Anatolia, just as Greek Orthodox Turks (Circassians and Kurds) ended up in Greece. On both sides of the exchange, it took the refugees on both sides of the Aegean generations to acculturate, establish family roots, and reach a stage where they considered themselves finally to be at home.

The Nazi Attack on the Jews

On August 22, 1939, shortly before the Nazi invasion of Poland, Hitler spoke to a gathering of Wehrmacht generals and Nazi leaders in Obersalzburg. This would be the first serious test of the German army in battle, and Hitler wanted to make sure they understood that this would be a war like no other. "Our war aim," he stated, "is not to attain a particular line [in the east], but the physical destruction of the enemy." Then, according to some accounts, he added: "Who, after all, speaks today about the annihilation of the Armenians?"[1] We cannot be absolutely certain that Hitler referred to the Armenians at all on this occasion.[2] But if he did, he used the Armenian example to encourage his generals to accept the murderous work of destroying the Polish nation (not to justify the killing of Jews, as is sometimes indicated in the literature). There is no question that Hitler and the Nazi leadership were well aware of the Armenian genocide and its relatively innocuous effect on international affairs during the Great War and after. The Germans themselves had played a central role in the Young Turk administration, and a number of Wehrmacht generals had earlier served as advisors to the Ottoman forces during the war. Some German officers may even have played a role in the Armenian genocide itself.[3]

With the connivance of German military officers, a number of Young Turk leaders, indicted by the Ottoman government for the attacks against the Armenians, fled to Germany in 1918 to avoid arrest and internment. Among them was Talat Pasha, the chief architect of the genocide, who was gunned down on the streets of Berlin in 1921 by an Armenian nationalist. The jury trial of Talat's assassin ended in his acquittal, which precipitated a great uproar in the German press. Not surprisingly, Hitler and a number of leading Nazis admired the Turks for their resoluteness in ridding themselves of an alien nation.[4] But the Nazi attack on the Jews grew out of other conditions, some similar to and some different from those that fostered the Armenian genocide. These conditions included an ideology that blended extreme German nationalism, racism, and anti-Semitism; a modern state and government that initiated anti-Jewish legislation and sponsored mass murder; and World War II, which, like World War I for the Turks, provided the formal justification and cover for genocide.

The historiography of the Holocaust is vast and growing by the day. At least 100,000 books, articles, and essays have been written on the "Final Solution," and the many institutes, journals, university chairs, and documentation centers devoted to the subject suggest that plenty more will be forthcoming.[5] Fortunately for historians of twentieth-century Europe, the Holocaust has preoccupied an unusually talented group of scholars: Omer Bartov, Yehuda Bauer, Christopher Browning, Saul Friedländer, Raul Hilberg, and George Mosse, to name just a few in the English-speaking world. The reason for so much scholarly attention to this event is clear: the Holocaust has become the dominant historical metaphor of our time. The way we talk about issues as diverse as free speech, intermarriage, abortion, or intervention in the Balkans is framed in terms of the Jewish experience of the Holocaust. Especially since the early 1960s, the Holocaust has been ubiquitous in our intellectual, moral, and spiritual universe;[6] and indeed, if the lessons of the Holocaust are applied with restraint and subtlety, they can appropriately serve as signposts for action in the contemporary world.[7] While one can sympathize with Robert Hayden's frustration when ethnic cleansing in Bosnia became so quickly interpreted in terms of the Holocaust, no consideration of ethnic cleansing or genocide can be free from the images, language, and insights provided by the Nazi attack on the Jews.[8] The discourse of the Holocaust is unavoidable; the task is to apply its lessons—when appropriate—to our understanding of the past and future.

Nazi Ideology

In the Nazi world view, the Aryan—the German—occupied the position of the good, the healthy, the altruistic, and the natural. Counterposed to the German was the Jew—a sham, a fake, a cultureless Asiatic. According to German demonology, the Jew was a liar, a dissem-

bler, a sponger, and a parasite—terms used in Hitler's *Mein Kampf*—
and no amount of assimilation could alter the eternal, fundamental evil
carried in the blood of the Jewish race. Long before the Nazis reached
the decision to murder the Jews of Europe, eliminationist rhetoric filled
the pages of their newspapers and highlighted their speeches, documentary films, and leaflets. The Jews were disease-carrying lice, vermin, bed-
bugs, or fleas that had to be exterminated lest they infect the healthy
body of German society.[9] They were tumors that had to be cut out.
They were a racial tuberculosis that had to be isolated and removed.[10]
The task was a surgical and clinical one, Goebbels never tired of repeating. "One had to make incisions, to be sure very extreme ones," he
wrote in his diary on November 2, 1939. Otherwise Europe would die
of "the Jewish disease."[11]

According to Nazi ideology, the mere existence of the Jews posed a
threat of serious contagion to all healthy European nations. But by their
overt actions, Jews also directly threatened the survival of German men
and women. They seduced and impregnated innocent German girls,
thereby weakening the Aryan blood of the nation. Every German
housemaid and cook in a Jewish household was seen by the Nazis as bait
for Jewish sexual predators. Inherently immoral, Jewish men gravitated
toward pimping, pornography, and other forms of sexual deviance,
spreading syphilis and other sexually communicated diseases wherever
they went. Jewish women were no better, seducing racially pure German men into their depraved and degenerate subculture. The combination of repressed attraction, misogyny, and anti-Semitism that Nazi men
often felt toward Jewish women led to terrifying consequences later on,
as Nazi guards and camp commandants acted out their brutal sexual
fantasies on the bodies of Jewish women.[12]

In addition to its ubiquitous biological imagery, Nazi ideology comprised a set of political assumptions about the Jewish threat. According
to this line of argument, the Jewish race had done everything it could at
home, in Europe, and in the world to thwart the attainment of German
goals. The traitorous Jews were responsible for Germany's and Austria's
defeat in World War I; Jewish intriguers had delivered "the stab in the
back" to German interests and had stolen the German's real victory at
arms. Jewish conspirators had imposed the severe burden of reparations
and territorial sacrifices that was codified in the Versailles Treaty. The
creation of the Weimar Republic, which the Nazis considered alien to
the German nation and injurious to its interests, was also attributed to
the machinations of the Jews.

Such notions of Jewish conspiracy derived much of their imagery from the late-nineteenth-century Russian and European anti-Semitic literature, most notably the infamous *Protocols of the Elders of Zion,* which insisted that an international league of Jews had secretly plotted to seize the reins of power in the world. Fabricated by the Russian secret police in the mid-1890s, the *Protocols* revived ancient Christian mythologies surrounding "blood libel," whereby Jews were accused of killing Christian children and using their blood for ritual purposes. In the hands of the Nazis, the conspiracy theories of the *Protocols* were linked on the one hand to Soviet international communism, a Judeo-Bolshevik creation, and on the other to international capital, epitomized by Jewish control of Wall Street. The loyalty of Jews—all Jews—to this conspiracy was seen as complete. No amount of assimilation, no amount of Germanization, could cover up this inherent alienation from the country or countries in which they lived. For the Nazis, the Jews were an anti-nation, loyal only to their own nefarious attempts to undermine true civilization. Once the message of the *Protocols* is really understood by a people, Hitler wrote, "the Jewish menace may be considered as broken."[13]

Eugenics

Racialist thinking at the turn of the century was cast in the language of science. During this period, criminality was "discovered" to match cranial size, and social class to match skeletal structure. Great "advances" such as these in biology spawned the science of eugenics—the attempt to identify and, through selective breeding, to improve the racial characteristics of humans. If certain racial types were more genetically inclined toward criminal behavior, congenital diseases, or mental illnesses, they could be isolated from the healthy population and prevented from breeding, thus freeing the nation or race of its antisocial elements and its weak, disturbed, or infirm specimens. This had two ostensible advantages. The race would be eventually purged of its impurities, and the modern state would be relieved of the burden of caring for unproductive individuals.

At the outset, whether in Germany, England, or the United States, the science of eugenics was seen as a rational and modern process of dealing with the socially and biologically marginal. It fit the modern state's need to impose order and uniformity on its population. "Far from being a politically conservative and scientifically spurious set of beliefs that remained confined to the Nazi era," writes Frank Dikötter, "eugenics belonged to the political vocabulary of virtually every significant modernizing force between the two world wars."[14] In the hands of the Nazis, however, eugenics became a particularly dangerous tool for cleansing the race and dealing with asocial elements, the handicapped, the mentally ill—and the Jews. The eugenics component complicated the eliminationist imagery of race-thinking for Hitler and his lieutenants. The German nation would have to be cleansed by removing alien elements, in particular the Jews, from the country (and Europe). In addition, alien elements would have to be surgically excised from the body of the nation itself. And finally, the blood of the nation would have to be purged of its tainted strains. "'Pure blood', writes Uli Linke, "was the teleological goal whereby the German nation would win its salvation."[15]

German eugenics had practical as well as ideological consequences which accelerated the Nazi attack on the Jews. Especially after Hitler came to power in 1933, medical doctors and researchers found that they could get grants, receive professorships, and advance their work by focusing their investigations on problems of racial hygiene.[16] One academic of the period bragged that the Nazi regime was "biology in action."[17] The Nazis sought to strengthen the Aryan race by selective breeding and by isolating the weak and infirm. Almost immediately after the Nazis came to power, German doctors and nurses practiced forced sterilization on mentally retarded and physically handicapped women of child-bearing age. According to a law passed on July 14, 1933, persons could be forcibly sterilized if they suffered from: congenital "feeble-mindedness," schizophrenia, manic depression, hereditary epilepsy, Huntington's disease, hereditary blindness, hereditary deafness, and serious physical deformities. Added to the list was "anyone who suffers from chronic alcoholism."[18]

During the winter of 1938–39, Nazi medical personnel began dealing with badly handicapped infants by cutting off life-support or using lethal injections or poison. This state-run euthanasia program was expanded in October 1939 after the outbreak of war in Poland, when Hitler authorized a wide-ranging policy of "mercy death" for "those suffering from illnesses deemed to be incurable."[19] A target figure of 65,000 to 75,000 deaths was established, in part to clear sanatoria and clinics so that returning German settlers from the Baltic region could be housed in Himmler's "Heim ins Reich" (Home to the Reich) program.[20] Nazi propaganda began to call for euthanasia and mercy-killing on an even wider scale, decrying the costs of maintaining the physically and mentally handicapped. But protests by relatives and friends of the children and other patients who had mysteriously disappeared or died while in the hospitals and sanatoria of the Third Reich sparked angry denunciations from clergymen and social activists. Hitler was forced to rescind his order in August 1941. But, as many scholars point out, the killing continued, only on a quieter and more selective basis.[21]

Some of these people were simply taken out of their clinics and hospitals by the SS and shot. Most, under the codename Aktion T-4, were gassed, sometimes in gas chambers disguised as showers, with fake shower heads and drains. By December 1941 in Chelmno, Jews were being killed in vans specially adapted for the intake of carbon monoxide gas.[22] The technology of the gas wagons was arranged by medical personnel who had already been part of the program to kill mental patients. Richard Breitman calls Chelmno "in effect, the first death camp in operation."[23] The gas that was turned on the Jews was the same used in the euthanasia killings, and the idea was the same. In some senses, then, eugenics provided both the theory and the mechanism for the radical solution to the Jewish "problem"—mass killing by means of gas.

Emigration

Hitler's theories and goals remained remarkably consistent throughout his career. George Mosse put it succinctly: "The extermination of the Jews must be the final aim of his [Hitler's] government, yet he was always ready to adjust his political timing to the necessity of the moment."[24] From Hitler's point of view, the Jews must be destroyed, though the actual meaning of destruction (*Vernichtung*) seemed to have different concrete notions behind it, depending on chronology and context. Sometimes it meant destroying the ability of Jews to affect their fate; sometimes it meant destroying the presence of Jews in Germany (and eventually in Europe); and sometimes it meant the physical destruction—that is, murder—of Jewish men, women, and children. Some scholars think that before the summer and fall of 1941 *Vernichtung* meant the destruction of the Jewish community in Europe through forced emigration, but afterward it meant mass killing.[25] That Hitler and his lieutenants used the words *Verbannung* (banishment) and *Entfernung* (removal) interchangeably with *Vernichtung* reinforces the interpretation that at least initially *Vernichtung* could have meant the mandatory deportation of the Jews. The word *Ausrottung* had the less ambiguous meaning of "extermination," though in some contexts it might be interpreted to mean "elimination"—from sight, from society, and physically from the country.

Even the word *Endlösung* ("final solution") had multiple meanings in Nazi discourse. Christopher Browning argues, for example, that it meant a different thing after the attack on the Soviet Union in June 1941 than before.[26] Christian Gerlach is even more insistent that during the war *Endlösung* did not mean the immediate elimination of the Jews; it took on that consistent meaning only after World War II, he argues.[27] Nevertheless, one can easily associate mass murder with all of these commonly used words. Whatever Hitler's official policy toward the Jews might have been at any given moment, somewhere down the line he meant to strike a final blow against them. Ian Kershaw, Hitler's most recent biographer, puts the problem in the following terms: "For Hitler, whatever the tactical considerations, the aim of destroying the Jews—his central political idea since 1919—remained unaltered. He revealed his approach to a meeting of party District Leaders at the end of April 1937, in immediate juxtaposition to comments on the Jews: 'I don't straight away want violently to demand an opponent to fight. I don't say 'fight' because I want to fight. Instead, I say: 'I want to destroy you!' And now let skill help me to manoeuvre you so far into the corner that you can't strike any blow. And then you get the stab in the heart."[28]

The rhetoric and even long-term goals of Nazi leaders were at some level eliminationist throughout the 1920s and 1930s. At the same time, however, Hitler consistently called for policies that would force the Jews to leave Germany and Europe. "Out with the Jews," insisted Hitler, June 24, 1920, "[those] who poison our people."[29] In an August 13, 1920, speech entitled "Why We Are Anti-Semites," Hitler again made clear that the Jews would have to go, "not because we begrudge them an existence," he added sarcastically, "[but] we [want] to congratulate the whole rest of the world on the occasion of their visit."[30]

The first step in driving out the Jews was to isolate them and turn them on themselves, both at home and, even better, abroad. This strategy derived from Hitler's consistent allegation that Jews lived as parasites off of healthy nations. He wrote in *Mein Kampf*: "If the Jews were alone in this world, they would stifle in filth and offal; they would try to get ahead of one another in hate-filled struggle and exterminate one another."[31] Once isolated from German society, they could more easily be driven from the country through a simple and straightforward policy of, in the memoirist Victor Klemperer's words, "oppression, oppression,

oppression."[32] In essence, in the 1930s Hitler was engaged in a form of forced deportation and ethnic cleansing, using the power of the state and the belligerence of the Nazi party to force the Jews out of German territory. In this case, the "ethnos" involved were the Jews, defined in purely racial terms by the Nuremberg Laws. Again, to use Klemperer's words: "One is an alien species or a Jew with 25 percent Jewish blood, if one grandparent was Jewish. As in 15th Century Spain, but then the issue was faith. Today it's zoology and business."[33]

Initially the Nazi goals were indeed like those of the Jews' fifteenth-century Spanish persecutors—to drive Jews from their territory forever. However, unlike the Spanish, the Nazis had quite specific views of what would happen to the Jews who left. Western countries would understand what the Germans had already learned about the Jews' pernicious qualities. The fever of anti-Semitism would rise everywhere, and the Jews would be proclaimed pariahs throughout the world. It also mattered to the Nazis where the Jews went. Hitler was convinced that the Jews had tried to use their influence inside Germany and out to prevent the Nazis from coming to power and gaining ascendancy in Europe. When protests against Nazi violence and anti-Semitism arose in London, Paris, and New York, the Nazis directly attributed it to Jewish influence there. German Jews expelled from the Third Reich might well raise the clamor of anti-Nazi agitation coming from Western cities, and the Nazis increasingly sought to direct Jewish emigration away from the West (though on this issue, like so many others, they were self-contradictory).

Initially, the Nazi destination of choice for Jewish emigration was Palestine. Like the Polish ultranationalist government of the late 1930s, the Third Reich was ready to make an alliance of sorts with the Zionists to get the Jews to leave Germany and Europe for Palestine. For Hitler, this was a perfect place to dump the Jews. It was isolated, economically insignificant, and lacking natural resources. Even better, Palestine was controlled by the British, who, Hitler felt, would never allow the Jews to construct their own state. He and the Nazi leaders wanted to keep the Jews away from the centers of power in the West, but they also worried about the Jews pulling the strings of world capital from the Middle East, if they were allowed to develop control over their own affairs. If the Palestine solution could be implemented, the Nazis thought, Germany and all of Europe would be freed of the Jewish menace, and Great Britain would serve as the guarantor of European racial purity by keeping Jewish Palestine under firm control. The Haavara (Transfer) Agreement of August 27, 1933, between the Nazi government on the one side and the Anglo-Palestine Bank and the German Zionist Union on the other put in motion a mechanism to foster emigration.[34] Over the next five years, some 60,000 German Jews emigrated to Palestine under a program that left half of their property in Germany as capital to finance German exports to Palestine.[35]

The Haavara Agreement failed to satisfy the Nazis' mania to expel the Jews and was not pursued with sufficient tenacity by any of the parties involved—the German Jews, the British, or the Nazis. The vast majority of Jews in Germany were disinclined to emigrate and had little or no interest in Palestine or Zionism. Saul Friedländer notes that neither the German Jewish leadership nor ordinary German Jews really grasped the "essentially unpredictable" future.[36] While the British encouraged the immigration to Palestine of relatively well-off German Jews, the Haavara Agreement was unsuited to the immigration of poor and working-class Jews as well as recent Polish-Jewish immigrants to Germany; neither group had any possibility of bringing capital into Palestine or leaving half behind in German government deposits. Even more important was growing Arab opposition to an influx of European Jews into Palestine. By the end of the 1930s, the British closed down the possibility of Jewish emigration to Palestine altogether, effectively ending the Zionists' hopes for saving European Jews by moving them to the Middle East.

Independently of the project of finding a destination for the emigrants, Hitler and the Nazis increased their pressure on the Jews to get them to leave. Vicious and humiliating attacks in the press and in public were part of the Nazi strategy. "The Jew-baiting and pogrom atmosphere grow day by day," Klemperer wrote in his diary on July 21, 1935.[37] The Nazis also undermined the legal position of the Jews, particularly with passage of the Nuremberg Laws in July 1935. Not only did these statutes define Jews according to hereditary ("racial") criteria, but they deprived Jews of German citizenship and thus of civil protection and legal recourse. According to the diaries of his military adjutant, Gerhard Engel, Hitler later regretted that the Nuremberg Laws had not been sufficiently draconian to drive all the Jews from Germany. "On August 13, 1938, the Führer spoke to a small group again about the Nuremberg laws and their consequences. If he considered them in retrospect, then these laws actually were far too 'humane.' One took away certain rights from the Jews and distanced them from the life of the state; but what was left over, was their activity and their work in the free market, and that is exactly what the Jews are attracted to . . . Now he would have thought of additional laws that would have so provocatively restricted Jewish life in Germany that the masses of the Jewish population simply would not want to stay in Germany. That would have been the best way to get rid of them."[38]

Goebbels also documents the legal restrictions the Nazis put on the ability of Jews to earn a livelihood, with the intention of forcing them to leave the country. In connection with new prohibitions against the practice of medicine by Jewish doctors, Goebbels wrote in his diary on August 4, 1938: "The Jews are being systematically driven back." Noting on August 31 that Berlin Jews would be henceforth required to declare all their property and transfer it to the state and/or Aryan owners, Goebbels insisted that the policies should continue despite protests from Jews and non-Jews alike.[39] Finally, so many Jews were emigrating from Berlin in large numbers, he wrote on October 13, that other countries were complaining about their arrival. "So the Jews will be driven from country to country and thereby harvest the fruits of their eternal intrigues, agitational campaigns and vileness."[40] Göring, Goebbels, Heydrich, and other Nazi leaders were ingenious at thinking up various measures to restrict Jewish movement within Germany, separate Jews from the "healthy" German population, and deplete the Jewish community's economic and moral resources.[41]

Ultimately, however, leading Nazis concluded that the pressure of discriminatory legislation, anti-Semitic hate propaganda, and torchlight demonstrations was insufficiently threatening. The Jews were not fleeing Germany fast enough, and those who stayed were not being adequately punished for their arrogance in remaining. In another of those odd and volatile contradictions in Nazi rhetoric and practice, the German Jews, though pressured to emigrate, were also used as hostages to protect Germany from the nefarious conspiracies of their fellow Jews in those countries that resisted Nazi incursions. But whether hostages or potential emigrants, the Jews deserved to be punished. The severe violence of Kristallnacht (the night of the broken glass) reflected this double vision.

Kristallnacht began with an incident on November 9, 1938, when Herschel Grynszpan, in protest against the forced deportation from Germany of his fellow Polish Jews, shot and mortally wounded the German diplomat Ernst vom Rath in the Third Reich's Paris embassy. Goebbels, incensed by the audacity of the act, incited anti-Semitic demonstrations to punish German Jews—and with them world Jewry—for the heinous act. Demonstrators in Kassel and Dessau set fire to Jewish synagogues and attacked Jewish stores. According to his diary of November 10, Goebbels presented to the Führer the useful possibilities built into the situation: "He [Hitler] decided: the demonstrations should be allowed to go on. Pull back the police. This time the Jews should feel the hatred of the people."[42] Goebbels—ecstatic about a reckoning with the Jews—gave the corresponding orders. "We will not allow this cowardly murder to go unanswered. For once things will be allowed to take their course." But by the next day, Hitler and Goebbels were already worried about the plundering getting out of control and gave orders to end the "action." Göring, who was in charge of the Third Reich's economy, was angry and upset about the wanton destruction during Kristallnacht. Yet he concluded that there were positive effects, as well; everyone can see that "the entire emigration issue has become acute"; the whole world now knows "the Jew cannot live in Germany."[43] From the leading Nazis' point of view, after Kristallnacht they had an opportunity once again to turn up the pressure on the Jews. Hitler told Goebbels he wanted to introduce "very strict measures" against the Jews to get them out of Germany.[44]

And, indeed, out of Europe as a whole. Grynszpan's assassination of vom Rath underlined again the European, not to mention international, dimensions of the Nazis' perception of the Jewish problem. The European issue became much more concrete at the end of the 1930s, when the Third Reich annexed Austria and the Sudetenland, assumed control over the Czech protectorate, and absorbed lands from the newly partitioned Poland. Hitler's dedication to creating *Lebensraum* (living space) for the German people dramatically increased the number of Jews within his territory. They, too, would have to be driven out of the Third Reich. For the Nazis, then, race and *Lebensraum* were interconnected concepts.[45] Himmler used the related notion of *völkische Flurbereinigung* (cleansing the soil in the fields) to describe what would happen to Jews, gypsies, Poles, and other alien elements in these new German territories. The impure races in the east would be replaced by good Germans, some "called back" to the Reich from the Baltics, Ukraine, or elsewhere, some racially "reclaimed" from having been superficially denationalized in a sea of Slavic peoples. Deciding who was a German and who was not was a decidedly unscientific process, even by the low standards of Nazi "racial science."[46] Himmler would often judge by face shape, hair and eye color, and stature whether a person was a Pole, a Ukrainian, or a German. But no such impressionistic resolution was afforded Jews or people who were part Jewish. Jews could not be reclaimed. Wherever the Nazis went, Jews would be driven out.

After the union with Austria *(Anschluss)* in March 1938, Himmler and the SS set up a special office in Vienna—the Central Office for Jewish Emigration—whose task was to expel all the Jews as quickly as possible from the so-called Ostmark. Here, too, the Jews were not just to be thrown out of Austria but punished. They were arrested and brutalized, their stores were attacked, their synagogues were taken over or destroyed. Heydrich tried to rein in some of the most extreme violence, but only because it interfered with the systematic expropriation of Jewish assets, which were to be Aryanized.[47] Under the direction of Adolf Eichmann, the operation to rid Austria of Jews went smoothly. Jewish organizations were called in to help raise the foreign currency to pay for the deportation. Within six months, approximately 40,000 Jews were forcibly driven out of Austria.[48] Jewish industries and stores were either closed down altogether or, in rarer cases, handed over to "Aryan" owners.

More Jews could have left Austria if there had been places for them to go. By the end of the 1930s, Palestine was out of the question, and Hitler was not interested in pushing Jews out to neighboring countries, which would not have accepted them willingly in any case. Emigration quotas from Germany were strictly enforced in the United States, Canada, South Africa, Great Britain, and Australia. The French colony of Madagascar continued to be mentioned as a potential destination for the Jews, as were other colonies in subequatorial Africa. At the Evian-les-Bains conference in July 1938, sponsored by the League of Nations, representatives of twenty-five major countries and a series of relief organizations met to discuss the problem of Jewish emigration. This effort came to naught, and the Evian conference can only be described as a tragic failure. No country big or small, densely or sparsely populated, liberal or dictatorial, was willing to accept masses of Jewish refugees. It is hard to avoid the impression that anti-Semitism around the world played a central role in this decision, despite protestations about the practical problems of accepting large numbers of immigrants. On the fringes of the Evian conference, the Nazis sought to earn currency from the growing desperation of potential Jewish emigrants and Jewish agencies abroad. According to Yehuda Bauer, they offered to sell a half-million Jews to the West at a rate of $250 per head.[49]

Hitler's determination to pursue the Jewish question to its conclusion increased with his diplomatic and military successes on the continent. The Third Reich reoccupied the Rhineland, absorbed Austria, and swallowed up Czechoslovakia without serious opposition from the European powers. Despite his successes, Hitler was enraged by the growing criticism of appeasement in France, Russia, the United States, and especially Great Britain. These propagandistic complaints about Nazi anti-Semitism and Hitler's treatment of the Jews also irked him deeply, and of course he blamed all of the uproar on the Jews. In his much-quoted speech before the Reichstag on January 30, 1939, Hitler threatened the Jews with mass extinction if they aroused world condemnation of Germany's steps to assert its rightful domination of Europe: "I have very often been a prophet in my life and have mostly been laughed at . . . I will again be a prophet today: If international financial Jewry in and outside of Europe should succeed in driving the peoples once more into a World War, then the result will not be the Bolshevization of the earth and therewith the victory of the Jews, but it will mean the destruction of the Jewish race in Europe."[50]

That Hitler and others in his entourage repeatedly recalled this threat in the years to come is often cited by historians as evidence for the continuity of Hitler's genocidal purpose.[51] He promised to kill off the Jews if they started a world war, and after the war started, he did. However, as Hans Mommsen points out, the context of the speech gave the "prophecy" a quite different character, as a "rhetorical gesture" to get the world powers and refugee committees to accept his financial demands for deporting all the Jews.[52] Later references to the speech, Mommsen adds, were used rhetorically by Hitler to justify the "cumulative radicalization" of Nazi policy.[53] Other parts of the Reichstag speech support Mommsen's contention that Hitler simply wanted to blackmail the West into making a deal about Jewish deportation: "Europe will never come to rest unless the Jewish question is taken care of. It is very much in the realm of possibility that sooner or later an agreement in Europe can be reached between such nations which otherwise do not so easily find a way to get on with each other. The world has plenty of space for inhabitation; one has to break once and for all with the idea that the Jewish people are determined by the Almighty to be the beneficiaries at a specified percentage of the bodies and of the productive work of other peoples. Jewry will have to develop as much of an ability to build their own lives as the other peoples do, or sooner or later they will suffer a crisis of unimaginable proportions."[54]

Palestine, Alaska, the Dominican Republic, Honduras, Australia, or Madagascar—all were mentioned at one time or another as potential destinations for Germany's and Europe's Jews, and in this speech it was all the same to Hitler. The important point was this: get the Jews out fast, or something untoward is going to happen. Alfred Rosenberg's speech to the diplomatic community in Berlin on February 8, 1939, followed up on Hitler's initiative: if the West is serious about its "friendship for the Jews," then they have to make up their minds in the near future which territory will be designated as a "Jewish reservation."[55]

The diplomatic entente with Stalin represented by the Nazi-Soviet Non-Aggression Pact of August 23, 1939, came as a shock to the West and served as the preliminary move in Hitler's attack on Poland. Beginning on September 1, a combined air and land assault overwhelmed the Poles. Warsaw was surrounded by September 9 and would hold out only a few more weeks. By September 17, when the Soviets, in turn, moved quickly to seize their designated part of Poland, nothing was left of, in Molotov's words, "this ugly offspring of the Versailles Treaty."[56]

England and France promptly declared war. The British fought more determinedly and held out much longer than Hitler ever expected, but the quick defeat of France in June 1940 presented the Führer with a continental empire that stretched from Paris in the west to the Nieman River in the east. There were still nettlesome problems in the Balkans that would undermine his agreement with the Soviets,[57] and Judeo-Bolshevism, his self-imagined arch-enemy, remained in power in Moscow. But still Hitler could and did congratulate himself on a remarkable series of victories.

Hitler's triumphant subjugation of the continent spelled catastrophe for the Jews. For the three million or so Polish Jews, hundreds of thousands of whom resided in areas of Poland incorporated directly into the Reich, the situation was particularly critical. In the Wartheland, Danzig, and west Prussia, Jews were driven out of their homes and forcibly deported to the Generalgouvernement, the Nazi-run territory of rump Poland, initially to make room for Germans returning from the Baltic and Ukraine. By June 1941 some 250,000 Jews and 600,000 Poles had been moved to this region, much to the consternation of its governor general, Hans Frank.[58] But at the outset, Frank lost this bureaucratic battle to Himmler and the SS, who had insisted on cleansing the newly annexed territories of Jews and Poles.

The Jews were confined to ghettos, as in medieval times, in order to segregate them from the rest of the population, both Poles and Germans. However, the ghettos were meant to be merely way-stations on the road to expulsion from the continent. Consistent with the Nazis' overall racial policy, the ghettos provided yet another form of punishment for the Jews. Rations of food and water were kept at minimal levels. Living conditions were abysmal, due to overcrowding and inadequate goods and services. The SS guards and their Jewish police helpmates treated the ghetto dwellers with murderous brutality.

Christopher Browning suggests that two models dominated the Nazi conception of the ghettos, and both operated simultaneously and in different mixes during the first few years of their existence. Some Nazi officials thought of the ghettos as no more than holding pens, in which natural attrition from starvation and disease would eventually finish off the inhabitants. Others sought to solve the Reich's growing labor problems by putting the residents to work, which required supplying minimal foodstuffs and providing a basic standard of living.[59] The Warsaw ghetto generally was administered according to the former model, the Lodz ghetto according to the latter.

But the ghettos could not hold all the Jews who were streaming into their quarters. The SS responded by creating a large reservation (Reservat) for the Jews in the region of Lublin. Surrounded by barbed wire and Nazi guards, the Reservat near Nisko on the San River turned into "a vast concentration camp, with congestion, stench, poverty, disease, and chaos unparalleled on earth."[60] Even if its Nazi architects intended for Jews to die in vast numbers on the reservation, it was still far too limited a solution to the problem of removing all the Jews from Europe.[61] Philippe Burrin suggests that conditions were so bad in the Lublin "ghetto of the Reich" that plans to develop it further were abandoned in mid-March 1940 because of potential adverse publicity abroad, especially in the United States.[62] Because of its importance as a staging area for potential military operations into the Soviet Union, the Wehrmacht opposed using the Lublin region as a destination for vast numbers of Jews. Hans Frank also kept up the pressure on Berlin to find a resolution to the Jewish question that would remove them from the Generalgouvernement altogether. As a result, the Madagascar solution, which had been bandied about by anti-Semites in Germany and Poland for at least a decade, once again came to the fore.

After the destruction of Kristallnacht, which both Göring and Hjalmar Schacht (Nazi economics minister from 1934–1937 and president of the Deutsche Bank from 1933 to 1939) felt did little else but injure the Nazis' economic interests, Schacht turned his attention to the possibility of deporting all the remaining German and Austrian Jews—

600,000 people altogether—to Madagascar. Schacht's plan, which was initially approved by Hitler in December 1938, called for Jewish institutions in the West to put up the capital for the forced emigration of Jews of working and child-bearing age and their families.[63] (The old and infirm would be allowed to stay.) In negotiations with George Rublee of the International Committee on Refugees, he worked out a formula for transferring Jewish assets to a fund to support German exports, not unlike the Palestinian arrangement of three years earlier. In no case would the transfer of Jews cost the Third Reich any money; on the contrary, Jewish assets would essentially subsidize the German economy. The critical difference between the Madagascar and Palestine arrangements was that Zionists rejected the Madagascar plan out of hand, and world Jewish organizations were not at all interested in supplying the capital to force European Jews to move to a desolate, disease-ridden island.

Still, the Nazi invasion of Poland and the limitations of the Lublin reservation resuscitated the notion among German bureaucrats that Madagascar offered a solution; the huge number of Jews concentrated in the Generalgouvernement made the Nazis nervous. Himmler was anxious to implement his Generalplan Ost, which called for redrawing ethnic borders in the east, moving millions of people, and eliminating Jews from the region.[64] The war itself seemed to make this vast undertaking possible, since, as one of Heydrich's lieutenants stated, "one could proceed relatively vigorously without taking into account the mood of world opinion."[65] To be sure, the Nazis would have to await the conclusion of the war and the defeat of the British to be able to transport the Jews through British-controlled shipping lanes. But particularly after the defeat of France in the summer of 1940, the Madagascar plan began to receive serious attention from the German Foreign Ministry. At this point, Hitler was said to be anxious to be rid of the Jewish problem and put it in the hands of the French.[66] Initially issued in early July 1940, the Foreign Ministry report was revised and expanded by Heydrich and Eichmann and reissued on August 15, 1940. This plan was not terribly different from Schacht's basic conception, except for the overwhelming number of Jews—four million altogether—to be transported to the Jewish reservation on Madagascar.[67]

Christopher Browning writes that the Nazis were quick to pick up on the Madagascar solution during the early summer of 1940 because of "a measure of frustration that had built up over the bottlenecks of demographic engineering in eastern Europe."[68] The hated Jews were taking up valuable space and consuming precious resources. There was no room to resettle the *Volksdeutsche* from the east until the Jews were removed. Those Germans who had been called "home to the Reich" often lived in hungry and helpless conditions in transfer camps.[69] The Generalgouvernement was already overcrowded with both Poles and Jews. The Madagascar plan was a way out of this dead-end, and hopes were high for a quick solution. Even the Jews had been alerted to the Madagascar option. On July 1, 1940, Adam Czerniakow noted in his Warsaw ghetto diary that he had heard from the Nazis that "the war would be over in a month and that we would all leave for Madagascar."[70]

In all of its Nazi iterations, the Madagascar plan was part of the "Final Solution" of the Jewish question; it was most definitely not an attempt by the Nazis to find a congenial home for Europe's Jewish population. Goebbels wrote in his diaries on July 26, 1940, that after the war Madagascar would become "a German protectorate under a German police-governor."[71] The Jews would not be allowed to have their own state or their own institutions; the considerations behind the earlier Palestine plan already made that clear. Their exhaustive investigations of the conditions on Madagascar made the Nazis aware that the climate was difficult and a good part of its land mass consisted of malarial swamps uninhabitable "for Europeans." The Jews would not be allowed to take more than the minimum of goods with them, although some artisans and professionals would be permitted to take the tools of their respective trades. Jewish capital would remain in Germany. Tropical diseases and unfavorable conditions on the island would wipe out the Jews. From Hitler's perspective in particular, the Jews would have no one else to exploit but one another, and they would perish as a just punishment for the evils they had inflicted on the healthy races of Europe.

Barbarossa

Like much of Nazi rhetoric, the Madagascar plan had a fantastic quality to it. The British did not surrender, the sea lanes remained dangerous for Nazi shipping, and the Petain government held on to its claims to the island, as it did to the remainder of its colonial empire. In any case, there was hardly any way to transport four million Jews to East Africa and little chance the world Jewish community would contribute to such an exile. Nevertheless, the Nazis continued to talk about the possibilities of banishing the Jews to Madagascar even after planning the attack on the Soviet Union (Operation Barbarossa) in the fall of 1940 and actually invading on June 22, 1941.

As pressure continued to build in the Nazi hierarchy for a "Final Solution," the projected attack on the Soviet Union provided the Nazis a potential option for dealing with the European Jews. Heydrich had been given the task of devising a plan during the winter of 1940–41, and Barbarossa gave him the idea of pushing the Jews even further east.[72] They could simply be dumped beyond the Urals in Siberia, far away from the Third Reich's natural *Lebensraum,* which included the Ukraine and Crimea. Hitler calculated that the victory over the Soviets would take four months at most; Goebbels said it would take "much less" than that.[73] In some senior German army circles, as Gabriel Gorodetsky writes, "the possibility of Russian resistance was dismissed out of hand" and "the common belief was that the Red Army would collapse within eight days."[74] With victory complete, the eastern Jews could be sent off to Siberia and the Arctic north. The British would lose heart as a result of the Soviet collapse and sue for peace; the western Jews, including those in North Africa, could then be shipped off to Madagascar.[75]

No favor was meant to the Jews by sending them beyond the Urals. It was assumed they would sooner or later expire in the Arctic or in the mosquito-infested swamps of Siberia. Heydrich and Goebbels carried on long conversations at the end of September 1941 about sending Jews to the Gulag, a particularly appropriate destination, they felt, because the Jewish-Bolsheviks were responsible for constructing this system of "corrective" labor camps and prisons in the first place.[76] As late as February 1942, Heydrich spoke to NSDAP high party officials in the Czech Protectorate about the Gulag of the north being the "perfect future homeland for Europe's 11 million Jews."[77] Thus leading Nazis were still talking of deportation for months after Einsatzgruppen were murdering Jews by the tens of thousands in the summer and fall of 1941.

Historians of the Holocaust justifiably point to the Commissar Order of June 6, 1941, as an important designator for the escalation of violence against the Jews during the campaign against Russia. Hitler made it clear to Himmler and his generals Keitel and Jodl that the coming conflict was not simply "a battle of weapons"; more significantly, it was a "conflict between two ideologies." In this conflict, "the Jewish-Bolshevik intelligentsia . . . must be eliminated." Hitler let his generals know that Himmler and the SS would be in charge of securing the newly conquered areas. This was because of "the necessity immediately to neutralize all Bolshevik leaders and commissars." That "neutralize" meant kill was made clear in subsequent sentences in which Hitler indicated that there would be no need for military courts and military justice. Himmler and the SS would take care of everything.[78]

As Barbarossa was implemented, Einsatzgruppen and regular Wehrmacht troops shot captured officers, alleged partisans (and their supporters), and large numbers of Jews. A slogans of the campaign from the very beginning was: "The Jew is a partisan, and the partisan is the Jew."[79] Jews were considered a genuine security risk and therefore targeted for elimination by both SS and army units.[80] In this fashion, the killing of Jews worked on both the rational and irrational mind of Germans at the front. As Ulrich Herbert puts it: "Because the Jews were murdered as alleged saboteurs, the assumption that one was dealing with enemies of Germany was confirmed—otherwise they would not have been so severely punished. By the deed [of murder], prejudice became fact."[81]

In their rhetoric and ideology, the Nazis melded the Soviet enemy and the Jews into a combined vision of evil. The German attack on Russia was not like the attack on Britain or France, though the Jews were blamed for those conflicts as well. In the Nazi mind, the internationalism of the Bolsheviks blended with the Jewish world conspiracy in a dangerous potion that mortally threatened the German nation and its right to rule Europe. Barbarossa was a crusade to slay the Jewish-Bolshevik demons and remove them from the face of the earth. As Jews were routinely murdered, the scenes on the Russian front confirmed an interpretation of reality that permeated the Nazis' crusading ideology.

Omer Bartov has written that even the ordinary troops of the Wehrmacht were led to believe that the Russian and Jewish enemy represented the devil incarnate. One of the many propaganda leaflets and circulars distributed to the troops stated: "Anyone who has ever looked at the face of a red commissar knows what the Bolsheviks are like. Here there is no need for theoretical expressions. We would insult the animals if we described these mostly Jewish men as beasts. They are the embodiment of the Satanic and insane hatred against the whole of noble humanity. The shape of these commissars reveals to us the rebellion of the *Untermenschen* against noble blood. The masses, whom they have sent to their deaths by making use of all means at their disposal such as ice-cold terror and insane incitement, would have brought an end to all meaningful life, had this eruption not been dammed at the last moment."[82] The propaganda worked well. Wehrmacht officers and men willingly participated in the massacre of the Jews. Indeed, they were responsible, directly or indirectly, for killing between 1 and 1.5 million victims.[83]

Mass slaughter took place on the front and behind the lines. The brutality of the killers—SS men, police, and regular troops—knew no bounds.[84] Not just Jews but Russian POWs were starved and beaten, if not immediately killed. The genocidal actions of the Germans only made the Red Army soldiers and partisans fight all the harder, knowing what would happen if they fell into German hands. Wehrmacht generals made this fact known to their superiors in Berlin. Perhaps even more important, the hierarchy of the Third Reich had counted on captured POWs to serve as a labor force to keep the German economy going. Goebbels wrote in his diary on December 12, 1941: "Our hope to employ to a great extent in the German economy the nearly 4 million Bolshevik prisoners will not be possible. In addition to the 900,000 of these prisoners who have already died of hunger, weakness, and disease, a huge number of the others will die in the next weeks and months. The greatest part of the Bolsheviks in POW camps have already descended to such a starving condition that even with the best care they cannot be revived."[85] As a result, the Commissar Order was rescinded on May 6, 1942, though by this point the killing of the Jews had been turned over to the SS and their newly constructed system of death camps. However, as Omer Bartov has written (and the recent Wehrmacht exhibition in Germany has demonstrated), the propaganda of hate, the inculcation of stereotypes of the *Untermenschen* into regular soldiers, and the mentality of the habitual killing of civilians contributed to the continued execution of Jews and other noncombatants by both the army and police.[86]

The Last Stage

During the summer and fall of 1941, Nazi attacks on the Jews took on genocidal proportions. The murderous actions of the Einsatzgruppen were dutifully reported by their commanders. The number of executions by Strike Commando 3, with headquarters in Kovno and responsible for parts of Lithuania and Latvia, totaled some 133,000 men, women, and children, the vast majority of whom were Jews. In July, Strike Commando 3, together with "Lithuanian partisans," killed mostly men and some women, but by late August many women and children were included in the death toll. On December 1, 1941, SS Colonel Jäger reported on the genocidal actions of his group: "Today I can confirm that Strike Commando 3 has reached the goal of solving the Jewish problem in Lithuania. The only remaining Jews are laborers and their families. The implementation of such actions is in the first instance an organizational problem. The Jews had to be collected in one or more towns and a ditch had to be dug at the right site for the right number . . . The Jews were brought in groups of 500, separated by at least 1.2 miles, to the place of execution . . . Only careful planning enabled the Commando to carry out up to 5 actions a week and at the same time continue the work in Kovno without interruption."[87] Colonel Jäger was not in the business of fighting a war against Jewish partisans. He was an ardent Nazi who thought he was following Hitler's and Himmler's orders to destroy the Jews. Even if one can't shoot the Jews designated for labor battalions, he concluded, "I am of the opinion that the male work Jews should be sterilized immediately to prevent any procreation. A Jewess who nevertheless becomes pregnant is to be liquidated."[88]

The mass executions of Jews in July and August 1941 in Galicia, Belorussia, Lithuania, and Ukraine institutionalized and legitimated the habitual killing of Jews, even if the decision to murder all of the Jews had not yet been reached. The pattern of mass murder in each area was also somewhat different, indicating a lack of direct orders from Berlin. In Galicia the executions started in June with Jewish men believed to be among the "intelligentsia." By the beginning of October women and children were also being routinely murdered.[89] In Belorussia during the invasion in mid-July, the entire "intelligentsia class" was "cleansed" from the rest of the population, and the Jews among them were only sometimes shot.[90] By the beginning of August 1941 Einsatzgruppen were shooting women and children in Belorussia as well. Between mid-August and mid-September, for the first time whole communities of Jews were wiped out.[91] But the executions in Galicia and Belorussia were not as systematic as those in Lithuania. In neither case was the local population quite so heavily involved. The spread of mass murder to include Jewish women and children in the late summer can be related to Himmler's visits to occupied territories in Russia in mid-August 1941.[92] Moreover, the shortage of food in the occupied areas steadily worsened from the late summer on, contributing to the sense among Nazi officials that "useless eaters," the Jews above all, should be eliminated.[93]

Jews were being massacred at the front and were dying of hunger and disease in detention camps and in the ghettos of Poland. In the Warsaw ghetto, hundreds of Jews died every day from hunger and disease. Adam Czerniakow writes in his diary on December 4, 1941: "Typhus is raging. Friends and acquaintances are dying all around me."[94] Meanwhile, Goebbels wrote on June 20, 1941: "The Jews of Poland are gradually dying out." He then added the familiar refrain: "A just punishment for their agitation among the peoples and for starting the war. The Führer predicted this to the Jews."[95] Goebbels made these notes in conjunction with his own wish to deport all of Berlin's remaining Jews to the Polish ghettos. Not just in Berlin but in Prague, Vienna, and the newly incorporated Wartheland, Nazi leaders took steps in the summer and fall of 1941 to deport the Jews to the east. Hans Frank in the Generalgouvernement insisted that his territory be "cleansed" of Jews, who should be sent further east, out of sight, where they could do no harm to developing German industries. Siberia now seemed a distant possibility; Madagascar appeared even more elusive. Instead, the transports from the Reich unloaded tens of thousands of Jews into the newly constructed ghettos of Riga, Kaunas, Vilna, and Minsk, as well as into the existing ones in Warsaw, Lodz, and Lublin. Some of these transports fell victim to Colonel Jäger's death squads, but most were crowded into the stultifying ghettos. Goebbels visited the Vilna ghetto at the beginning of November 1941, as it was becoming increasingly clear that the war would go on and as the Jewish problem remained unsolved: "The initial picture on a short tour through the ghetto is horrifying. The Jews are all over each other, obnoxious figures, not to be looked at, not to mention to be touched . . . The Jews are the lice of civilized people. One has to somehow exterminate them [*ausrotten*] . . . Only if one goes after them with the necessary brutality, will we be done with them. If one protects them, one will always later on be their victim."[96]

On July 31, 1941, Göring assigned Heydrich and the SS the duty "to make all necessary preparations—organisational, technical, and material—for a total solution of the Jewish question throughout the German sphere of influence in Europe." A few days earlier, on July 28, Göring stated "that Jews residing in regions under German rule have no further business there."[97] Henry Friedlander calls the July 31 order a "retroactive sanction" for the Holocaust, one that compelled the German bureaucracy to cooperate with Himmler and the SS, who already had been charged by Hitler to deal finally with the Jewish question.[98] But it seems more likely that Göring continued to have in mind deporting all of the Jews to Soviet territory, with many of them dying in the process.

During the late summer of 1941, the SS and the Einsatzgruppen turned to more radical solutions—mass executions—which increased in intensity through the late fall of 1941. Then, on December 8, 1941, the SS began experimenting with gassing the Jews in Chelmno. They sometimes wore white coats and stethoscopes "to dupe their victims." Within a fifteen-month period, some 145,000 Jews were killed in mobile gas vans there.[99] The program was "judged a success," writes Martin Gilbert, "and was continued on an ever widening scale."[100] Although the Nazis continued to talk and think about the forced deportation of the Jews, mass murder gained momentum as the war on the eastern front continued unabated. The fall brought no relief, and Hitler's realization that the war would continue through the winter increased his resolution to be done with the nettlesome Jewish problem.[101] Einsatzgruppen, SS commanders, and ardent Nazi Gauleiters in the east supervised the murder of tens of thousands of Jews, with little or no reaction that we know of on Hitler's part. In fact, the solution of mass murder was accelerated by the fact that no one seemed to object: not the military, nor civilian officials, nor non-Jewish local populations, nor the authorities in Berlin. There seemed to be both approbation and satisfaction among all the parties involved in the killings.

Hitler himself was riveted to day-to-day battlefield reports and military planning; fashioning himself a military genius in the tradition of Napoleon, he had little time and remarkably little interest in dealing with the Jewish nemesis himself. However, with the surprising resilience of the British, the unexpected resistance of the Soviets, and the entry of the United States into the war in December after the bombing of Pearl Harbor, Hitler finally decided to deal with the Jewish question once and for all, to get it out of the way. Himmler and the SS would be given the go-ahead to finish off the Jews.

Goebbel's report of Hitler's speech to the Gauleiters on December 12, 1941, makes clear that the Jews would suffer the ultimate punishment for Germany's increasingly painful war: "As far as the Jewish question is concerned, the Führer has decided to clear the table of the matter. He had prophesied to the Jews that if they once again bring about a world war, they would experience their destruction. Those were no mere phrases. World War has come, the destruction of the Jews is the necessary consequence. This question should be looked at without any sentimentality. We are not here to take pity on the Jews, but only to have sympathy for our German people. If the German people has again sacrificed in the eastern campaign at present 160,000 dead, so the originator of this bloody conflict should have to pay with their lives for it."[102] Some German scholars call this the fundamental decision *(Grundsatzentscheidung)* for initiating the Holocaust.[103] Up until this point, the Nazis had talked about killing Jews in terms of fighting Bolshevism, gaining living space, crushing the black market, and eliminating "useless eaters." Now, the "Final Solution" was about nothing else but mass extermination. Frank's report to his leading lieutenants in the Generalgouvernement of December 16, 1941, supports this conclusion. He let it be known that the Jews "must leave . . . must disappear." "Here are 3.5 million Jews that we can't shoot, we can't poison. But there are some things we can do, and one way or another these measures will successfully lead to liquidation."[104] The Polish scholar Bogdan Musial also notes that the mass murder of the Jews in the Generalgouvernement as part of the "Final Solution" was slated from the beginning of December 1941.[105]

World War II served as a perverse excuse for genocide. It provided a cover for mass murder of the Jews, much as the World War I gave the Turks the opportunity to destroy the Armenian nation. The killing had already begun by the Einsatzgruppen and the Wehrmacht in the summer and fall, without serious protest or opposition at home or abroad. Jews were dying by the thousands in ghettos and in transport. The Nazis' self-fulfilling prophecies of world war came true with the Japanese attack on Pearl Harbor on December 8, 1941, and the entrance of the United States into the war. There was no place to send the Jews where they would not endanger the Germans. The horrible treatment of the Jews at the front and in the ghettos dehumanized them in the Nazi eyes even further.

According to the research of Christopher Browning and Götz Aly, communications between Hitler, Himmler, and Heydrich gave every indication that the Nazi leaders had decided in October 1941 that none of the deportation schemes were going to work and that mass murder was the only answer.[106] Heydrich called a meeting of leading members of the Nazi party and government for late November 1941 to deal with the Jewish question in this spirit. The meeting was delayed until January 20, 1942, when, at a Nazi villa on Wannsee on the outskirts of Berlin, the assembled party and state representatives discussed the physical extermination of Europe's Jews. Theirs was a cold-blooded plan of industrial murder that involved the transportation of Europe's Jews to SS-supervised concentration camps. There the Jews would either be sent to the gas chambers or worked and starved to death. This was the plan for effecting the "Final Solution"; all of Europe's Jews were to die.[107]

Yet at the same time that plans for the Holocaust were being completed at Wannsee, Hitler continued to talk about emigration and forced deportation. On January 23, 1942, in the presence of Himmler and a few other collaborators, the Führer insisted that "the Jew must clear out of Europe. Otherwise, no understanding will be possible between Europeans. It's the Jew who prevents everything . . . For my part, I restrict myself to telling them they must go away. If they break their pipes on the journey I can't do anything about it. But if they refuse to go voluntarily, I see no other solution but extermination."[108]

Four days later, on January 27, 1942, Hitler again talked about the Jews leaving Europe: "The Jews must pack up, disappear from Europe. Let them go to Russia. Where the Jews are concerned, I'm devoid of all sense of pity."[109] But, typically, a month later, on February 22, 1942, in a conversation with Himmler and a Danish SS leader, Hitler's emphasis shifts back to genocide: "The discovery of the Jewish virus is one of the greatest revolutions that have taken place in the world. The battle in which we are engaged to-day is of the same sort as the battle waged, during the last century, by Pasteur and Koch . . . We shall regain our health only by eliminating the Jews."[110]

Much as before the Russian campaign, Hitler's "table talks" (and Goebbels' accounts of Hitler's monologues at meetings and discussions) oscillated between what we would today classify as invocations for genocide, mass murder, and the Holocaust, and demands for ethnic cleansing, the forced deportation of Jews from Germany and all of Europe. On the level of state policy and its implementation, the mania for deporting, isolating, and banishing the Jews to some remote corner of the world seamlessly evolved—almost without the Nazi authorities noticing or talking about the difference—into a campaign of mass murder and industrial killing, the Shoah.

The Holocaust and the Armenian Genocide

The Nazi murder of the Jews shared a number of important characteristics with the Armenian genocide, while also differing in profound ways. In both cases, the political leadership—Young Turks and Nazis—ordered the mass murder, and the states they controlled created the institutions and circumstances for the killing. In both cases, the leaders sought to conceal their acts and to deny the horror of their deeds. There can be no question of the direct responsibility of Hitler or the Young Turk triumvirate for the mass murders; yet, especially in the case of the Young Turks but also of the leading Nazis, there are no direct orders and few unambiguous documents that prove beyond question that the leadership intentionally ordered mass murder. Despite this lack, bureaucrats in both the Ottoman and German states claimed they were following orders and fulfilling their duties. In that sense, the evidence for state-organized mass murder is overwhelming.

In both cases, too, the process of genocide was cold and efficient. These were not predominantly pogroms or massacres in the sense of explosions of hatred and violence against the Jews or Armenians. They were organized and planned acts of mass extinction, justified by reasons of state and promoted by ideologies of modern integral nationalism. Both genocides also originated in ethnic cleansing; the Nazis initially sought to expel the Jews from Germany and then from Nazi-occupied Europe before the decision was reached to eliminate them from the continent through mass murder. Although the evidence is more ambiguous in the case of the Young Turks, it seems that their initial intention was to drive the Armenians from eastern Anatolia into the Syrian desert. In both cases, there was an escalation of and habituation to violence; genocide, in other words, was as much the completion of a contingent process as a blueprint for action.

The categories of "functionalism" and "intentionalism" so often debated in the literature on the Holocaust do not fit either case very well.[111] Functionalism emphasizes the impetus within the systems themselves toward taking increasingly radical measures against the hated minority. Intentionalism underlines the long-term plan—whether Hitler's or the Young Turks'—for the elimination of the Jews or Armenians. In both cases, context and contingency are critical to the increasing radicalization that occurred. Shifting choices under evolving circumstances determined both tragedies. There was nothing inevitable about them.[112]

The utter indifference to the sufferings of the victim peoples may be the hardest similarity to explain; in fact, the worse the conditions of the Jews or Armenians, the greater seemed to be the cruelty and harshness of their respective persecutors. That the genocides took place under the cover of war is important in the sense that soldiers in the armies and paramilitaries were habituated to following orders, to killing, and to accepting suffering, both of their comrades and their victims. A Wehrmacht soldier wrote home of his experiences on the eastern front: "One becomes cruel and without feelings. One is no longer one's self."[113] World war in the twentieth century meant total war; in World War II, twice as many civilians—old and young, women and children—would suffer and die as would soldiers and officers.[114] But in both genocides, the power of state ideologies to create the "other," the hated and the despised, the enemy within, proved essential in developing the potential for mass murder. In both cases, the victims were dehumanized ideologically and physically. Their degradation by their persecutors proved their "otherness" and inhumanity.

The incessant barrage of Nazi anti-Semitic rhetoric and imagery resonated with traditional German anti-Semitism, creating a cultural context in which the elimination of Jews by one means or another seemed all too natural. The crowding of Jews into ghettos and camps, the reduction of the Jewish population to passive, gaunt-eyed, disease-ridden skeletons, seemed to make the gas chambers all the more reasonable to the Nazis. Similarly, the actual physical deterioration of the Armenians, as they were forced to march through the desert, starving, begging, and diseased, contributed to the Turkish rationale for mass murder. The elimination of the Armenians, as well as the eventual attack on the Greeks, also took place in the realm of state ideology—in this case a distortion of Islamic ideas of superiority and a devaluation of traditionally tolerant, protective relations with non-Christian peoples. Modern Turkish nationalism also took an increasingly anti-Armenian turn in the period after the Adana massacres of 1909 and the outbreak of the war in 1914. The culture of periodic Armenian massacres at the end of the nineteenth and beginning of the twentieth centuries did not help.

Both the Holocaust and the Armenian case highlight the central place of women as important objects of ethnic cleansing and genocide. Unlike war, even the totalistic wars of the twentieth century, ethnic cleansing and genocide focus almost exclusively on unarmed civilians rather than armed military populations, on women and girls rather than on men and boys. Men tend to be those who emigrate or flee, join partisans or foreign armies to resist, or are required to work in labor battalions or special industries. Women usually, though not always, stay at home with the young and the aged and are vulnerable to attack. The ideologies of genocide and ethnic cleansing also focus on women as the cultural and biological repository of the nation. Women pass on to their children the memory, the codes, and the symbols of nationhood. They perpetuate the nation by bearing and nursing the nation's children. Women are assaulted, therefore, because they are there and because they are females.

Armenian women were deported, attacked, raped, killed, and sometimes denationalized through forced conversion to Islam and absorption into Muslim families. Nazi racial theory made the latter "solution" untenable for Jewish women. Especially before mass murder became the Nazis' means of solving the Jewish problem, they directly assaulted Jewish women's ability to bear children by developing methods of forced sterilization.[115] After Wannsee, the Nazis focused their attention on killing off the future of the Jewish people by murdering women and children. Mary Felstiner emphasizes the unequal victimization of Jewish women by noting that the women and children were usually the first to be sent to the gas chambers. Jewish men, though also slated to die, were more often selected out for hard labor and a variety of camp duties.[116] But many scholars and survivors are reluctant to draw distinctions between the fate of men and women in circumstances in which being Jewish under the Nazis overwhelmed gender differences.[117]

The intensity of Nazi racial ideology and its maniacal pseudo-biological underpinnings in the end distinguishes the Holocaust from the Armenian genocide in quite profound ways. The Nazi state and its loyal bureaucracy was capable of industrializing murder in ways the Ottomans could not imagine. But it was the creation of an "anti-race," the Jews, "infectious" anywhere and everywhere, that pervaded the Holocaust. If banished to Palestine, Madagascar, or the Arctic north of Siberia, they would eventually destroy one another and expire, as parasites deprived of the bodies on which they feed always do. If the Third Reich and Europe could not be ethnically cleansed of the Jews, then Hitler meant to hunt them down and destroy them wherever they lived and breathed. The Nazis also indicated that Jews around the world would not be safe after the victory of the Third Reich.[118] Although the Young Turks considered the Armenians a "race" and indeed threatened them and their existence outside Turkish borders in the Caucasus, the central issue remained their removal, one way or another, with as much death and suffering as required, from Ottoman Anatolia. Only because *so much* death was finally required by the Young Turks to carry out their plans do we label the Armenian case genocide. The Holocaust was conducted at a different level of magnitude altogether. The appropriately labeled Nazi *Rassenwahn*—racial madness—saw ethnic cleansing mutate into a kind of mass murder unknown before or since.

Soviet Deportation of the Chechens-Ingush and the Crimean Tatars

From its inception, the Soviet state sought to mobilize its citizens and, at the same time, to control them. These dichotomous goals plagued the Soviet system until its very end. One of the ways of mobilizing the large non-Russian populations of the Soviet Eurasian land mass was to grant them autonomy and a measure of self-government. With their success in the 1917 revolution, the Bolsheviks quickly reneged on promises to the nationalities of independence and the right of secession. Instead, in the 1920s and early 1930s, Soviet nationality policy encouraged the subject peoples to develop their national self-consciousness within the finite borders of a geographical unit.[1] The Soviet state built up indigenous national elites within these units and provided them with a structure of governance over their respective peoples. Where it was impossible to provide measures of self-government for nationalities at the lowest level of organization—that is, in the autonomous regions, or oblasts—the Soviet government instituted ethnically based collective farms (kolkhozes) and state farms (sovkhozes). Thus, in the Crimean region, which was part of the Russian federation, there were Jewish, German, Armenian, Tatar, and Bulgarian collective and state farms, which were encouraged to foster their respective ethnic heritage and culture.[2]

As the first commissar of nationalities and a native of the Caucasus, Stalin recognized the inherent power of nationalism to destroy the new Soviet multinational state. Therefore, under his leadership, this elaborate hierarchy of formalistic autonomy for individual ethnic groups was created to harness the national strivings of the peoples of the Soviet Union to the newly constructed authority. The idea was that the USSR would be "national in form and socialist in content" until that time when national differences would fade away. Meanwhile, the Communist Party would carry on its propaganda to inculcate the lessons of socialism among the less progressive nations of the union, and any sign of rising nationalism—which could only be bourgeois and reactionary—would be crushed.

At the same time, the Soviet state was determined to exert centralized control over the movement of its population, despite the country's vast territories and multinational character. The process of recording population statistics and channeling the migration and resettlement of vast numbers of people had already been initiated by the imperial government. Nineteenth-century military statisticians and planners developed elaborate models for dealing with the empire's far-flung nationalities.[3] The All-Russian Imperial Census of 1897, the first complete census in Russian history, was designed to speed the process of modernization by creating a numerical basis for taxation, military service, and citizenship. During the First World War, in particular, the Russian authorities used these nationality categories to deport over a million subjects of the empire: Jews, Germans, Muslims, Chinese, and Koreans, among others.[4]

Soviet statisticians and census planners built on the imperial foundations, but with an even more lively interest in identifying and categorizing national differences for the purposes of population management.[5] In being counted, classified, and ordered by region, town, and nationality, the Soviet population was homogenized in its diversity and placed at the mercy of what Richard Stites labels "administrative Utopianism."[6] Central planners identified and transported hundreds of thousands of young people and workers to build new cities in Siberia and construct dams and canals in hitherto inaccessible reaches of the country. Nickel mining and processing plants were built in the Arctic region and steel factories in the Siberian tundra. Peasants from Ukraine were sent to farm vast stretches of land in Kazakhstan and western Siberia. Meanwhile, national minorities were kept in place or moved as the state saw fit. In his history of the building of the city of Magnitogorsk, entitled *Magnetic Mountain,* Stephen Kotkin describes this process as integral to the civilization of the Soviet Union. The Soviet state, he writes, sought to reconstitute "the demographic makeup of the country, person by person." As a Magnitogorsk newspaper stated the issue: "The population is a matter of utmost political importance."[7]

Soviet nationality policy, central planning, and an ideology of high modernism were not enough to manage a population as diverse in its interests and background, and at such different stages of development, as the Soviet one. Police control and surveillance were critical to the process. The establishment of the secret police system started with the Cheka in 1918 as a "Special Commission" for fighting "counterrevolution and sabotage." But these "repressive organs" (GPU, OGPU, NKVD, and later KGB) were crucial for the maintenance of Soviet power and the management of nationalities in their discrete republics or autonomous units. With the establishment of an elaborate program of residency permits and the institution of the passport system at the end of the 1920s and beginning of the 1930s, Moscow's control over the population tightened, making it possible to move large numbers of people for purposes of regional development, construction, punishment, or a combination of all three.[8] If the goal was to mobilize the country for the attainment of socialism, then—in theory anyway—no one could opt out or disappear. Control of the borders, control of population movement, and control of the workplace were intended to ensure full participation.

The Communist Party of the Soviet Union, its institutions, and its leadership—first Lenin and then Stalin—sought to complete and make perfect these various mechanisms of control. The party insisted on unity and hierarchy, accountability and reporting. But as much of the new research on Stalinism demonstrates, local institutions, groups of individuals, and communities of one sort or another found ways to participate in the system to their own benefit and to resist party rescripts by indirect methods.[9] The system, in other words, was used against itself; high modernism, as James Scott points out in a number of other cases around the world, often trips on the obstacles of local economic systems and human preferences.[10] This was especially true of the Sovietization of the nationalities. Their own interpretation of their rights and needs were in subtle but very real conflict with the expressed wishes of the Soviet state.

In a system motivated by Marxist-Leninist ideology, mobilization depended on successful combat with and defeat of the system's enemies. The aristocracy and bourgeoisie were the initial enemies of the new Soviet state, but they were roundly defeated, according to Soviet conceptions, in the Civil War. The kulaks—supposedly wealthy farmers and their families—were identified as enemies of the state in the late 1920s and, in 1932, they were deported en masse—some 1,100,000 people altogether—to the Far North, Central Asia, and Siberia.[11] Engineers, technical specialists, and other remaining bourgeois enemies were similarly dealt with at the beginning of the 1930s.[12] Amir Weiner has suggested that a critical moment in this history of attacks on class enemies came in 1936, with the promulgation of the new Soviet ("Stalin") constitution, which proclaimed the attainment of socialism and the creation of the legal category of "enemies of the people." From this point forward, Weiner argues, national (or "biological") enemies tended to replace class ones, and deportations focused on enemy peoples rather than enemy classes. In some senses, the categories of class and nation were conflated into one.[13]

After 1937, for the first time in Soviet rhetoric, the "Great Russian" nation was elevated above all of the others. The Russians became the "first among equals," to whom the others looked with deep regard and a sacralized "feeling of friendship, love, and gratitude."[14] Around the same time, many smaller national units and subunits were eliminated as reactionary and unnecessary.[15] In 1937, 1938, and 1939, large nationality groups were subjected to forced deportations.[16] A significant percentage of the Finnish population was deported from the border regions of Karelia.[17] The Koreans and Chinese were removed from the Pacific region, supposedly for security reasons, and deported to Kazakhstan. Poles and Germans were removed from homelands in the west and deported to Central Asia as well. In particular, the fall 1937 deportation of the Koreans from the Far East to Kazakhstan served as a valuable precedent for similar large-scale operations that followed.[18] Soviet planners learned lessons about how to conduct military-like operations against their own people, using surprise and speed as their most valuable weapons to uproot masses of unsuspecting citizens. They developed techniques for transporting large numbers of people by rail and trained NKVD special units to do the business of deportation, both at its starting point and at its destination in Kazakhstan.[19] Perhaps even more significantly, the Soviet government deported for the first time an entire nation: all the Koreans, the young and the old, workers and peasants, party members and not.

Up to this point, the Soviet deportation of nations focused on the borderlands, where, the authorities believed, national minorities were vulnerable to enemy penetration. Germans, Poles, Ukrainians, Finns, and Estonians were cleansed from the western border regions and sent to the east as a way to prepare for the eventuality of war and for potential treachery on the part of the nationalities. Eventually, 1.2 million out of some 1.5 million Soviet Germans were moved to the east—by far the largest single group of exiles in the history of Soviet deportations.[20] Similarly, Koreans and Chinese were cleared out of eastern border areas and moved to the west. These were essentially preventative deportations, rather than punitive ones, and the scale of violence and loss of lives was much less than the punitive deportations of the kulaks earlier, or of the nations of the northern Caucasus during the war.

The Background to the 1944 Deportations

Ethnic cleansing and genocide often take place against the background of war or during the transition from war to peace. World War II exacerbated in every way Stalin's fears regarding national enemies at home and abroad. In the process of fighting a war and suffering occupation by the Germans, the Soviet population itself became much more nationalistic. Both officially and unofficially, the language of class all but disappeared, while ideas of racial affinity for other Slavic nations grew markedly and racial stereotypes of Germans, Jews, Caucasians, and Central Asians hardened. If Hitler considered the German attack on the Soviet Union as a colossal "struggle of two world views against each other," Stalin viewed the war as a fight to the death between Slavs and Germans.[21] Both sides saw it as a race war: for the Nazis, against the Judeo-Bolsheviks; for the Soviets, against the Teutonic invaders.

Soviet propaganda about the clash with the Germans exalted the Russian people above all others. In his first great wartime speech, on November 7, 1941, Stalin invoked a series of historical defenders of the Fatherland to inspire his nation in war: the Princes Aleksandr Nevskii and Dmitrii Donskoi, who fought Teutonic knights and Tatars; the heroes of the "Time of Troubles," Kuzma Minin and Dmitrii Pozharskii; and the great generals of the Napoleanic Wars, Aleksandr Suvorov and Mikhail Kutuzov. Very few could miss the fact that all of them were Russians. The newspapers were full of Russian nationalist rhetoric. "On the eve of a bitter battle, we say to ourselves, as Suvorov said at such moments to his marvelous fighters: 'We are Russians!'" wrote a *Red Star* journalist. "Patriotism is a feeling formed in our people over centuries," wrote another. "Now, in wartime, we even more warmly and closely sense our blood tie with the founders and creators of Great Russian culture."[22]

Especially as a wartime leader, Stalin looked at his role as that of a Russian tsar, conflating his own Soviet and Russian identity as *vozhd—*

leader.[23] One should not make too much of this; Stalin would and did use almost any persona to achieve his goals. Still, he did not appeal to the "freedom-fighting" traditions of the Ukrainian Cossacks or peoples of the Caucasus, since too often those traditions were developed during their struggles against the Russian tsars.[24] To be sure, some local nationalist patriotism was invoked by Ukrainian and Belorussian party leaders as a way to bolster resistance. But this was extremely rare among the non-Slavic peoples of the USSR. Soviet propaganda made it all too apparent that, in the end, the inherent superiority of the Russian people and the Slavs was responsible for the victory in the war.[25]

It may be too much to suggest that Stalin and Hitler learned from one another during the war. Certainly, Hitler and other leading Nazis repeatedly expressed admiration for Stalin's ruthlessness in eliminating political enemies and unflinching willingness to sacrifice countless lives and valuable materiel to military victory.[26] In the spring of 1940, Hitler told Mussolini that "the Georgian Stalin had succeeded in gaining the upper hand and suppressed Jewish influence; the Soviet Union was now reunited with eternal Muscovy."[27] For Hitler, Stalin was variously a "crafty Caucasian," "a barbarian of genius," "a tremendous personality," "a beast, but a beast on a giant scale." Hitler saw Stalin, writes Trevor-Roper, "as his only worthy enemy."[28] Stalin's thoughts about his Nazi opponent were more opaque and, given the paucity of sources, hard to know. But there were times when Stalin clearly admired the Nazi dictator. Robert Tucker notes that one such moment was Hitler's 1934 purge of Ernst Roehm. "Have you heard what happened in Germany? Some fellow [*molodets!*] that Hitler. Knows how to treat his political opponents."[29] Even after the war was over, Stalin rued the end of a valuable partnership. According to his daughter, Svetlana Alliluyeva, he often remarked: "Ekh, together with the Germans we would have been invincible."[30]

By the end of the war, Stalin shared many aspects of Hitler's anti-Semitism. Nazi-inspired racial thinking, including vicious stereotyping of the Jews, also permeated Soviet society in the immediate postwar period. Especially those Ukrainians, Belorussians, Balts, and Russians who had lived under Nazi occupation absorbed much of the propaganda and saw the consequences of anti-Semitism. In this case, the views of society and of the leadership meshed. Stalin and his lieutenants increasingly looked at Jews and at the Jewish Anti-Fascist Committee with a jaundiced eye. Its leaders were forbidden to publish the *Black Book of Soviet Jewry*, which documented Nazi crimes against the Jews. Any mention of special Jewish suffering during the war was denounced as anti-Soviet and suppressed. The committee itself was finally closed down in 1948, accused in the most dangerous terms of anti-Soviet activities and of supplying information to foreign intelligence. On January 12, 1948, the famous Jewish actor and leader of the committee, Solomon Mikhoels, was found brutally murdered in Minsk, repeatedly run over by a truck. Recently released Soviet documents provide proof that the order to arrange for a "speedy liquidation" of Mikhoels came directly from Stalin to his secret police functionary Viktor Abakumov.[31]

Vicious, Nazi-like anti-Semitic caricatures appeared in the Soviet press accompanying the January 1953 announcement of the so-called Doctors' Plot. A group of Kremlin doctors, almost all of Jewish background, were accused of plotting the death of high government and party officials, Stalin included, in association with CIA and Zionist collaborators. A wider and wider ring of Soviet leaders was implicated in the plot. Before Stalin's death on March 15, 1953, rumors spread all over Moscow that the entire Jewish population of Russia would be transported en masse to Siberia.[32] Scholars are still debating the veracity of the reported deportation plans.

Although determined to refute obvious comparisons between the Nazi regime and its own, the new postwar Soviet state continued to foster an ideology that maintained the domination of the Russian (and, to a lesser extent, Ukrainian and Belorussian) nations over the others. The multinational Soviet state was to take its cues from "the most outstanding [nation] of all," the Russians.[33] In film, the popular press, and in accounts of the war, the Russians were lauded as the senior and most important nation of the Soviet Union. If, in the 1930s, history books reversed the earlier Soviet condemnation of Russian imperialism in Central Asia and the Caucasus, historians of the period of postwar "high Stalinism" unabashedly lauded the Russian nation for bringing civilization and development to the backward peoples of the Russian Empire. During the war and after, Stalin also emphasized a strong neo-pan-Slav element in the foreign relations of the Soviet Union. The Soviets' East European allies were similarly encouraged to foster Slavic consciousness in their policies at home and abroad. However, like pan-Slavism in the nineteenth century, Russia was the big brother, the senior partner, the most important of the Slavic peoples. The others—the Czechs, Slovaks, Bulgarians, Serbs, and so on—were there to foster Russia's aims and support its policies.

In this context, the new Soviet man (and woman) was to look like a

Russian (Belorussian or Ukrainian), speak like a Russian, and—if not actually be Russian or Slavic—to recognize the inherent superiority of the Russians in the historical development of the lands in which he or she lived and in contemporary affairs. Soviet patriotism, as it emerged from the war, tried to absorb the experiences of the subject nations into that of the Russians.[34] After all, numerous non-Slavic soldiers served shoulder to shoulder with Russians, Belorussians, and Ukrainians during the war. Many learned Russian for the first time and felt a sense of accomplishment and pride in common victory. However, any nation that stood in the way of this melding of Soviet and Russian patriotism was imperiled. The deportations of Chechens-Ingush and of the Crimean Tatars in 1944 can be understood only as part of this story.

Chechens and Ingush

Joanna Nichols tells us that the Chechens and Ingush are "distinct ethnic groups with distinct languages, but so closely related and so similar that it is convenient to describe them together."[35] The history of these peoples in the northern Caucasus goes back almost six thousand years.[36] The strength of clan ties to their neighbors and their villages in the mountains and valleys of the region are deep and abiding, more so than to any idea of Chechen or Ingush "nationhood," separately or individually, or to particular territorial boundaries.[37] Known in the period up to the 1917 revolution simply as *gor'tsy* or "mountaineers," the Chechens and Ingush operated as clans and groups of clans, sometimes more closely tied to other "nations" in the region than to their own "people." This was true of the neighboring Muslim peoples of Daghestan, as well as the Karachaevtsy and Balkars, who, together with the Chechens and Ingush, endured deportation during World War II.

With the Russian penetration of the Caucasus in the first half of the nineteenth century, Chechens and Ingush—like other Muslim mountaineers—found themselves the object of Cossack raids and incursions into what they thought was their homeland, and they fought bitterly to preserve the integrity of their customs and law. When the Cossacks established settlements and forts in the lowlands and foothills, the Chechens and Ingush pulled back to the mountains and engaged in periodic raids and forays against the new Russian settlers. Chechens and Ingush participated widely in the uprising led by the great Daghestani warrior Imam Shamil which dominated the northern Caucasus from

1840 to 1859 and held such a deep fascination for nineteenth-century Russian writers like Lev Tolstoy and Nikolai Lermontov.

Despite Bolshevik rhetoric about liberating the peoples of the region from Russian colonialism, the most severe trials of the Chechen and Ingush peoples were to come during the Soviet period. Chechens and Ingush fought in the Civil War to maintain their autonomy. It took the Bolsheviks and the Red Army until 1925 to crush the resistance of the mountaineers and begin the process of Sovietization. But even then, resistance continued. The Chechens and Ingush fought collectivization, which even Soviet scholars noted simply did not fit the migratory agricultural economy of the majority of the people.[38] Chechens and Ingush would kill their animals and burn their grain before they would turn it over to procurement officials. In 1932 and 1933 they fought pitched battles with Red Army and police officials, killing a substantial number before succumbing to inclusion into collective farms.[39] Throughout the 1930s, Chechens and Ingush withstood the onslaught of Soviet "civilization," whether it was forced industrialization, collectivization, mandatory agricultural deliveries, or more benign policies like literacy campaigns, secularization programs, and mass education initiatives. Chechen women and girls continued to stay in their homes, with their flocks, or in the fields; Chechen men increasingly turned to the Sufi brotherhoods that provided shelter and relief from Sovietization campaigns.

As with the other small nations of the northern Caucasus, the Soviet authorities promoted forms of territorial autonomy for the Chechens and Ingush, while pressuring them to conform to socialist norms and institutions. Initially, the Soviets set up a Soviet Mountain Republic in 1921 that comprised most of the peoples of the northern Caucasus, including the Chechens and Ingush, with the exception of those who were living in the Daghestan Socialist Republic. But in 1922 the Soviets decided to break up the Mountain Republic in favor of smaller national units, including a Chechen autonomous *oblast*. In 1925, after repeated skirmishes with the Chechens, Moscow focused a major military effort—including air power and artillery—on the region in an attempt to disarm the Chechens and "remove the chiefs of counter-revolutionary banditry."[40] After a decade of struggle with the Chechens and Ingush, Moscow combined them in a Chechen-Ingush autonomous province, as part of the campaign to amalgamate the smaller peoples of the Soviet Union. Today, once again, there are separate republics of Chechnya and

Ingushetiya within the Russian Federation, incipient "countries"—like many others in the former territory of the Soviet Union—which were essentially created by Bolshevik nationality policy.

The Chechens-Ingush during World War II

Relations between the Soviet authorities and the Chechens-Ingush during the 1930s can only be described as deeply troubled. From the Soviet point of view, the region was infested with "counterrevolutionary bandits," who received sustenance from the local population.[41] The NKVD recorded incessant fighting between their units in the region and the Chechens-Ingush. At the outbreak of the war, the NKVD claimed to have liquidated 963 gangs in the northern Caucasus, with some 17,563 members; by far the largest number were Chechens.[42] From his work in NKVD archives, Nikolai Bugai has documented dozens of anti-Soviet conspiracies among Chechens and Ingush during the period 1941–1943, including the development of a "national socialist" party that allegedly planned an uprising to coincide with the invasion of the Chechen lands by the Nazis.[43] The Chechen émigré historian Abdurakhman Avtorkhanov believes that the reports of counterrevolutionary bandits were purposely inflated by members of the NKVD for careerist purposes; Aleksandr Nekrich also asserts that the battles of the 1930s were much exaggerated.[44] Nevertheless, when the Germans dropped parachutists, both Germans and émigré mountaineers, into the region in the late summer and early fall of 1942, they found some support from local groups. Large numbers of Chechens and Ingush joined up, like other members of the nations of the northern Caucasus, to fight for the Soviet Union in "the Great Patriotic War." But many resisted induction, and those who enlisted were often not trusted. As a consequence, mandatory military service was suspended in the region in late 1942.[45]

World War II provided the immediate background for the deportations of the Chechen and Ingush peoples. The official justification for the deportations emphasized the collaboration of the Chechens during the fighting: "Many Chechens and Ingush were traitors to the homeland, changing over to the side of the fascist occupiers, joining the ranks of diversionaries and spies left behind the lines of the Red Army by the Germans. They formed armed bands at the behest of the Germans fighting against Soviet power."[46] While it is unlikely that the Chechens were any more enthusiastic about the Soviet war effort than other Muslims of the northern Caucasus or Central Asia, it is also unlikely that they were less so. The issue of the exact extent of Chechen-Ingush collaboration cannot be fully answered without a thorough investigation of relevant Soviet and German archives. But available evidence indicates that they did not collaborate in any significant way. Moreover, they participated in the war effort at a level similar to that of other non-Russian peoples who were not subjected to removal from their homelands.[47] John Dunlop confirms the observations of the first historians of the Chechen-Ingush deportations, Aleksandr Nekrich and Robert Conquest, that there were no more than a hundred recorded instances of "aiding and abetting" the enemy.[48] Even an NKVD report from the period stated that no more than 335 "bandits" were in the republic.[49] Why then were they deported? The explanation is two-fold and goes back to rationalizations of state (shaping the "body politic") and rationalizations of history (settling old scores), both of which were more easily dealt with during wartime.

Although hardly the collaborators portrayed by the Soviets, the Chechens and Ingush were unquestionably a thorn in the side of Moscow authorities. As Muslim mountain peoples, nearly a half-million altogether, the Chechens and Ingush maintained much more cultural and religious autonomy than the Soviets liked. Aleksandr Iakovlev suggests that the Soviet authorities felt particularly threatened by the "anti-Soviet" Sufi Muslim brotherhoods that flourished in the mountains during the war.[50] Documents from the regional party organization (*obkom*) speak of the resiliency of the Chechen clan leadership in the face of Soviet education and propaganda campaigns and of the difficulty of recruiting Chechens into Grozny's working class, associated almost exclusively with the local oil industry.[51] Chechen women were particularly hard for the party to reach, primarily because their fathers and husbands, inside and outside the party and government, refused to allow their participation in public affairs.[52]

Stalin and Beria would not forget easily how the Chechens and Ingush resisted pacification during the Civil War and after. Also fresh in Soviet leaders' memories was Chechen and Ingush resistance to collectivization, which included pitched battles with armed units.[53] The attachment of the Chechen and Ingush to their homelands, the difficulty of imposing modern state forms on a resilient traditional society, and the ability of the Chechens and Ingush to resist both direct pressures from Moscow and the modernization expected from the granting of national institutional forms made the Soviet leadership determined to deal with them once and for all. This was a Soviet-style final solution to an ongoing and scabrous problem of national antagonism.

The Deportations

Beria was in full charge of the operation in the northern Caucasus. When the Red Army liberated the Caucasus from the last Wehrmacht units in January and February 1943, Beria initiated the first discussions of operation Chechevista.[54] In October 1943 he sent his deputy Bogdan Kobulov to the region to collect information about the potential deportation of the Chechens and Ingush. By the end of 1943, the government had bivouacked Red Army and NKVD troops in Chechen and Ingush towns with the explanation that the units were taking a rest from the war and would soon be returned to the front. Some of the soldiers engaged in the charade of practicing for mountain warfare. The troops mixed easily with the villagers, often eating and living in their homes and joining them in their customs. On the night of February 23–24, 1944, Beria ordered the operation to start.[55] He called in Chechen party leaders and told them about the fate of their people. Comrade Molaev, the representative of the Chechen Autonomous Republic to the Sovnarkom, wept bitterly but in the end offered his services to make the deportations proceed more smoothly.[56] Troops went from house to house informing the residents that they had a half an hour (in some cases a bit more, in some less) to get themselves ready for transport. Many of the men were rounded up at work or in the fields and taken directly to the railheads.[57] Non-Chechen students were sent out from Grozny to the most important of the depopulated collective farms to keep them functioning until new settlers arrived.[58] Troops assembled villagers and townspeople, loaded them onto trucks—many deportees remembered that they were Studebakers, fresh from Lend-Lease deliveries over the Iranian border—and delivered them at previously designated railheads.[59] Anyone who resisted was shot, but the NKVD reported only sporadic cases of resistance.[60] From the railway stations, the Chechen and Ingush nations were loaded into boxcars and sent off to Kazakhstan and Kirghizia, which were to be their domiciles until the mid-1950s.

The NKVD ordered all Chechens and Ingush out of their homelands. No exceptions were allowed. Party leaders, war heroes, and famous writers and artists were sometimes sent separately under somewhat better circumstances, but everyone had to go. Those who could not be moved were shot. In one particularly grisly case in the snowbound village of Khaibakh (Galanchozhskii district), NKVD troops herded some 730 villagers from the area into a horse barn, set it afire, and shot those who tried to break away from the inferno, their hair and clothes in flames.[61] Despite the careful planning and NKVD claims to a flawless operation, significant numbers of Chechen fighters escaped to the high mountain passes of the Caucasus. Chechens who somehow managed to avoid deportation joined them; but any Chechen or Ingush identified after the deportations was treated as a "bandit" and shot on sight or sent off to hard labor.[62] These few fighters aside, the entire Chechen and Ingush nations, 496,460 people, were deported from their homeland.[63] In theory, all the Chechens and Ingush living within the borders of the USSR were designated for deportation. Some 30,000 Chechens living in northwestern Daghestan were deported, as were Chechens and Ingush living in northern Ossetia.[64] Whether they were serving in army units or laboring in NKVD camps in the north, Chechens and Ingush were sent with their brethren to Kazakhstan and Kirghizia.

As in every case of ethnic cleansing and forced deportation of peoples, large numbers of Chechens died in the process. Some 3,000 perished even before being deported.[65] The NKVD readily supplied precise (and unquestionably low) figures about the numbers who died during transport, mostly the old, the infirm, and the very young. One can extrapolate from these separate figures that roughly 10,000 died from disease, hunger, and cold.[66] The rail cars were sealed; there was no food or water; sanitation was nonexistent. Typhus left thousands dead and dying. The trains stopped periodically to dispose of corpses, but the locals were forbidden to help. Archival documents are filled with regrets on the part of health officials that the ostensibly scheduled stops for food and medical care never seemed to be observed or were forbidden by the NKVD.[67]

The largest death toll came in the days and months after arrival—roughly 100,000 in the first three years (again extrapolating from NKVD statistics).[68] The local authorities were simply not prepared for the influx of these "special settlers," a classification previously reserved primarily for kulaks.[69] Despite NKVD orders to Kazakh and Kirghiz communist parties to make building and working materials available to the settlers and to provide adequate food and clothing at the deportees' destinations, the Chechens and Ingush found themselves without work, food, clothing or shelter.[70] Women and children foraged for edible grasses. Ragged orphans wandered about aimlessly. Already fearfully impoverished, local officials were often unwilling to help. The Chechens and Ingush died by the tens of thousands in wretched poverty.

The Aftermath

Some Chechen and Ingush historians assert that the deportations of 1944 constituted genocide against their nations. But if it was genocide, it was genocide with a particular Soviet twist. Stalin and Beria's goal—as best we can tell—was to destroy the Chechen and Ingush nations without necessarily eliminating their peoples. Certainly, the fate of the Chechen-Ingush Autonomous Republic leads one to think that the Soviet leaders were in search of a permanent solution to the Chechen question. The region was officially dissolved in 1944, and neighboring Daghestan, northern Ossetia, Georgia, and Stavropol region eagerly seized and absorbed their designated sections of the Chechen and Ingush lands.[71] The new inhabitants renamed towns and villages, bulldozed graveyards and monuments, and erased any remaining signs of the Chechen presence in the region. No one spoke of the deportations in the newspapers, in meetings, or in public. Post-deportation records of Grozny *obkom* meetings never mention the peoples who had once lived there.[72] They disappeared even from history books and encyclopedias. In exile in Kazakhstan and Kirghizia, the Chechens and Ingush were forbidden from using their language in schools or from fostering their culture in any public way.

Even after the death of Stalin in March 1953, the Soviet authorities refused to allow the Chechens to return to their homelands, though a few began to make their way back to the northern Caucasus. After Khrushchev's secret speech in February 1956 called attention to the violations and "excesses" of Stalinist policy in the treatment of Soviet nationalities, thousands of Chechens and Ingush began the long trek back to the mountains. But unlike other nationalities, the Chechens and Ingush were explicitly forbidden to return to their homelands. Although their status as special settlers was dropped, "this does not mean that they have the right to the return of their property confiscated during their expulsion, nor do they have the right to return to the places, from which they were expelled," stated the directive of the Supreme Soviet.[73] In fact, the Soviet government intended to prevent the Chechens and Ingush from returning home and to create for them an autonomous region in Kazakhstan or in Chimkent in Uzbekistan.[74] But Chechen and Ingush party leaders and intelligentsia resolutely rejected any such solution to their problems.[75] There were mounting reports from the region of fighting, even armed clashes, between returning Chechens and Ingush and those people who had moved into their houses and villages after the deportations. Despite opposition from the new bosses of the Chechen-Ingush territory, in 1957 the Soviet government finally consented to allow some 17,000 Chechen and Ingush families to return to their homelands. Even more arrived in the region, but they refused "categorically" to go to those areas where they were told to settle. Instead, the Chechens and Ingush returned to their homes and drove out the inhabitants; shootings and even killings were reported.[76]

At the end of 1957 the Chechen and Ingush Autonomous Republic was reestablished, and all the Chechens and Ingush were allowed to return to their homes.[77] But problems with the Chechens were far from over. Between 1958 and 1972 the Ministry of Internal Affairs reported that nearly one out of six Chechen and Ingush adults, some 115,455 people, were brought before the authorities on charges of criminal behavior. In January 1973 serious armed confrontations broke out between Soviet authorities in Grozny and the Chechens and Ingush. The party attributed the problems to the clan and Islamic loyalties of the native population.[78] The superficial and incomplete Sovietization of the Chechen and Ingush nations and the repeated penalties they were forced to pay for this fact left them the most serious internal enemy of the Moscow regime.

The Crimean Tatars

The Crimean Tatars descended from the great Mongol khanates which ruled vast stretches of the Eurasian continent during the medieval and early modern periods. As one of the heirs to the Mongol empire, the Crimean khanate reached its apogee in the fourteenth and fifteenth centuries. Initially allied with the Ottoman sultan and then forced into being his vassal and client, the Crimean khans tried to maintain their independence by playing off Ottoman power in the region against the growing ambitions of the Russian Empire on the northern littoral of the Black Sea. The first serious Russian incursions into the region came at the beginning of the eighteenth century under the reign of Peter the Great (1698–1725). By the end of the century, the Ottoman Empire was in serious decline and the ambitions and armed victories of Catherine the Great (1762–1796) brought the Crimea and the northern Black Sea coast under Russian rule. In 1783, with great pomp and circumstance, Catherine proclaimed the Crimean peninsula part of Russia.

The fate of the Crimean Tatars in imperial Russia was different than that of the Chechens and Ingush, though both groups were Muslim. The Tatar aristocracy assimilated with the Russians, intermarrying and becoming part of the Russian estates hierarchy. Similarly, Tatar peasants, though unlikely to assimilate, became part of the serf system. Urban Tatars sold their labor at home in the Crimea or further to the north, as migrant workers. The remote farm lands of the northern part of the peninsula remained in the hands of Tatar agriculturalists, while the towns of the seacoast quickly became resorts and resting spots for the elite of imperial Russian society. Anton Chekhov had his summer home in Yalta; Russian noble families built tasteful mansions along the rocky coast. Unlike the northern Caucasus, where Russian colonization was limited mostly to Cossack stations in the lowlands, leaving the mountains and foothills to the Chechens and Ingush, the Crimea was quickly settled by Russian and Ukrainian peasants, as well as Jews (including native Karaites), Greeks, Armenians, and Bulgarians, some of whom had already established their first communities on the peninsula centuries earlier. With the influx of Russians and Ukrainians, social tensions between Tatars and non-Tatars episodically exploded in rioting and pogroms. But on the whole, the Crimea supported a relatively stable multinational culture.[79]

The Crimean War (1853–1856) marked an important stage in the development of Russian-Tatar relations. Because of their sympathies with the Turks, the Tatars were accused of collaborating with the British and French against the Russians, despite the fact that Tatar brigades fought loyally on the side of the imperial Russian army. The Russians survived the conflict with minimal territorial losses and held on to the Crimea as a result of the Peace of Paris (1856). As a consequence, Tsar Alexander II encouraged what he called the "voluntary emigration" of some 100,000 Tatars from the peninsula, most of whom ended up under Ottoman rule or fled persecution to other centers in the region.[80] The Crimean Tatars remained part of the remarkable civilization that flourished around the Black Sea, moving from town to town, even coast to coast, depending on the situation.[81]

As dictated by the new Soviet nationality policy, Lenin and Stalin established a Crimean Autonomous Republic in November 1921. This situation lasted until the German invasion in 1941. But despite considerable support for the Bolshevik revolution among the Tatar intelligentsia, the new Soviet state clashed repeatedly with the Tatars between the revolution and World War II. Alan Fisher notes that some 150,000 Tatars, half of the 1917 population, had either been killed or forced into exile during the revolution, civil war, and collectivization. In addition, the purges, as everywhere among the nationalities, took a terrible toll among the Crimean Tatars.[82]

Moscow was interested in the Crimea because of its natural harbors for the Soviet navy, such as Sevastopol, and its luxurious seaside resorts for the Soviet elite, such as Yalta and Alupta. The area quickly became dotted with special Pioneer Camps and Labor Union retreats. In conformance with Soviet nationality policy, the Crimean Tatars remained the titular nationality of the region. A Tatar was named head of the regional party organization; a Russian or Ukrainian was almost always his deputy. But this distribution of power was fictitious; the Crimea was completely at the mercy of Moscow's whims. Tensions between Tatars and Russians remained high in the 1930s, though the kind of outright armed clashes that occurred so often in the northern Caucasus were avoided.

The Deportation of the Tatars

As with the Chechens and Ingush, the Soviets justified their deportation of the Crimean Tatars to Uzbekistan and Tadjikistan in May 1944 by alleging the collaboration of Tatars with the Germans during the war. The Germans had actually set up an occupation regime in the Crimea from October 1941 until April 1944. Hitler's and Himmler's idea was to drive the Tatars out of the Crimea and turn the area into Gotland, an Aryan haven for Germans, especially from the south Tyrol. But the need to placate the Turks and use the Tatars for labor caused the Nazis to abandon this fantasy, as they had so many others. Nazi control of the Crimea quickly brought Tatar resentments of Soviet Russian rule to the surface, and evidence of collaboration is plentiful.[83] Tatars set up village home-guard units, which were part of the Nazi administration. The Nazis supported these Tatar "self-defense" units, which engaged in actions against Soviet partisans. But there is no evidence that the Tatars, as sometimes alleged, helped the Nazis wipe out the entire Crimean Jewish population.[84] Nevertheless, angry recriminations against Tatars permeate the memoirs of Russian partisans of the region collected by the Soviet Academy of Sciences after the war.[85]

From the Soviet side, trouble was brewing for the Tatars as early as 1943, when Russian partisan leaders A. N. Mokrousov and A. V. Martynov denounced local Tatars for collaborating with the enemy. V. Bulatov, head of the Tatar *obkom,* forced Mokrousov to recant his statement. Large numbers of Tatars were in the resistance, he insisted. Moreover, many Russian and Ukrainian partisan groups, like Mokrousov and Martynov's, would not allow Tatars to join, and, instead of seeking cooperation with Tatar villagers, they would attack them and steal their food, thus driving them into the camp of the enemy.[86] Even though Mokrousov and Martynov recanted, local Russians continued to complain about the Tatars and their friendliness toward the Germans.[87] Criticisms of Tatar collaboration under the Nazis found their way to Beria, head of the NKVD, who reported them to Stalin.[88] Although the Crimean Tatars did collaborate much more noticeably than the Chechens and Ingush, it is unlikely that their collaboration with the Germans was much different from that of many Russians or Ukrainians in the region.[89] Nevertheless, Stalin and Beria used these charges to deport the entire Tatar nation, roughly 189,000 men, women, and children, from the Crimea.

On the night of May 17–18, 1944, NKVD and Red Army troops, already experienced from similar operations in the northern Caucasus, surrounded Tatar villages and homes, demanding that the Tatars assemble for transport to the east.[90] As in the case of the Chechens and Ingush, every single Tatar had to go, whatever their position in society, whether married to a Russian or not (a much more common occurrence among the Tatars than among Chechens or Ingush). Non-Tatar husbands and wives could choose to go with their spouses or remain behind. Beria bragged to Stalin that the troops encountered only isolated cases of resistance and committed "no excesses at all."[91] Rail transport in sealed box cars, similar to those that transported the Chechens and Ingush, took a fearful toll in Tatar lives.[92] The Tatars died of thirst by the thousands. "We Tatars call these Soviet railcars 'crematoria on wheels,'" recalled Ayshe Seytmuratova, who managed to survive the ordeal and write about it. "So we were transported for weeks without proper food or medical attention. There was not even any fresh air, for the doors and windows were bolted shut. For days on end, corpses lay alongside the living. And only out in the sands of Kazakhstan did the transport guards open the doors, so as to toss out the corpses alongside the railway. They did not give us time to bury the dead. Many people went insane."[93]

Although an educated and highly adaptable people, the Tatars suffered terribly in the special settlements designated for them in Central Asia. After the transport, they were in no condition to work and therefore could find no way to support themselves and their families. Like the Chechens and Ingush—as well as Balkars, Karachaevtsy, and Kalmyks—the Crimean Tatars were told they were exiled "in perpetuity" and "without the right to return to their previous place of residence." If they tried to leave their places of exile, they were liable to as much as twenty years of hard labor. Anyone who helped them escape or gave them refuge in their home territory could be sentenced to five years of prison.[94]

The indigenous population refused to help and treated them with brutality and disdain, and the local NKVD warders sometimes beat and exploited them.[95] Tens of thousands died before the situation stabilized at the beginning of the 1950s.[96] According to Tatar historians, the losses from the deportations and settlement reached up to 45 percent of the entire Tatar population.[97] The victims were mostly women and children.[98]

Undoubtedly, long-term reasons of state as defined by Stalin and Beria lay behind the deportations. The Soviet leadership wanted a Crimea without Tatars, thus fulfilling a goal of Russian statesmen ever since the incorporation of the Crimea into the Russian Empire during the reign of Catherine the Great.[99] Now, after the liberation of the Crimea in 1944, Stalin and his lieutenants were determined to clean out the Crimea of *all* foreigners, Tatars primarily but also Greeks (15,040), Bulgarians (13,422), and Armenians (9,621), who were deported soon after the Tatars.[100] While the deportations of the Tatars had racial overtones, as did those of the Chechens and Ingush, race was not the primary consideration on the Soviets' minds; Tatars from other parts of Russia were allowed to stay where they were. Tatar residents in the Crimea who were off fighting the war were, however, like their Chechen-Ingush comrades-in-arms, also sent into exile.

After the war, when a few hundred Tatars managed to return legally to the Crimea, the local authorities sharply protested to Moscow. Foreign espionage services would inevitably use the Tatar population for their nefarious purposes, they claimed. Thus, not a single Tatar should be allowed to stay in the Crimea. If released from the status of special settlers, then the Tatars should be allowed to settle in other parts of Russia, just not in the Crimea. Stalin met with Comrade Bulaev of the Crimean *obkom* and "gave the order not to allow Tatars in the Crimea under any conditions, because they serve as sources for foreign spies."[101] Although a few exceptions were allowed for family reasons, most of the Tatars who had filtered back to the Crimea were deported again to other parts of the country.[102]

Tatar monuments were destroyed, books and manuscripts were burned, and history was rewritten to suggest that Tatars had engaged in little else but banditry and thievery throughout modern Russian history and had made no contribution to the development of their homeland.[103] In a few postwar Soviet spy novels, Crimean Tatars figure prominently as traitors and evil Nazi agents. On August 14, 1944, the Crimean *obkom* issued an order to change all the Tatar names of towns, cities, regions, kolkhozes, and sovkhozes, "in connection with the changed circumstances of the Crimea."[104] After the war, the Crimean Autonomous Republic was abolished and replaced by the Crimean *oblast* (region) of the Russian Federation. In 1954 Nikita Khrushchev, in the name of "the friendship of peoples," gave the Crimea to Ukraine as a "present." Like the Chechens and Ingush, the Crimean Tatars were not mentioned in Khrushchev's "secret speech" at the Twentieth Party Congress in 1956. Nearly all those who tried to return to the Crimea in the mid-1960s were rebuffed by the authorities. Although a 1967 decree cleared the Tatars of charges of collaboration with the Nazis, the Soviet authorities let it be known that "citizens of the Tatar nationality formerly resident in Crimea" and "settled in the Uzbek and other Union republics" did not need to return to the Crimea.[105]

Unlike the Chechens and Ingush, the Crimean Tatars were never given permission by the Soviet government to return to the Crimea. In this respect, they were discriminated against as were no others of the "punished peoples." They were not even allowed to call themselves Crimean Tatars but rather were referred to by the authorities simply as Tatars or as "Tatars formerly living in Crimea." During *perestroika,* however, many did indeed return and sought to regain rights to their homes and lands, a struggle that continues to this day. Only in 1994, did the Crimean local government officially restore the name "Crimean" to the local Tatars who had returned.[106]

Conclusion

The deportations of the Chechens-Ingush and Crimean Tatars fit the definition of ethnic cleansing as it has been developed in this book. Stalin, Beria, and the Soviet leadership intentionally and forcibly removed these peoples from their homelands and deported them to regions from which they were allowed no escape. That tens of thousands died during the deportations and after they arrived at their destinations did not overly concern Soviet authorities, though killing off these nations in a genocidal attack was clearly not the Soviets' intention. Instead, policies were implemented to reeducate the Chechens-Ingush and Crimean Tatars—to force them to forget their homelands and their cultures. The "human material" was salvageable; just the nations—as nations—were slated to disappear through assimilation and detachment from their homelands. This was different from Hitler's attack on the Jews and gypsies, where humans themselves were inherently tainted and therefore doomed to extinction.

Unlike other cases of ethnic cleansing in the twentieth century, the Soviets did not designate a particular nation to take the place of the Chechens and Ingush in the northern Caucasus. Many different nations moved in to replace the deportees, including some Muslims from Daghestan. In the Crimea, however, the Soviets did try to ensure that Russians and Ukrainians controlled the destiny of the region. Still, the deportations were not aimed at creating ethnically homogeneous regions, as in the cases of ethnic cleansing in the Balkans. Still, the eliminationist attack on the Chechens-Ingush and Tatars was complete; alien elements were violently excised from the body politic.

Stalin used the cover of war to take care of unfinished business with the Chechens, Ingush, and Crimean Tatars. Nationalist sentiment and reasons of state impressed on him and on his lieutenant Beria the need to get the Chechens and Ingush (and Balkars and Karachaevtsy) out of the mountains of the northern Caucasus. From the available documentation, one can only speculate about Stalin's motives. He may have been interested, for example, in creating some form of "Christian"—if not purely Slavic—domination of the mountainous borderlands between Russia and the Caucasian region by turning the area over to Georgians, northern Ossetians, and Russians from the Stavropol region. Stalin's xenophobic reasoning in the case of the Crimean Tatars may have been much the same. The Crimea, perceived as vulnerable to Turkish and Western penetration, was to be cleared of the Tatars, as well as Bulgarians, Armenians, and Greeks. (The Germans had already done the job of dealing with the Jews and Karaites.) They would be replaced by Russians and Ukrainians. Stalin may have felt that he was finishing the job of clearing the Crimean peninsula of unreliable Muslims that Alexander II had started.

From the point of view of the Soviet leadership, Crimean Tatars and Chechens-Ingush were too attached to their cultures, mores, and histories to become effective Soviet nationalities. They were also small enough to be moved en masse without being missed as critical members of the labor force or as reliable masters of contiguous territory. For Stalin and Beria, these individual cultures—if not the peoples themselves— would perish in the vastness of their new and alien Central Asian special settlements. They would be assimilated into the Kazakh and Uzbek worlds, while their homelands would be renamed, given a new history, and absorbed by other, ostensibly more reliable, nations. This was less a racist concept than a Soviet nationalist one, though racism was never far from the surface in the Soviet authorities' treatment of these peoples. The peoples could survive, just not as claimants to their homelands. This was an important difference with the Turkish treatment of the Armenians and especially with the Nazi policy toward the Jews.

Politics in the Soviet Union was also much more subtle and difficult to discern than that of the Third Reich, especially given the paucity of documents and the limits of archival access. Stalin was not given to long ramblings like Hitler, whose stenographers and contemporaries recorded his utterances for the benefit of posterity. We do know that conflicts between Russians and Tatars in the Crimea obviously influenced the decision of Stalin and Beria to deport the Tatars. The northern Ossetians, Georgians, and Stavropol Russians had their eyes on Grozny's oil industry and pieces of Chechen-Ingush territory, and that must have made a difference to Stalin and Beria's decision to deport the Chechens and Ingush.

As anyone who follows contemporary events is aware, these stories are far from finished. The Chechens continue to resist Russian attempts to incorporate them into the new Russian state. Anatol Lieven writes that the memory of the 1944 deportations, even more than the wars of Shamil, has become "the central defining event in modern Chechen history."[107] Every Chechen fighter rehearses the story of the "betrayal" of his people by the Soviet (that is, Russian) authorities; the entire Chechen population repeatedly hears the tale of the terrible punishment their people endured.[108] As a result, the fighting continues, as it has for 150 years. Serious evidence indicates that the Russian government developed plans to deport the Chechens once again in the mid-1990s if they had lost the war.[109] During the outbreak of the 1999 war, the Chechens seemed unwilling to accept the borders cut out for them after their return in the 1950s; thus they carried the fighting into Daghestan.

But again, evidence has turned up indicating that the huge number of Chechen refugees in Ingushetiya may be sent off to the Altai region, a solution presumably not of the Chechens' own choosing.[110] There have also been episodic suggestions in the Russian press to disperse the Chechens throughout the Siberian north and east. Ethnic cleansing and even genocide remain a dangerous possibility.

The Crimean Tatars seek to regain their homes and villages through protracted political lobbying between rival Ukrainian and Russian parties in the Crimea. (Formally, the Crimea belongs to Ukraine, but the Russians continue to exert powerful influence in the region.) Progress has been stymied by the impasse between the Ukrainian government and local Crimean (Russian) authorities. About half the Crimean Tatars still live in Uzbekistan, while most of the rest have found their way back to the Crimea. They fight for their return in their own way, living in tent cities or makeshift shanties on the edge of towns whose houses and apartments formerly were inhabited by their own relatives.[111] They are subjected to attacks by local Russian and Ukrainian thugs, who attempt to drive them from the region. Some Tatars have been murdered.[112] Newly constructed mosques and community centers have also been attacked and, in some cases, destroyed. The Crimean Tatars have not forgotten the events of 1944, and that memory strengthens their resolve to reestablish their rightful place in their ancient homeland.

The Expulsion of Germans from Poland and Czechoslovakia

The Second World War had barely begun when both the Polish and Czechoslovak governments-in-exile began talking about the expulsion of the Germans from their respective countries after the victory. Both governments referred frequently to the ostensibly successful transfer of Greeks and Turks by the Treaty of Lausanne in January 1923. This was to be the legal precedent for their actions: the great powers had supervised this transfer and provided the financial backing to relocate the exchanged populations.[1] For the Poles and Czechs, the operative principle was the forced relocation of their minority populations under the auspices of international organizations. Indeed, the two governments, located in London during most of the war, talked to each other about the expulsions of their respective German populations and the need to lobby with Allied governments to ensure the acceptance of population transfer in principle.[2] Even in the postwar period, when tensions rose between the Polish and Czechoslovak governments because of the Teschen conflict, which involved armed clashes as well as mutual denunciations, both governments remained in perfect agreement about the need to expel the Germans and to pin down the Allies on terminal dates.[3]

The Polish and Czechoslovak governments-in-exile did not need to worry. The Allies were in complete agreement that the Germans would have to be moved out of both postwar Poland and the former Sudetenland. The vast movements of peoples during the war itself made further mass population transfers, especially ones involving the hated Germans, unproblematic. The Soviet Union's experiences with deporting large numbers of people before and especially during the war also made their officials quite receptive to the entreaties of the Poles and Czechoslovaks.[4] Newly published documents from the Russian archives make it clear that Stalin and Molotov were fully informed about the East Europeans' plans to deport the Germans. During their frequent meetings with the Czechs and Poles, the Soviet leaders stated that they not only had no objections "in principle" to the deportations but that they thought "positively" about them.[5] In a June 28, 1945, conversation with Zdenek Fierlinger and Vlado Klementis, Czechoslovak prime minister and deputy foreign minister respectively, Stalin unambiguously endorsed the deportations: "We won't disturb you. Throw them out. Now they will learn themselves what it means to rule over someone else." At the same time, Stalin was unwilling to accede to Fierlinger's request that the Red Army help with the deportations of Germans and Hungarians.[6] The Soviet dictator also let the Polish communist leader, Wladyslaw Gomulka, know that the deportations were the business of the East Europeans, not the Red Army. Still, he was ready to give Gomulka advice on how to get the Germans to leave: "You should create such conditions for the Germans that they want to escape themselves."[7]

Edvard Benes, president of the Czechoslovak government, repeatedly and justifiably claimed that he had received the blessings of Churchill and even Roosevelt for the transfers.[8] True, the Americans felt some unease about the potential effect of mass deportations on the economic viability of occupied Germany. Yet both the American and British governments were "sympathetic" to the Czechoslovak and Polish cases for expulsion of the Germans and, like the Soviets, had "no objection in principle."[9] Churchill was especially callous on the subject. Already on October 9, 1944, he remarked to Stalin that seven million Germans would be killed in the war, thus leaving plenty of room for those Germans driven out of Silesia and East Prussia to move into rump Germany.[10] During a conversation with Stalin at Yalta in February 1945, Churchill stated that he was not at all "shocked at the idea of transferring millions of people by force." The conversation continued:

> *Stalin:* There will be no more Germans there for when our troops come in the Germans run away and no Germans are left.
> *Prime Minister:* Then there is the problem of how to handle them in Germany. We have killed six or seven million and probably will kill another million before the end of the war.
> *Stalin:* One or two?

Prime Minister: Oh I am not proposing any limitation on them. So there should be room in Germany for some who will need to fill the vacancy.[11]

Churchill used Stalin's arguments to bolster his case for expulsion at home. On February 23, 1945, he complained to his junior ministers that people kept bringing up the "great difficulties" of transferring the German population to the west, but, he insisted, "most of the Germans in the territories now taken by the Russians had 'run away already,'" making the issue much more easy to resolve.[12]

Churchill repeatedly used the example of the Greek-Turkish transfer of populations mandated by Lausanne as a legitimate precedent for removing the Germans, the resolution of which also "at first seemed impossible." As Klaus Dietmar Hencke writes, Lausanne was an "idée fixe" for Churchill and other leaders of the anti-Hitler coalition.[13] It gave the British leader the confidence that the Allies could deal once and for all with the German minority problem in East Central Europe. Churchill's speech in the British House of Commons on December 15, 1944, put the situation bluntly: "For expulsion is the method which, so far as we have been able to see, will be the most satisfactory and lasting. There will be no mixture of populations to cause endless trouble as in Alsace-Lorraine. A clean sweep will be made. I am not alarmed at the prospect of the disentanglement of population, nor am I alarmed by these large transferences, which are more possible than they were before through modern conditions."[14]

Roosevelt, too, thought in terms of Lausanne. In a conversation with British Foreign Minister Anthony Eden, the American President stated: "We should take measures so that the Prussians will be removed from East Prussia in the same manner as the Greeks were removed from Turkey after the last war."[15] It was in the spirit of Lausanne, poorly understood by the Grand Alliance leaders, that Churchill, Roosevelt, and Stalin indicated during the war that they approved of transferring the Germans from Eastern Europe to occupied Germany.

Although all three Allies had agreed separately on the need for moving the Germans out of Eastern Europe, the discussions about the problem at Potsdam indicated that the Americans and British may have entertained second thoughts on the subject. Truman worried about where "nine million" Germans would go. Stalin reassured him that they had all already left. Later in the sessions, the Soviet leader noted that the Poles had retained some Germans to work in the fields, but once the harvest was in, the Poles would expel them: "The Poles do not ask us. They are doing what they like, just as the Czechs are."[16] Churchill inserted somewhat disingenuously that: "I have grave moral scruples regarding great movements and transfers of populations." He then added that perhaps those Germans who Stalin assured them had left Silesia should be allowed to go back. Stalin retorted: "The Poles would hang them if they returned." In the case of the expulsion of Germans from Czechoslovakia, Churchill suggested that perhaps the Allies should see Benes before discussing the issue further. Here, too, Stalin tried to convince his Allied partners that the problem had been taken care of. "The Czechs gave them [the Germans] two hours notice and then threw them out." As far as talking to Benes was concerned, Stalin asked: "But is this not serving mustard after supper? The Germans have already been driven out."[17]

For Stalin, the forced deportation of the Germans was a *fait accompli*. But the Americans and British increasingly fretted about the costs to their domestic budgets of feeding and housing Germans in their respective zones of occupation. This had an important effect on discussions about reparations from Germany, and it also aroused their worries about the continued influx of Germans from Poland and Czechoslovakia. Thus, the Western Allies insisted that the process of deportation be slowed down and regularized. The Soviets concurred, and Article XIII of the Potsdam Treaty canonized that agreement. It read: "The three Governments, having considered the question in all its aspects, recognize that the transfer to Germany of German populations, or elements thereof, remaining in Poland, Czechoslovakia, and Hungary, will have to be undertaken. They agree that any transfers that take place should be effected in an orderly and humane manner."[18]

By the time of the Potsdam meetings, 700,000 to 800,000 Germans had already left or been driven out of the former Sudetenland, and approximately the same number out of Poland. (In the Polish case, this does not include the 3.5 million or so German refugees who fled before the Soviet Army offensive, first into East Prussia in October 1944 and then into Silesia, eastern Pomerania, and the Neumark in January 1945.)[19] Most historians assert that after Potsdam the brutality of the forced deportations decreased markedly, once the transfers were sanctioned and made more orderly by the Allies and the Polish and Czechoslovak governments. No doubt, this was true in general, but the particulars of the deportations in both Czechoslovakia and Poland continued to exact a terrible toll in both German lives and property.

German Expulsion from the Sudetenland

Although the cleansing of Germans from Czechoslovakia at the end of the war and beginning of the peace was as total and merciless as the Soviet cleansing of the northern Caucasus and the Crimea, the causes are much more transparent. In addition, in the Czechoslovak (and Polish) cases, the apparatus of state could not directly control the nature of the violence, and thus it tended to be much more haphazard and indiscriminate. The Germans in Czechoslovakia, like the Chechens-Ingush and the Tatars, were accused by the authorities of being traitors to the state.[20] This was more justified in the case of Czechoslovakia, given the activities of the Germans in the interwar republic, not to mention the widespread Sudeten German sympathy for and participation in the Nazi occupation. The overwhelming success of Konrad Henlein and his Sudeten German Nazi party had succeeded in giving all the Germans in the region a reputation for virulent anti-Czechoslovak and pro-Hitler sympathies. As Benes reportedly put it: "Our Germans . . . have betrayed our state, betrayed our democracy, betrayed us, betrayed humaneness, and betrayed humankind."[21]

It is also important that in both the Soviet and East European cases, the governments acted to eliminate the rights of a national minority in the name of the modernization of the state. In the Soviet cases against the Chechens-Ingush and Tatars, this rationalization was muted and implicit in the removal of these peoples from their traditional homelands in the Caucasus and Crimea, where they had allegedly held back Sovietization and socialist mobilization. In the Czechoslovak and Polish cases, democratic governments justified the elimination of minority rights because they were an impediment to the smooth functioning of a citizen government. During the war, the Czechoslovak government-in-exile was ready to grant Czechoslovak citizenship to those Germans with proven antifascist credentials as long as they swore fealty to the new Czechoslovak republic. There were serious efforts by Masaryk and Benes to ally with the Sudeten German antifascists abroad.[22] But to the consternation especially of the Sudeten German Social Democrats, who worked closely with the Czechoslovak government-in-exile in England, the Czechs refused to grant any minority rights to the Germans, meaning they would shut down their schools and special institutions, the German university would be closed, and the same would happen to Hungarian schools and institutions in Slovakia.[23] Benes told Molotov in March 1945 that more than two million Germans would have to be transferred but that approximately 800,000 workers would be allowed to mix among the Czech population and assimilate.[24]

Given the history of the Comintern's support for minority rights in Eastern Europe, the Czechoslovak communists—and other communists as well—found themselves in a difficult position when it came to the question of expelling the Germans. During the war, the communists' position, articulated by Georgi Dimitrov in Moscow, was that those Germans responsible for the war and its crimes should be tried and sentenced, while the German workers and peasants should be re-educated. But the Czechoslovak communists quickly realized that the "German question" had tremendous political resonance in the country, and by the end of the war the communist leader Klement Gottwald, like Benes, called for the expulsion of the Germans from the Czech lands and of the Hungarians from Slovakia.[25] Gottwald framed the attack on the Germans in revolutionary terms, but the policy was the same: "Power passed from the hands of the oppressive nation, the nation of occupiers, the German nation, into the hands of the formerly oppressed nation, the Czech and Slovak nation—in this sense our revolution is a national revolution."[26] Benes also exalted the expulsion as a "great revolution."[27] The Soviets readily confirmed the policy of the communists and Benes in this regard. Stalin accepted the fact that nationalist states would be set up everywhere in East Central Europe; Hungarians, Czechs and Slovaks, and Poles would not want to share sovereignty with other nationalities.[28] In the end, there was virtually no difference between noncommunist and communist politicians on the issue of the expulsions of Germans in postwar Czechoslovakia or Poland. When it came to the issue of the forced deportation of the Germans, Benes and Gottwald, Mikolajczyk and Bierut, Stalin and Churchill all danced to the same tune.

Benes and the Czechoslovak government-in-exile announced from the very beginning of German rule in Bohemia and Moravia that the postwar state should be reconstructed in its former borders.[29] Yet they were more insistent about maintaining the western borders than the eastern, meaning they would have to deal in one fashion or another with the 3,200,000 Germans who resided in the west. (The Czechoslovak leaders eventually gave in without much resistance to Stalin's patient but insistent demand for annexing the Carpatho-Ukraine in the east.[30]) During the war, the Czechs discussed a variety of approaches to dealing with the German question, some of which had their roots in the late Habsburg period. In this connection, federalization and assimilation were considered.[31] But once the Czechs recognized the full impact of Richard Heydrich's regime in the Protectorate and suffered the aftermath of his assassination during the Lidice massacre of May and June 1942, the plans of the Czechoslovak government focused exclusively on expelling the Germans. Initially, Benes called for the expulsion of one million German fascists, Henleinists, and their sympathizers. Later, he spoke of expelling two million Germans.[32] In 1943 his deputy, Edvard Taborsky, devised a plan that made it possible for German antifascists, Social Democrats, and those who had suffered at the hands of the Nazis to stay in the new democratic state. Small-holding German peasants would also be allowed to remain if they had neither involved themselves in politics nor exploited their Czech neighbors.[33] However, in a meeting with Stalin on December 16, 1943, Benes stated that he wanted to solve the German problem once and for all and create a Slavic Czechoslovak state free of Germans and Hungarians. "The defeat of Germany presents us with the singular historical possibility to clean out radically the German element from our state . . . The future republic should be a state of Czechs, Slovaks, and Carpatho-Ukrainians. It should be a state of Slavic nations. From Czechoslovakia should be obligatorily expelled all German teachers, professors, SS types, Gestapo-men, members of the Hitler youth, all active members of the Henlein movement and the entire German bourgeoisie, all rich Germans."[34]

Transfer (Odsun)

Here and elsewhere during the war, Benes and his advisors talked about some "good" Germans being able to stay in Czechoslovakia. By the end of the war, however, no Czech politician or political party could resist the rising wave of anti-German Czech nationalism that demanded revenge and retaliation for the insults of Munich, the loss of Czech sovereignty, and the trying circumstances of the war itself. The reverberations of Lidice and Theresienstadt were simply too strong. Survivors of the small Czech resistance demanded revenge. Benes received recommendations from his advisors to pursue the expulsions to the end; otherwise it would be possible, some argued, that a demagogue could seize the issue for his own purposes.[35] In a foreign ministry communiqué to the State Department dated July 5, 1945, the Czechs noted that the expulsion of the Germans was the most important postwar task, "the most burning of all the problems that the Czech government is attempting to resolve."[36] Until this issue was dealt with, Vlado Klementis wrote, none of the other important social, economic, and institutional problems of the country could be addressed.[37]

Czechoslovak government propaganda purposely raised the temperature of anti-German feeling in the country. The massacre in Lidice figured prominently in the press. "The entire German people are responsible for Lidice," proclaimed the headline of one such article.[38] To be sure, some of the attacks on the Germans were highly self-interested, as Czech looters arrived from other regions of the country to seize and carry off booty. But the greatest part of the depredations were perpetrated in the name of the state and its nationalist agenda. A communist party proclamation of May 13, 1945, demanded that its members "cleanse the Fatherland of the agents of a treachery without equal in the history of our people!"[39] In the same spirit of urging Czechs on to violence against the Germans, *Novo Slovo* wrote on August 18, 1945: "The German possesses no soul, and the words that he understands best, are—according to Jan Masaryk—the salvos of a machine gun."[40] Prokop Drtina, leader of the "liberal" National Socialist Party, declared on May 17, 1945, that the primary task for Czechs was "to clean out the republic as a whole and completely of Germans . . . Everyone of us must help in the cleansing of the homeland."[41] Even the Czech Catholic Church got into the act. Monsignor Bohumil Stasek, the canon of Vysehrad, declared: "Once in a thousand years the time has come to settle accounts with the Germans, who are evil and to whom the commandment to love thy neighbor therefore does not apply."[42]

With this kind of propaganda in mind, as the German armies retreated before the Soviet advance, the Czech militia (many recruited from Prague after the uprising), communist action groups, and the so-called Svoboda army moved into German areas and attacked civilians in their homes and on the streets. These armed fighters drew few distinctions between antifascist Germans, plain farmers, or Henleinist sympathizers. In a paroxysm of violence that shocked even experienced Soviet tank commanders and political officers, Czechs beat up Germans, shot at them, forced them to do humiliating and life-threatening tasks, and showed them no mercy. People were randomly killed, and villages were torched and burned to the ground. Germans were hung by their heels from trees, doused in petrol, and set on fire.[43] In outright pogroms, Czech militia rampaged through towns and villages, shooting Germans at will.[44] Thousands of German refugees from the Sudetenland later documented the unprovoked brutality in great detail, though only in the rarest cases did they show any understanding at all for the reasons the Czechs felt the need for retributive justice.[45]

One of the worse cases of wanton violence against the Sudeten German population took place in Usti nad Labem (Aussig) on July 31, 1945. Fires started by a series of explosions in the local munitions warehouse killed twenty-eight people and wounded many more, both Germans and Czechs.[46] The explosions were blamed on "Werewolf" organizations—gangs of German youngsters who allegedly sabotaged Czech installations and planned to assassinate Czech officials.[47] Despite the fact that no proof of sabotage was demonstrated, Czech militia and civilians accepted the rumors as true and massacred Germans in the town. The rampagers threw women and children off the bridge into the Elbe River below and took potshots at them until they no longer surfaced. A German Red Cross sister reported that "the Czechs stormed through the streets, beat the Germans to the ground, and shot at them, if they tried to run away."[48] The police and military not only did not hinder the violence, another eyewitness reported, "they took part."[49] The number of victims in the massacre has been variously estimated at anywhere from several hundred to 2,700.[50] Just as important is the fact that the Czech government used the events in Usti nad Labem to urge that the Germans be deported more resolutely. Minister of Foreign Trade Hubert Ripka, stated on the radio: "One should understand the feelings of our people who are being consistently attacked by Werewolf organizations and whose property is still being destroyed . . . Many of our people still do not feel safe until they know the Germans will go away."[51]

In some regions, the Red Army was the first to arrive after the Wehrmacht retreat. Soviet soldiers did a great deal of damage and were especially brutal in their dealings with German women and girls. As in other heavily German-populated areas, the Soviets exacted their revenge for the fearsome war through assaults, rapes, mass rape, and rape murder.[52] One eyewitness remembered that the Soviets arrived in his town on May 10 and, "on May 19 came the long wished-for arrival of the Czech military. Now there would be order, or so we all hoped. But what disappointment! Now real hell broke loose. Often we had to appeal to the Russians to help us against the Czechs, which they often did, when it wasn't a matter of hunting down women."[53] Just as in Poland, the Germans considered Soviet military personnel much more humane and responsible than the native Czechs or Poles. Russians occasionally fed hungry German children, while the Czechs let them starve. Soviet troops would occasionally give the weary Germans a ride on their vehicles during their long treks out of the country, while Czechs looked on with contempt or indifference. Soviet officers were also sometimes offended by the Czech practice of painting swastikas on the backs of Germans or forcing them to wear white armbands marked with an "N" for *Nemec,* or German. The Soviets even interfered with the Czech regulations, though generally they tried to stay out of the Czechs' way.[54]

It quickly became clear that all of the three million Germans in Czechoslovakia would be forced to leave their homes and that the Three Powers would not stop the process. The Germans were given very little time to pack up and leave, sometimes no more than fifteen minutes, and they were allowed to take only the barest minimum of things with them. They lost their livelihoods and jobs, and they were threatened with violence by the new rulers if they refused to vacate their homes, which were, in any case, open territory for Czech plundering.[55] The cumulative distress among the Germans led to mass suicides in towns and villages throughout the former Sudetenland. One doctor reported that these suicides were sometimes well-planned. Whole families would dress up in their Sunday finest, surrounded by flowers, crosses, and family albums, and then kill themselves by hanging or poison.[56] On June 8, 1945, General Serov wrote to Beria from Germany that the wave of suicides among Sudeten Germans continued even after they arrived in the Soviet zone of occupation: "Daily, up to 5,000 Germans arrive in Germany from Czechoslovakia, the majority of whom are women, old folks and children. With their futures ruined and having no hope for anything better, many of them end their lives by suicide, cutting their wrists." In one region alone, Serov continued, on June 8 they found seventy-one Germans dead with slit wrists.[57]

The "wild" deportations that took place in the spring and early summer of 1945 forced Germans to flee the Sudetenland for safer territory (or so it was thought) in Silesia, Austria, Bavaria, and Saxony. The Potsdam agreement, concluded in August 1945, sanctioned the transfers from Czechoslovakia and Poland but called for them to take place in "a humane and orderly fashion." It is possible that this injunction cost more lives than it saved and caused more suffering than it spared. The flow of refugees was temporarily stopped at the borders in order to ensure that they would be taken care of when they arrived at their destinations in occupied Germany. With no place to flee and no way to go back home, the Germans were easy targets for Czech retribution.

The largest number of Sudeten Germans were designated to reside in Bavaria in the American zone, and the Americans slowed down the transfers for months, hoping to guarantee decent rail transportation to Germany and housing and food when the refugees arrived. The problem was that despite Allied protests, the Czechs continued to hound the Germans, removing them from their homes and villages to work camps, where many thousands were brutalized, took sick because of the lack of decent food and hygiene, and died.[58] Tomas Stanek, the leading Czech historian of the transfers, puts the situation tersely: "The acts carried out against the Germans in the immediate postwar period were in many cases extremely hard, often even inhuman."[59]

At the former Nazi camp at Theresienstadt (Teresin), the interned Germans worried openly about what would happen to them if the local Russian commandant did not protect them against the Czechs. One secret Soviet report sent back to the Central Committee in Moscow noted that the Germans repeatedly begged the Russians to stay: "'If the Red Army leaves, we are finished!' We now see the manifestations of hatred for the Germans. They [the Czechs] don't kill them, but torment them like livestock. The Czechs look at them like cattle."[60] The horrible treatment at the hands of the Czechs led to despair and hopelessness. According to Czech statistics, in 1946 alone 5,558 Germans committed suicide.[61]

The conditions for the Germans in the fifty or so labor camps to which they were sometimes confined by the Czechoslovak authorities were fraught with danger.[62] It was clear that the Czechs savored the chance to pay back the Germans. One survivor of the camps wrote: "The sadism knew no boundaries."[63] A sign was nailed onto the entry of one camp in Budweis (Budejowice), which read, "An Eye for an Eye—A Tooth for a Tooth," and the Czech camp commandant made sure the inmates suffered accordingly. They were constantly abused, beaten, and yelled at. One man wrote of his experience in a camp: "We were often roused from our bunks at night, we had to assemble in the camp courtyard, then we were forced to dance, sing, slap each other about the head, crawl about on all fours, and so on." After being forced to work twelve hours every day on minimal rations, many inmates simply gave up and killed themselves.[64]

By far the largest population in the camps were German women and girls. As is so often the case in ethnic cleansing, the women were generally separated from the men and sexually abused and exploited in violent and obscene ways. They were constantly called "pigs" and "Nazi whores" and sometimes were stripped and beaten merely for the entertainment of the guards.[65] German women who reported their experiences could barely talk about the details. "Every time of the day we women were raped and our shirts torn from our bodies . . . I cannot speak in public about the kinds of animalistic perversities that the German women had to endure in disgust."[66] Another woman writes about rape and sexual abuse: "What all that happened in this connection is hard for me to talk about. If one would imagine the worst, then it remains far behind the truth."[67] While the Soviet soldiers are often praised by Sudeten German memoirists for the pity they took on them, especially when contrasted with the Czechs, this praise ends when the issue of rape and sexual exploitation is discussed. Soviet soldiers picked out the handsomest women from the labor battalions and raped them repeatedly before returning them to their work. Czech camp commandants let in groups of Soviet soldiers to the women's barracks to grab German women and girls in a sometimes nightly routine of rape and gang rape.[68] German women often described their situations as *"Freiwild"*—fair game—and in some sense that is exactly how they were treated by the Russians and Czechs.

The threat of being sent to one of these labor and detention camps loomed over the Germans who remained in the cities and towns of the former Sudetenland. Their lives highly restricted, they kept their heads down as best they could and stayed out of the way. They were not allowed to sit on park benches or walk on the sidewalks. They were not to use the trains, and they could shop at stores only at certain hours of the day. They could not frequent taverns and restaurants or go to movie theaters. Some Czechs took pity on the Germans and tried to help them.[69] Sometimes, especially after Potsdam, the deportations were conducted in a normal and decent fashion, without the beatings, robbery, and chicanery that so often accompanied the earlier transfers. Plenty of Czech officials behaved well toward the Germans and were "honest, loyal, and just, according to their best lights."[70] But too often the Czechs used the opportunity of the deportations to take out their frustrations and anger on the Germans. During the famous death march of Brünn (Brno), the entire German population, some 30,000 people altogether, was rousted from their homes on May 30, 1945, and beaten mercilessly as they trudged on foot to camps on the border with Austria.[71] Around 1,700 Germans died as a result.

According to Sudeten German sources, some 272,000 Germans (about 8 percent of the total German population in Czechoslovakia) died in the process of being driven from their homes. This includes a very large number in the category of "missing."[72] These figures have been challenged by Czech and German historians, who insist that these claims are wildly exaggerated and that only roughly a tenth of this number died as a result of the transfer of the Germans. The recent Czech-German historical commission, for example, states that the number of deaths is between 19,000 and 30,000.[73] The number of 30,000 is used by the Marburg historian Hans Lemberg in his description of the commission's work.[74] Philipp Ther settles on the number of 40,000.[75] Derek Sawyer states that the death toll "may be as high as a quarter of a million." He appropriately adds, however, that "all such figures, in this matter, are uncertain and contested."[76]

The numbers often depend on who is being counted—sometimes Czech and/or German Jews are included—and how the missing are dealt with.[77] Disease was the biggest killer; many Germans died en route and after arrival in occupied Germany of a variety of maladies. Suicide, hunger, and exposure also took a serious toll. In other words, the lower numbers may well accurately reflect the number of Sudeten Germans murdered and killed in the course of their deportation; the higher numbers would include the number who died from other causes during the uprooting, detention, transport, and resettling. In thinking about the costs of ethnic cleansing, whether of the Greeks, Armenians, Chechens, or Sudeten Germans, the losses of life during the total process should be considered. The consequences of ripping people from their homes reverberate throughout their entire lives. The price of ethnic cleansing is paid not just at the point of departure but also on arrival.

By the fall of 1947, almost the entire Sudeten German population had been transferred to Germany. Over a million Germans, including a large number of antifascists, communists, social democrats, and their families, were transferred to the Soviet zone of occupation.[78] After January 1, 1946, some 1,239,000 Germans were transferred to the Western zones, primarily to the American zone. The bulk of the three quarters of a million Germans who were deported or fled during the "wild" deportations before Potsdam also ended up in the American zone.[79] Those Germans who remained in Czechoslovakia, some 200,000 altogether, were primarily industrial workers (40,000) and their families, Germans in mixed marriages, and scattered German antifascists who committed themselves to Czech culture.[80]

There was great pressure placed even on those relatively few Germans to leave. Czechs had the right to apply for the jobs of any German worker or employee, and, if an employer rejected the Czech applicant, the employer had to justify, in writing, his decision to maintain the German employee.[81] On the margins of nationality, it was not quite so easy to separate Czechs from Germans. Early on in the deportations, the Czech marauders paid little attention to the niceties of documentation and proof, while local Czech courts found it inconvenient to hold up the transfer of Germans by enforcing legal norms. "Expulsion, not prosecution, was the government's primary concern," writes Benjamin Frommer.[82] In the post-Potsdam period, however, the Czech government attempted to enforce a more cultural definition of Czech nationality, allowing those Germans to stay who had been sufficiently assimilated into Czech culture. Jeremy King notes the shift in policy from "Once a German always a German" to "Once a Czech, always a Czech."[83] New regulations demanded that those who were German by "ethnicity" but had declared themselves Czechs or Slovaks during the Nazi occupation should not be forced to leave. The Ministry of Interior issued a circular on August 24, 1945, which insisted that the courts pay attention to "customary [not necessarily 'racial'] perspectives through which national identity is determined." Subjective factors should be taken into account: How did individuals register in prewar censuses? How did they identify themselves at the communal level, when applying for rations cards, enrolling in school, or registering with the police? Did they belong to Czech or German political parties, clubs, unions, and church groups? To which heritage did their parents adhere? The circular concluded: "In addition to this, such discrete facts must be evaluated in relationship to each other, and one cannot be satisfied with just one such indicator [of nationality], especially when we are dealing with circumstances that easily change over time."[84] Even though the Czech authorities wanted to make a clean break with the Germans and separate radically Czech from German nationality, they did not want to do so using Nazi racial criteria. Benjamin Frommer's work on intermarriage in this period demonstrates, as well, that after the bulk of the Germans had left, the Czech government was ready to think in terms of "elected" nationality.[85]

Flexibility at the margins of nationality did not mean that the Czechs would tolerate any continuity of "Germanness" in the reconstructed republic. As in other cases of ethnic cleansing, the authorities did everything possible to erase the physical remnants and even memory of German culture and civilization in the former Sudetenland. Benes made it clear that not just the Germans would have to go but also their civilization: "Let our motto be: to definitively de-Germanize our homeland, culturally, economically, politically."[86] Place names were changed, German monuments destroyed, and graveyards defaced. All German property was seized and in some cases turned over to Czech settlers from urban areas. Derek Sawyer writes that the glories of German Prague were also erased from the Czech view. The neo-Renaissance Neues Deutsches Theater, which was built by the Prague Germans in 1886–87, became the Smetana Theater. The Casino, which, "for over seventy years was the social hub of German Prague," was renamed the Slavonic House. Sawyer concludes: "What was left was a denuded landscape, shorn of its ethnic and social complexities and ripe for the imposition of a unitary national script."[87]

The ethnic cleansing of Bohemia and Moravia, like the other cases discussed in this book, represented the culmination of long-standing rivalries and resentments, in this case against German domination of the Czechs going back to White Mountain and including ill-treatment at the hands of the Habsburgs.[88] Communists and noncommunists alike approved, indeed urged, the expulsion of the Germans as part of a new stage in the development of the Czechoslovak social and economic order. To be sure, the national enmity that surfaced naturally as a consequence of the war gave the expulsions the character of a spontaneous wave of nationalist revenge for the German occupation. But the Czech political leadership framed this national upheaval in terms of a social revolution to remove German landowners and factory owners from positions of power and seize their properties in the name of a radical democratic, antifascist state.[89] "We are finished with the Germans in Czechoslovakia," Jan Masaryk stated. "There is no possible way to get us to live under the same umbrella again."[90]

Polish Wartime Plans

The case of the expulsion of the Germans from Poland is both more and less complicated than that of their expulsion from Czechoslovakia. It is less complicated because the nature of the German occupation of Poland, in which the Poles were exploited, brutalized, humiliated, and subjected to mass murder, puts their lust for revenge and their fearsome attacks on the Germans in a more understandable context. The Czechs, after all, did not suffer terribly at the hands of the Germans, certainly not in comparison to the Poles. Their economy remained in decent shape; their losses in the war were comparatively small; they were often able to maintain their communal lives without excessive interference from the occupiers.[91] None of this could be said about Poland.

Yet the situation of the Poles was more complicated than that of the Czechs for several reasons. First, Polish demands for the expulsion of the Germans were related to the shifting calculus of Polish territorial claims during the war. The Soviet Union was increasingly insistent on incorporating eastern Poland (western Belorussia and western Ukraine) into its territories, much as it had done as a result of the Nazi-Soviet Pact of 1939. As Allied concessions to this demand became ever more likely, and as Soviet plans for the absorption of this territory were put into effect, the Poles more resolutely sought compensation in the West from the Germans. At the same time, Polish claims on Danzig (Gdansk), East Prussia, and German territories east of the Oder were presented to the Allies long before it became apparent they would lose territories in the east. Internal memoranda of the Polish government-in-exile in 1942 indicate that the Poles were interested in territory east of the Oder but were ready to settle for the eastern Neisse as the southern section of the western border with Germany. The Poles worried about the overwhelming number of Germans living between the western and eastern Neisse rivers, who would be impossible to incorporate into the new Polish Republic given their "fanatic anti-Polish views" and who could not be expelled because—it was thought—public opinion in Great Britain in particular would not tolerate it.[92] But as the war progressed, Polish ambitions grew. The almost completely German city of Stettin (Szczecin) and the adjacent islands in the Oder were claimed as "the key to Central Europe." The Poles went so far as to demand occupation rights along the Baltic as far as Rostock-Warnemünde and Rügen and sought to participate in the occupation of the Kiel Canal.[93] Lower Silesia, inhabited by nearly three million Germans, also eventually became a central focus of Polish war aims.

Although the Polish case is also complicated by the fact that the Soviets broke off relations with the London government-in-exile in April 1943, ostensibly over the Katyn affair, there remained few differences between the communists and noncommunists on the issue of expelling the Germans. As early as February 1940, Polish Foreign Minister Zaleski included the deportation of Germans from prewar Poland and East Prussia as a major Polish war aim.[94] After his return from Moscow in 1941, General Sikorski, the Polish president, insisted that "the German horde, which for centuries had penetrated to the east, should be destroyed and forced to draw back far [to the west]."[95] In exile, the Polish government worked out legal procedures that would deprive the Germans of Polish citizenship and of their property.[96] They also engaged the difficult problem of defining who was a Pole and who was not.[97] But the end result was to be the same: the total expulsion of the Germans from the western territories. Poles and Germans cannot live together in one country, states an internal London Government memorandum in August 1944. "The Germans, who do not leave the territory of Poland themselves after the war, will have to be expelled."[98] The Polish underground supported these policies with its actions against the Germans, applying the precepts of collective guilt to all manner of Germans. "Now they will know what collective guilt means."[99]

When Stanislaw Mikolajczyk returned to Poland in June 1945, to join the new Government of National Unity agreed to at Yalta, his speeches were as militant about ridding the country of Germans as were those of Wladyslaw Gomulka, communist minister for the "recovered territories." As deputy prime minister of the new government and head of the Polish Peasant Party, Mikolajczyk saw the expulsion of the Germans as a social as well as national act. German exploiters, the German middle class, German landowners would be expelled and replaced by Poles. The Polish peasantry would no longer suffer at the hands of the German upper class.[100] Just as in Czechoslovakia, the expulsion of the Germans was seen as a revolutionary act. Meanwhile, Gomulka sent out orders to party officials to get rid of the Germans: "We must expel all the Germans because countries are built on national lines and not on multinational ones."[101]

Expulsion

The situation of Germans in the western territories was much more fluid and uncertain than that of the Germans in the Sudetenland. The Red Army reached the Oder in January and February of 1945, halting for a strategic regrouping before the final assault on Berlin in April. Many hundreds of thousands of Germans fled before the advancing Soviet armies, only to return to their homes after the capitulation in early May. In Wroclaw (Breslau) for example, some tens of thousands of Germans returned after the signing of the armistice, assuming that their native city would remain German, as it had been for centuries.[102] Between May and the Potsdam conference in late July, tens of thousands of Germans were moving in both directions, west and east, both groups warning the others of what awaited them.[103] (One is reminded of the sad plight of the Jews after the Nazi-Soviet Pact in August 1939. They crossed the river Bug between the Soviet and Nazi zones heading in both directions from the opposite banks, those going to Soviet territory and to German territory frantically gesticulating to the others that they were crazy.) The Germans who returned to their Silesian and Pomeranian homes counted on the fact that these lands, temporarily assigned to Polish occupation by the Yalta Conference, would be returned to Germany by the eventual peace conference. The Polish secret police worried that many Poles also assumed that these territories would be returned to the Germans.[104]

Even after Potsdam, where the Allies agreed to the transfer of Germans from territory occupied by the Poles, the Germans continued to hope that either a peace conference would return these lands to German control or that Allied cooperation itself would break down and German sovereignty over the territory would be restored.[105] The Potsdam Conference had left in question the right of the Poles to the newly occupied territory in the west. The situation that the Germans encountered when they returned to their homes was horrible. Their animals had been slaughtered; the houses were robbed; they faced hunger, anarchy, and chaos. "In our home village," wrote one returnee, "we found empty and destroyed homes and farms. All the farm machinery had disappeared, the cattle were slaughtered or taken away."[106] No sooner did many repair their homes and begin to rebuild their lives than the new Polish administration forced them to leave again. As the war came to an end, Gomulka set up police detachments along the newly claimed Oder-Neisse border. Their job was to make sure that the Germans went one direction only—west into Soviet-occupied Germany. "As for those Germans who are still there," Gomulka wrote, "the kinds of conditions should be created so that they won't want to remain."[107]

Those who fled west did so under severe Polish pressure. By their own actions, the Germans had engendered the fierce hatred of the Poles. This was evident from the very beginning of the German occupation, as attested to by Gerhard Hauptmann, a German writer who had lived for years in Silesia. Hauptmann wrote in his diary as early as December 30, 1939: "After waking up, the terror of the war pressed in my chest: Poland! How much hate has been released there. We destroyed Poland, delivered up half of it to the Russians, calling forth all the spirits of revenge on us for a century. Why is it that this pitiless nationalism has been aroused everywhere and in everything."[108]

Over the course of the occupation, this hatred of Poles for their Ger-

man oppressors became so deep and natural that it was barely articulated. There was no need. When the war ended, the hatred of the Germans was part of society; there would be no pardoning of their national
oppressors.[109] As a result, no less than the Czechs, the Poles attacked,
subdued, and humiliated German civilians, seizing their property and
goods and sometimes throwing them out of their homes. Germans
were beaten senseless and murdered; German women and girls were
raped and abused; Germans—more often than not whole families—
committed suicide by the thousands. The suicides were sometimes precipitated by news of the arrival of the Red Army, sometimes by Polish
notification of deportation.[110]

How many Germans died in the process of being driven from their
homes by the Poles is hard to know. Hunger and sickness took countless lives; the Russian offensive was costly for civilians, as was the Polish
takeover and forced deportations. Large numbers of Germans died en
route to hard labor in the Soviet Union as well as in Soviet and Polish
detention and work camps in Poland itself. Probably half a million died
as a direct result of the deportations; in all likelihood, at least twice that
many lost their lives during this period as the result of the ethnic cleansing of Poland.[111] Some studies based on local records provide a sense of
the many different kinds of mortal dangers faced by the Germans at the
end of the war and the beginning of the peace. According to the historian Piotr Madajczyk, in the village of Bojkow (Schönwald), 250
Germans suffered casualties during the war, 180 members of the
Wehrmacht died, 30 civilians died, 200 were murdered in January
1945, no doubt as a result of the Russian offensive, 30 died or were
killed in Polish camps, 70 died while fleeing, and 100 were transported
to the Soviet Union. A second author, estimating the cause of German
mortality in Byczyn (Prudnicki region), divides the 219 total deaths as
follows: 18 killed in battle, 11 killed during the occupation as *Volksturm*
(hastily assembled local guard units), 7 by suicide, 1 during deportation, 69 while taking flight (in Dresden), 2 in the camps.[112]

Much as in Czechoslovakia, the Germans in Poland were absolutely
petrified of the Soviet occupation and suffered terribly in its wake.
Rape, gang rape, and rape murder were part of everyday life.[113] The Soviets robbed Germans and invaded their homes without the least hesita-
tion. Still, as countless German memoirists report, the Poles were considered much more relentless in their persecution of the Germans than
the Soviets.[114] The Russians were considered more tolerant of the use of
the German language, which they seemed to know better than Polish,

and they were less interested in changing place names and street signs into Polish. They relied heavily on their German maps and on their German food suppliers.

Moreover, the Soviet armed forces needed economic contributions from the Germans; they were far less motivated than the Poles to drive the Germans off of prosperous farms and out of functioning factories and workshops. Rudolf von Thadden writes: "It is hardly surprising that the withdrawal of the Russians often resulted in the parallel deportation of the last Germans from a particular locale."[115] The Russians themselves were often astonished by the Polish actions. The Political Section of the Red Army reported back to Moscow on August 30, 1945: "The German population is starving in many places, in other areas they are under the immediate threat of starvation in the near future. Not only does the plundering of the Germans on the part of the Poles not stop, but it gets stronger all the time. There are more and more frequent cases of unprovoked murders of German inhabitants, unfounded arrests, long prison confinements with purposeful humiliation."[116] Things were so bad, the report continued, that Red Army soldiers had to step in sometimes to keep the Poles in line, leading in a number of cases to conflict between Soviet soldiers and the Poles.[117]

In this Polish "wild west," gangs of marauders, usually from central Poland, stole as much as they could from the Germans before returning to their homes laden with loot—furniture, clothes, valuables, and foodstuffs.[118] Rape and pillage were common; it made no difference to the Poles whether the Germans they attacked had been antifascists or not. German homes were open territory; the Poles could go into any German dwelling and take what they wanted, even the dwelling itself. If the Germans attempted to defend themselves, they were often beaten and sent off to the feared internment camps.[119] To denounce a German as a Nazi was enough to gain access to their property: Piotr Madajczyk writes in this connection that the main investigative methods of those days was to beat the Germans.[120]

To make matters worse, the police and civilian Polish authorities were weak and ineffective in face of these depredations, and they were generally unwilling to interfere. The secret police stayed out of the fray; they felt they had enough to do in fighting underground bands of anti-government Poles (and sometimes Germans).[121] As a result, the regular militia used the very real threat of internment to bully the Germans themselves and extract food and money from them. In Silesia, noted one Soviet report, "the Polish authorities do absolutely nothing to stop the plundering of the [German] population." In fact, they sometimes joined in.[122] The lawlessness was ubiquitous. In the entire district of Opole Silesia, wrote a Polish party official, "Terrible arbitrariness is the rule; the people have lost all feeling for right and wrong, no crime arouses any sense of surprise. The militia and in part also the security forces rape and pillage the population, so that people break out in terrible anxiety if they even see a militiaman." It was often the case that women simply ran for cover the moment they saw a Polish policeman.[123] The Soviets episodically protected Germans against the Poles, but very inconsistently.[124]

By the end of 1945, tens of thousands of Polish settlers from the eastern lands given over to the Soviet Union arrived in the western territories in search of homes and farmsteads. The settlers themselves were often in terrible shape, having endured violence and privation during their deportation and transport. They arrived with little or nothing themselves.[125] The results were predictable; the pressure on the remaining Germans increased even more. If possible, the Germans tried to gain access to the rail transports to occupied Germany provided by the Allies. Severe backups in the rail system meant, however, that huge crowds of Germans could not leave right away. Many were placed in labor battalions or in camps. In some cases, Germans camped out at various rail stations and waited for weeks. In other cases, the transports by rail were interrupted by problems with the equipment or lines. With no food or shelter, and their currency worthless, many Germans died.[126] Rail transports in the winter of 1945–46 had to be suspended when freight cars arrived at their destinations full of corpses—Germans who had died of the cold. The winter of 1946–47 was even more bitterly cold than the one before. Despite somewhat better heating facilities at the gathering points and in the rail cars, the fierce cold still claimed many lives.[127] One rail transport that left Wroclaw (Breslau) on December 23, 1946, arrived at its destination with sixty-six Germans dead and another 141 who had to be hospitalized from frostbite, pneumonia, and shock.[128]

In some instances, the Germans were moved out of their homes into ghettos—the worst areas of towns, cities, and sometimes villages—provided with little work and minimum rations, and left under miserable conditions.[129] As in the Czech case, the Germans were forced to wear the letter N for *Niemiec* (German) on their sleeves; they were forbidden to appear in restaurants, theaters, or taverns; and they were placed by the Polish authorities outside the law. "We will treat the Germans like work animals," stated the Polish chief of Walbrzych (Waldenburg), echoing Nazi-like statements about the desired treatment of the Poles. "They should interest themselves in nothing. They should know only where they should work and their bunks."[130] There were to be no German newspapers, and virtually every German school was closed down.[131] Orders from the central government to regularize relations with the German population and abandon the practice of labeling them with an N fell on deaf ears at the local level.[132]

The Poles also turned the former concentration camps and detention facilities of the Third Reich—Auschwitz, Birkenau, Lamsdorf, Jaworzno, Swietochlowitz, Potulitz, and others—into labor camps for Nazis and suspected Nazis. Some of the camps were used simply to house Germans scheduled for transfer. According to Bernadetta Nitschke, of the 235 penal institutions (camps, detention jails, and prisons) in Poland in this period, many were used to house Germans. These do not count the labor camps for Germans associated with the mining industry.[133] The Germans who were inmates in these prisons and camps—105,000 or so men and women, boys and girls—suffered from disease, malnutrition, and fearsome beatings. Even before they got to the camps, the Poles abused the Germans, sometimes giving them no more than fifteen minutes to pack up their allowed ten kilos of goods for the march to the camp. In the end, the fact that the Germans were often not allowed to take anything with them didn't matter very much. Whatever they had was stolen by camp officials.[134] Small children were sometimes taken from their mothers and sent off to orphanages and homes for wayward children. The rules in the camps about discipline and procedure were often adopted directly from the Nazi example. Rations were at the same level.[135] Stomach typhus was the biggest killer. Venereal disease was rampant and uncontrollable, given the lack of penicillin and sulfa drugs.[136]

According to some reports, camp directors were often Poles of Jewish origin who sought revenge for the fate of their people by abusing the inmates.[137] True or not, the camps were without doubt sometimes run by sadists, who picked out especially Aryan-looking Germans for abuse. Salomon Morel, the notorious camp commander at Swietochlowic, was known to strut about the grounds, routinely pistol-whipping the inmates.[138] In the camps, Germans were made to sing the Nazi "Horst Wessel Song" and engage in all kinds of demeaning behavior.[139] Thomas Urban estimates that about three-quarters of the total number of prisoners (8,064) in one of the most notorious of the camps, Lambinowic (Lamsdorf), southwest of Opole, including large numbers of women and children, did not survive through the spring of 1946. Other estimates of the death rate are much lower.[140] Zygmunt Woznicka concludes that the death toll in all the camps ranged between twenty and fifty percent of the inmates.[141] However many died, there is little reason to doubt Urban's list of the causes of death: starvation, disease, hard labor, physical injury, infection, and execution.[142]

The director of the camp at Lambinowic, Czeslaw Geborski, was indicted by the Polish authorities in 1959 for his wanton brutality toward the German prisoners. He admitted at his trial that his only goal in taking the job was "to exact revenge" on the Germans for his own treatment by them during the war.[143] In the most notorious case of abuse, on October 4, 1945, Geborski ordered his guards to shoot down anyone trying to escape a fire that engulfed one of the barracks buildings; at least forty-eight people were killed that day, perhaps many more.[144] The guards at Lambinowic also routinely beat German prisoners and stole from them. Party inspectors noted that "bouts of drunkenness and violence are the daily routine in the camp."[145] A large part of the problem was that the camp personnel in Lambinowic, as in most of the other camps, were not paid a regular salary. The result was that they brutally extracted their wages from the prisoners.[146] Lambinowic was a sad and horrible place. People died of hunger and disease in droves; guards recalled heartrending scenes of children begging for scraps of food and crusts of bread.[147]

How the Germans were treated varied considerably, depending on their status on the *Volksliste* (People's List)—the racial hierarchy of Poles and Germans established by the Nazi administration of the Generalgouvernement. Those Germans who had been a minority in pre-1939 Poland were categorized as *Volksdeutsche* (local Germans), category 2 on the Volksliste. Their rights and property were taken away and they were treated as traitors, sometimes immediately executed or sent to prisons and camps. *Reichsdeutsche* (Germans from the Reich), category 1, were either prosecuted as war criminals or deported immediately. Some 100,000 Volksdeutsche and Reichsdeutsche were transported for forced labor to the Soviet Union. Those in categories 3 and 4 on the Volksliste, including most of the Silesians and other so-called autochtons, could apply for "verification" as Poles.[148]

There was also considerable geographical variation in the way Polish officials dealt with the Germans.[149] In anticipation of Potsdam, several hundred thousand Germans living in the border regions of the Oder-Neisse were moved out in June and July 1945, in a military-like action, and forced across the border into Soviet-occupied Germany. Germans who lived in prewar Poland, including large numbers in the parts of Upper Silesia that had been included in the Second Republic, were treated especially harshly. They were deprived of all rights of citizenship, interned, and forced to work in labor battalions. Some 100,000 of them were deported to the Soviet Union. Forced deportation to occupied Germany was the fate of most Germans who lived in the new areas that were designated for Polish occupation: Lower Silesia, formerly German Upper Silesia (Opole/Oppeln Silesia), eastern Pomerania, eastern Brandenburg, and the southern part of East Prussia. The Soviet forces did most of the damage in southern East Prussia; those Germans who did not flee or perish at the hands of the Red Army were attacked and humiliated by the new Polish administration.[150] Because of their status as autochtons, some Mazurian Germans managed to stay on during the deportations and proved particularly adept at keeping their traditional village lives and economies intact.[151] In those seaports used for the transportation of German war booty to the Soviet Union, like Stettin (Szczecin) and Danzig (Gdansk), the Germans were allowed to stay long enough that their deportations, after Potsdam, took place in a relatively orderly fashion.

That reasons of state lay behind the wholesale expulsion of the Germans is apparent from the important exceptions that were made. Both communist and noncommunist Polish leaders understood perfectly well that their ability to hold on to the "reclaimed lands" depended on contradictory needs: first, to expel Germans from the occupied territories so that German claims to them would be weakened and, second, to make these lands economically useful to Poland and the rest of Europe. One simply could not expel all the Germans and hope to keep industry, mining, transportation, and manufacturing from grinding to a halt. The result was that while continuing to insist in principle that all Germans be expelled, the Poles also applied a liberal definition of nationality when deciding who was, after all, a German. Many Poles who had taken on German citizenship as a way to survive the war in their homes were allowed to become Polish citizens. The autochtons—Mazurians, Silesians, Kashubians, and others—were also designated as Germanized Poles and encouraged to "re-Polonize" and remain.[152] Moreover, many thousands of German workers who were critical to rebuilding the economic infrastructure of Poland were kept in place by the authorities and given special rations and housing privileges.[153] Mikolajczyk encouraged the government to undertake training programs for Polish peasants and workers resettled from the east, so that they could move into jobs occupied by the Germans, but he also was determined to rid Poland of every last German; "for us there can be no doubt that every German is before anything else a German nationalist."[154]

The Poles were less concerned than the Czechs with the negative role played by the German minority in the interwar republic, though they too were not unhappy to see minority rights disappear. Like the Czechs, during the new stage of state-building after the war, the Poles envisioned a homogeneous population unimpeded by large "alien" minorities like Germans, Jews, and Ukrainians. The Germans were driven out. The 225,000 or so Polish Jews, who managed to survive in Poland or return there after the war, were shocked by the high level of Polish anti-Semitism, which manifested itself in a series of pogroms, the worst of which took place in Kielce in 1946. In Kielce and elsewhere, there was evidence of government connivance with or, at the very least, indifference to the attacks.[155] In a "population exchange" arranged between the Soviet and Polish governments, some 480,000 Ukrainians in southeastern Poland were moved to Ukraine, while 2.1 million Poles from Ukraine, Belorussia, and Lithuania were moved to Poland.[156] But the extremely violent Polish-Ukrainian fighting that erupted during the war continued in the postwar period, as Ukrainians resisted being removed from their homes. In the spring of 1947 the Polish government launched a military campaign, Operation Vistula, to remove the remaining 140,000 Ukrainians from the region and scattered them in the "recovered lands" in the west and north. Some 5,500 Ukrainians were killed during removal and transfer. The ethnic cleansing of the Ukrainians in southeastern Poland was complete.[157]

Ironically, through their actions the Polish communists ensured that Roman Dmowski's ultranationalist dream of "Poland for the Poles" would be accomplished. Yet equally important to the Poles when thinking about the expulsions was the fact that Allied recognition of the incorporation (versus occupation) of the recovered lands could take place only if the territories were thoroughly Polonized and integrated into the new Poland.[158] The Poles also used strategic arguments to advance their claims. The Baltic coastline of Poland had to be secured from German control and influence from East Prussia to the Oder. Mikolajczyk argued, moreover, that German domination of East Central Europe depended on their control of the Oder and its tributaries to the south. Therefore, the Oder and western Neisse border was critical to depriving the Germans of their expansionist routes.[159]

De-Germanization and Polonization

The flight and deportations of Germans and their incarceration in labor camps only began the long and complex process of the "de-Germanization" of the new People's Poland. Unlike the Czechoslovak case, the Polish government acquired large new swaths of territory that had been German for centuries. The task of de-Germanization mirrored that of Polonization—or in the language of the time, re-Polonization—and was of the highest priority, since much of that territory had been given over to Polish occupation and administration by Yalta and Potsdam but was not yet *de jure* recognized as part of Poland (and would not be fully recognized under international law until 1990). Polish sensitivities about this issue were understandably extreme, given the revanchist statements coming from the Federal Republic of Germany, in particular from politically influential associations of deportees. As late as the 1970s, signs on the formerly German territory near the Baltic coast stated: "This land was and always will remain Polish."

Polonization and de-Germanization meant first of all the elimination of the German population and the immigration of Poles from both central Poland and the east. Campaigns were initiated by both communists (PPR) and socialists (PPS) to make sure their local party activists participated in the great cause of expulsion. They signed petitions and popularized slogans for the relentless deportation of the Germans. PPS slogans from Bialystok in January 1946 were typical: "All Germans have to leave Poland at once!"; "Not one Prussian on Polish land from the Bug to the Neisse"; "Poland for the Poles"; "There's no room for Germans in Polish lands"; "Punish anyone who delays the time of expulsion."[160] These campaigns were often accompanied by force. The Germans were intimidated by the threat of incarceration in the camps if they did not leave.

Aleksander Zawadzki, the first governor of Opole Silesia (and later Polish interior minister), was a fierce proponent of deporting the Germans by any means necessary. He felt the Poles needed to cultivate their hate for the Germans, "for we stand before the problem of, it's either them or us. There is not time at this moment for any kind of sentimental weakness, [any] empathy for the Germans . . . Germans are our mortal enemies and we have to fight them with any means at our disposal."[161] He was especially suspicious of the German clergy, whom he saw as dangerous purveyors of German culture. They were quickly chased away or sent to detention camps. (Catholic priests managed to stay in place somewhat longer than the Protestant pastors.) He simply wanted no more Germans around, and he did everything he could to expel them from Silesia. "Every citizen has the right to arrest a German and doesn't have to wait for the militia . . . And if anyone sees some woman or child being friendly with these Germans, then [they should] grab that German and that woman."[162] Zawadzki swore by the slogan of verification: "We will not give up a single Polish soul and we don't want a single German one."[163]

Following closely on these measures came the predictable attempts to de-Germanize the land. Towns and streets were renamed; German storefront signs were taken down; "Prussian-Hitler" memorials were removed; German inscriptions were chiseled off of buildings, church interiors, and gravestones.[164] German books were removed from the shelves, and there was an attempt to purge Polish of its many German usages. In connection with the actual burning of German books and archives, one Polish memoirist stated: "We went about the task of eliminating the remainders of Germandom in the western territories barbarically, without much subtlety. One can think about this today only with great shame."[165]

Even those autochtons who were designated as Poles—some 850,000 people altogether—were forbidden to speak German, though many, especially in Silesia, knew only a few words of Polish. From April 17, 1946, on, the government forbade the use of the German language in public places and even at home. The police were ordered to arrest anyone using German as "provocateurs to [our] national feelings."[166] Those designated as Poles were also placed under great pressure to change German first or last names into their Polish equivalents—Hans to Jan, Georg to Jerzy, and so on. Last names were Polonized by adding - ski, - wicz, or - zik.

The most difficult task for the Polish authorities was to try to get the local populations to think of themselves as part of a unified Polish nation. Silesian governor Zawadzki complained that the inhabitants of the region looked at themselves as a distinct nationality, not exactly Polish and not exactly German. That would have to end, he insisted. In a series of extremely nationalist speeches (and accompanying measures), Zawadzki made it clear that anyone who continued to think of themselves as German should clear out of the territory or else they would be imprisoned. Those Silesians who were "verified" should forthwith re-Polonize themselves. Socializing between Poles and Germans and mixed marriages were forbidden. He was unhappy, as it was, with the mixed marriages that had been "verified" when the German partner expressed devotion to the Polish state and promised to raise children in the spirit of the Polish nation.[167] "We won't allow any covering over of German meat with Polish gravy. We must tell ourselves firmly that in Opole region the exclusive and only rulers are the Poles."[168]

The problem in the region was not just the Silesians. Those Poles who had been transferred from Ukraine and Belorussia, the *kresy*, to the western territories—some 2.1 million altogether—also thought of themselves as different from the Poles of Warsaw, Krakow, or Lublin. They, too, would have to be reclaimed and remade into citizens of the new integral Poland. This was no mere exercise in teaching language, customs, and law. Jozef Dubiel, an official in the Ministry of Recovered Territory, talked about population management in the following manner on March 22, 1945: "The task of carrying out the full re-polonization of Opole Silesia cannot consist simply of the verification of Poles [Silesians] . . . and not only in the bringing in of another several trainloads of repatriots [from the east]. Now the task consists of the shaping of these two distinct biological groups into a single entity."[169]

The attempts of Zawadzki, Dubiel, and other officials to Polonize Silesia and other formerly German parts of People's Poland were often frustrated by the continued cultural identification of the Silesians, Mazurians, Kashubians, and other autochtons with their special heritages and culture. Many Mazurians held ferociously to their German nationality. The women, in particular, feared that if they received Polish papers, their "German" husbands in POW camps would not be allowed to rejoin them.[170] Despite the terrible war, many Silesians still felt themselves closer to German culture than to Polish, but they hid their feelings in order to be able to stay in the towns and villages of their birth. Their local ties were stronger than any national ones, Polish or German.[171] They knew well that conditions in the occupied zones of Germany were worse than in Poland; if they could be verified as Poles, then the Silesians, even those who identified with the German nation, acceded to the formalities of Polonization.

Many Silesians feared the Poles from the central region of the country and felt alienated from those newly arrived from the east. Both groups tended to treat them with disdain. In fact, the oppression at the hands of the Polish authorities sometimes made the Silesians feel even closer to the Germans, though most were not interested in living in Germany itself.[172] It certainly did not help matters any that many Silesians were driven from their homes and sent to internment camps before it was determined that they were eligible for "verification."[173] "It is a painful fact," wrote Zawadzki, that "the cleansing of Germans from the reclaimed lands" included the incarceration in deportee camps of many Poles who know the Polish language and "now consider themselves Polish." Zawadzki recognized that the Silesians were handled in this manner because the newly arrived Poles wanted their land and homes.[174] The bitterness and resentment among the Silesians against the outsiders expressed itself in continuing use of German at home and, eventually in the 1970s and 1980s, in widespread applications for emigration to the Federal Republic of Germany.

In September 1947, three years after anti-German laws were introduced in Silesia, Zawadzki was still annoyed that so much German was being spoken on the street and in private, despite laws against it. He suggested a renewed offensive against the German language that would include intrusion into people's homes to remove German from inscriptions on albums, pictures, wall-hangings, and calendars. It was especially painful, he noted, that Polish (meaning Silesian) families continued to tolerate German writing on the gravestones of their deceased family members.[175]

Conclusions

The Czechs and Poles used the cover of war and the transition from war to peace to expel the Germans from their countries and to settle old scores. The problem of the German minority had plagued both countries in the interwar period. Nationalist sentiments and the understandable desire for revenge permeated the Polish and Czech populations, as they eagerly and brutally turned the tables on their former German persecutors. Nationalist feelings had been exacerbated by the war and occupation. The Nazis themselves were the primary cause of spiraling nationalist resentments. In some fashion, then, it is fair to say that the Germans reaped what they sowed. That so many lives were lost and ruined in the ethnic cleansing of the Germans from East Central Europe should be attributed, in the final analysis, to the hatred wrought by Nazi policy in the region.

But a major motivation of the Czechs and Poles for expelling the Germans derived from the desire of the new postwar governments (and their predecessors in London) to rationalize and control their societies by making them ethnically homogeneous and fully responsive to the needs and goals of the dominant nationality. Unresolved interwar tensions between Czechs and Germans and Poles and Germans contributed to this outcome. In Poland, the Ukrainians as well as the Germans were sacrificed to the god of ethnic purity. Those Jews who did not fully assimilate into the new political culture of communist Poland were likewise unwelcome in the postwar Polish state. The bulk of those Polish Jews who remained—some 25,000—were eventually expelled in 1968. In the Slovak lands, the Czechoslovak authorities expelled the Hungarians until the Soviet military authorities in Hungary insisted that the forced deportations be halted. Throughout Europe and the Soviet Union, nationalism appeared to be the dominant motif of the new stage of state-building that accompanied the end of World War II. Recognition of minority rights, a principle that was at least formally accepted as part of the post-World War I settlement, had come crashing to an end. Wilsonian Europe had changed beyond recognition.

Politics played an even more important role in Poland and Czechoslovakia than it did in the Soviet Union, when Stalin and Beria decided to deport the Chechens-Ingush and Crimean Tatars. No communist or noncommunist political leader in Prague or Warsaw could hurt his or her chances for success by adopting a virulently anti-German stance. The desire of both communists and democrats to build and consolidate power through popular approval buried those isolated voices which argued that antifascist Germans—progressive citizens of interwar Poland or interwar Czechoslovakia—should be allowed to stay. It is hard to know what ordinary citizens thought of the deportation of the Chechens-Ingush and Crimean Tatars, especially since very few of them were even aware of the situation. The expulsion of Germans from Poland and Czechoslovakia was widely known and extremely popular. Strategic, historic, and economic arguments played their part; no one wanted the Germans to remain in territory that would assuredly be contested by a reunited German government in the future.

The trauma of the war, the Nazi occupation of Poland, and the subsequent expulsion of the Germans inflicted deep wounds that took a long time to heal. Willy Brandt took a major step forward in 1971 when he visited Poland and knelt in silent mourning at the monument of the Warsaw ghetto uprising. It took another two decades of patient diplomatic exchanges for the Poles and Germans finally to sign a treaty that put an end to the nagging uncertainty about the incorporation of the western territories into Poland. Only then were the Poles willing to apologize for the bitter fate they had inflicted on the Germans after the war; and the Germans, in their turn, begged the Poles' forgiveness for the horrible events of the occupation. Both sides are coming to terms with their responsibility for the suffering of the other.[176] Relations between the two nations have markedly improved as a result.

The Czechs and the Germans have taken much longer to come to the same kinds of agreements concluded by the Poles and Germans earlier in the 1990s. Politics explains much of the difference between the Polish and Czech cases. The powerful Sudeten German lobby, centered in Bavaria and able to influence the CSU, made it very difficult for the ruling CDU to engage in dialogue with the Czechs. But the Czechs themselves were not entirely blameless. Denial of the brutality of the expulsions and a lingering sense of guilt about their inconsequential resistance to the Nazis after Munich and during the war came into play. The president of the Czech Republic, Vaclav Havel, has consistently done his best to get his countrymen to recognize the moral costs of denial. His efforts paid off in part in January 1997, when a treaty was signed between the Czechs and Germans, by which both sides apologized for brutalities during and after the war and both sides agreed to recognize the finality of the expulsion. But many issues remain unsettled, and much healing remains to be done between the nations.

The Wars of Yugoslav Succession

Ethnic cleansing in former Yugoslavia and the genocidal attacks that have accompanied it are inextricably linked to the failure of the Yugoslav idea of the nineteenth century, the collapse of the Yugoslav state in the twentieth, and the recent wars of Yugoslav succession. Even more directly, ethnic cleansing is tied to the creation in the 1990s of new states—Serbia, Croatia, Slovenia, Macedonia, Bosnia-Herzegovina—that have succeeded the old Yugoslav federation. The process is far from complete, and additional new states—Montenegro and Kosovo, for example—could emerge from the rubble of former Yugoslavia. Both the breakdown of Yugoslavia and the creation of new nation-states in its wake are rooted in the twentieth-century history of nationalism and war in the Balkans, not—as so often proclaimed in the popular literature and press—in six hundred or more years of conflict. To be sure, as they developed in the nineteenth century, modern national movements in the Balkans contained exclusivist elements. But ethnic cleansing in former Yugoslavia is not a necessary corollary of nation-state building; it is a path chosen by governmental elites with concrete political goals in mind. The conscious choices of a Milosevic or Tudjman, backed by their political supporters in Serbia and Croatia, are as critical to ethnic cleansing as the more abstract processes of disintegration within the former Yugoslav state and the reconstitution of its national components in a multistate system.

The Background

In the twentieth century, two Yugoslav states have failed to meet the challenges presented by their multinational composition. The first—the Kingdom of Serbs, Croats, and Slovenes—was created in December 1918 at the conclusion of World War I. Following the collapse of the Ottoman Empire and the Habsburg monarchy, the frontiers in the western Balkans were redrawn and a completely novel South Slav entity was created. After King Alexander's royal coup in 1929, this country was officially renamed Yugoslavia. Between the world wars, Yugoslavia's two largest and most important component nations, the Serbs and Croats, failed to share power to the satisfaction of both, gravely weakening the country's unity. Some historians believe that the first serious attempt to compromise Croat and Serb interests, the Sporazum of 1939, might have saved Yugoslavia from destruction if the war had not quickly followed. But the Sporazum itself contained the seeds of future conflict by including large Serb and Muslim minorities in the newly created Banovina of Croatia.[1] In any case, the incursions of Italian fascists and the Third Reich into the Balkans at the onset of World War II destroyed the fragile country. The bloody fratricidal killing that characterized the war years ended when Tito and the Partisans forged a second Yugoslav state. Its decentralized federal structure and highly centralized political system was designed to resolve the ethnic tensions between the various nations of Yugoslavia that had festered during the interwar period and caused such destruction and death during the war.

The breakup of communist Yugoslavia at the end of the 1980s unleashed forces of national antagonism that recapitulated, in some ways, those of World War II. Even the language of combat in the wars of Yugoslav succession harked back to the struggles of the Second World War, long mythologized in Partisan lore. Serbs claimed to be fighting Croat Ustashas and Bosnian SS fascists; Croats and Bosnian Muslims saw themselves confronted by Serb Chetniks. Both Serb and Croat fighters donned the symbols and uniforms of their Croat Ustasha and Serb Chetnik predecessors of more than a half century ago. In so doing, they emphasized that the war in Bosnia was "a continuation of the Second World War," as the Bosnian Serb leader Radovan Karadzic expressed it.[2] The way nationalists in former Yugoslavia remembered World War II linked ethnic cleansing in Bosnia and Kosovo to the problems of this century.

Most scholars who have written about the recent war have questioned the assertion that it was produced by "ancient hatreds," centuries in the making, between the nations of the region.[3] As they point out, many of these "nations" were relatively recent creations with little or no premodern history of entrenched struggle with their neighbors. Even those nations with more venerable medieval origins—Serbs, Croats, and Bosnians, among them—have not been locked in struggle or mutual animosity for centuries. The widespread images in both contemporary Yugoslavia and the West of an age-old conflict between Turks and Serbs, Muslims and Orthodox, need considerable revision. The six-century-long Pax Ottomanica allowed the Balkan peoples to grow and develop within their own religious communities, the millets, even though they were under Ottoman domination. Before the end of the nineteenth century, a substantial percentage of the leadership of the Ottoman ruling class consisted of converted Christians from the Balkans—Albanians, Greeks, Serbs, Montenegrins, and others. Dozens of non-Turkish grand vezirs and countless Balkan generals, finance ministers, and regional governors, among others, played a critical role in the Ottoman administration. Conflicts and wars accompanied the Ottoman advance into the Balkans in the fourteenth and fifteenth centuries, and the Ottoman decline and exit from the region in the nineteenth and early twentieth centuries also precipitated clashes and unrest. But these confrontations were far less significant in their own right for the wars of Yugoslav succession in the 1990s than in the way they were commemorated and manipulated by politicians and ideologues.

The harnessing of historical memory to national causes did not begin, of course, with Milosevic, Tudjman, Karadzic, and leaders of their ilk. The rapid decline of the Ottoman Empire and the rise of national ideologies in the wake of the French Revolution gave Serbs, Greeks, Bulgarians, and other Balkan peoples the idea and the opportunity to seek control over their own affairs and to pursue state sovereignty over territories they claimed as their own. The claims came for the most part from "proto-nationalists" of the early modern period, who kept alive ideas of national distinctiveness during the period of Austrian and Ottoman Turkish domination.[4] Like the folk bards who passed on the oral epics of Balkan peoples, these literate priests, teachers, and writers cultivated the historical memory of the respective "great" Serbian, Croatian, Bulgarian, Albanian, Bosnian, and other medieval Balkan kingdoms and principalities.

During the nineteenth century, most of the peoples of the region began nation-building. Serbs and Greeks moved first to establish independent entities, while Albanians and Macedonians came much later; but the pattern was very similar. First, small groups of intellectuals conceived of a national entity. Second, national movements were formed with a narrow but significant social base in the population. Third, new political leaderships at the head of the respective national movements sought political power, either within a larger multinational entity or in an independence movement. Fourth, some form of autonomous unit or independent state was formed with concrete boundaries and an ethnonational identity. Finally, the new states sought to inculcate national values into populations that had been often isolated from the processes of nation-building.[5]

For the Serbs, the now world-famous epic poetry about the Battle of Kosovo, fought on St. Vitus Day (Vidovdan), June 28, 1389, provided the central metaphor for the heroism and self-sacrifice of the Serbian nation. On the Field of Blackbirds (Kosovo Polje), the noble Prince Lazar led a hopeless battle against the Ottoman sultan, Murad, electing to fulfill his sacred mission and that of his nation rather than sue for peace and thus compromise Serb honor. The Kosovo mythology remembers the perfidiousness of the Turks, the treachery of the noble Vuk Brankovic, and above all the heroism and self-sacrifice of Milos Obilic, who, though accused of being a traitor himself, steals into Murad's tent, stabs the sultan, and dies a martyr's death. In one of the most moving passages, the Kosovo Maiden—symbol of Serbian womanhood—wanders the battlefield "amongst bleeding heroes," seeking her betrothed, who had been killed.

> When she finds one living midst the wounded
> Then she laves him with the cooling water,
> Gives him, sacramentally, the red wine,
> Pledges with her fair white bread the hero.[6]

The epic poems commemorating the battle were passed on in fragments and parts through generations, their meanings shifting and changing with the needs of the Serb communities and the bards who recited to them.[7] The fact that Christians and Muslims fought on both sides of the battle—that Serbs, Croats, Albanians, and Turks could be found in both armies—was quickly forgotten. That the battle was probably a stand-off, a draw, and not the epiphany of a tragic defeat also disappeared in the searing light of national self-sacrifice. The Battle of Marica (1371) was historically much more significant for the history of the Serbs in the Balkans than the Battle of Kosovo. But that mattered as

little to the Serb bards and Church fathers, who fostered the consciousness of a common Serb fate, as it did to Milosevic, who gathered more
than a million Serbs on Kosovo Field on June 28, 1989, to commemorate the 600th anniversary of the battle.[8]

In the 1840s, the great "prince-poet" of Montenegro, Petar Petrovic
Njegos, used the Kosovo myth to construct his own vision of the history of Montenegro, "The Mountain Wreath."[9] Here, revenge for the
sacrifice of the Serbs at Kosovo served the cause of uniting Montenegrin
Serbs in their battle against the Turks. In Njegos's view, the problem
was not so much Islam from without but Islam within—the fact that
many Montenegrin clans had converted to Islam. In the poem, Metropolitan Danilo, who ruled Montenegro from 1700 to 1735, debates
with himself and his notables how to deal with the problem. In Njegos's
version, Danilo wavers and pounds his chest but in the end has no
choice but to order the massacre of the Montenegrin "Turks," who did
not flee at the threat of extinction. One of his generals reports back:

> Though broad enough Cetinje's Plain
> No single seeing eye, no tongue of Turk
> Escap'd to tell his tale another day!
> We put them all unto the sword
> All those who would not be baptiz'd:
> But who paid homage to the Holy Child
> Were all baptiz'd with sign of Christian Cross.
> And as brother each was hail'd and greeted.
> We put to fire the Turkish houses
> That there might be nor stick nor trace
> Of these true servants of the Devil!
> From Cetinje to Tcheklitche we hied.
> There in full flight the Turks espied;
> A certain number were by us mown down.
> And all their houses we did set ablaze;
> Of all their mosques both great and small
> We left but one accursed heap,
> For passing folk to cast their glance of scorn.[10]

Although by the end of the nineteenth century, a single Serb national
ideology is hard to identify, at the center of most of its variants was a
well-developed understanding of the special role of the Serbs in defending the South Slavs from the Turks (and Orthodox Christians from
Muslims). Over the course of the nineteenth century, the Serbian state
fought its way free from the Ottomans, expanded its borders, and

strengthened its army and bureaucracy. Using and developing the myths of Kosovo and Danilo, Serb leaders assumed the mantle of defending the South Slavs against the Ottoman Turks and Habsburgs. And within this ideology of "gathering the lands" of the Serbs, few Serb figures were as sanguinary as Njegos's Danilo.

As Ivo J. Lederer explains, the Serb national program was inherently expansionist. That "the frontiers of the Serbian state did not coincide with the boundaries of the Serbian nation lent a galvanic quality to the very notion of Serbian nationality while, politically and ideologically, every Serbian national program perforce looked to changes in the international status quo."[11] But in expanding its borders and including Serbs in a single state, Serbia inevitably would have to confront the presence of Croats and Muslims in Bosnia. The latter were slated in most Serb (and Croat) national programs for forced assimilation. But an uneasy tension existed in the Serb national program—represented, for example, in the 1844 *Nacertanije* (Outline) of Ilija Garasanin or the political program of Nikola Pasic's Serbian Radical Party—between a "narrow ideology" of Greater Serbianism, which excluded Croats, and a desire to include all South Slavs in a single state.[12] It is fair to say, as does Nicholas Miller, that even before World War I, "the ethnic model for political action defeated the civil model."[13] There were simply very few Yugoslavist thinkers among the Serbian political and intellectual elite.[14]

The very strength and intensity of national self-consciousness among the Serbian political elites and cultural producers in the nineteenth century tended to work at cross-purposes with the development of the Illyrian movement, which advocated a union of equal South Slav peoples in a single state. The Croatian lawyer and linguistic pioneer Ljudevit Gaj sought to create an Illyrian language that would unite the peoples of the region in a common movement. His proclamation of the year 1836 stated: "The discordant strings of this lyre are Carniola, Carinthia, Istria, Kranj, Styria, Croatia, Slavonia, Dalmatia, Dubrovnik, Bosnia, Montenegro, Herzegovina, Serbia, Bulgaria, and Lower Hungary . . . Let's stop each strumming on his own string, and tune the lyre in a single harmony."[15] The Balkan Wars and World War I exacerbated the underlying contradictions between the Serbian national idea and the hopes of the other peoples of the Balkans for a "single harmony." After a "Young Bosnian" (Serb) terrorist-patriot assassinated Archduke Franz Ferdinand in Sarajevo on June 28, 1914 (the anniversary of the Kosovo battle), the Serbs once again defied a superior and alien power, the Austro-Hungarian monarchy, and sacrificed their youth to the Moloch of war, suffering a bitter, if heroic, defeat. Meanwhile, the other South Slav nations, freed from Ottoman and Austro-Hungarian rule, developed their own mythologies of sacrifice and independence which insisted on an equal place in the newly constructed postwar Yugoslavia.

The first Yugoslav state was fatally flawed from the moment of its birth. The two largest and most influential of its component nations— the Serbs and Croats—looked at the new country through different historical and political lenses.[16] The Serbs saw the state's creation as a final reward for their long history of battle and sacrifice on behalf of the South Slavs, and they assumed Serbs would govern and rule it as a unitary, centralist polity, as befitted their history and experience. From the very start, Croats and Slovenes, among others, contested this vision, looking to protect their interests through decentralization and confederation, an equal union of equal peoples. The Serbs never quite lost the habits of rule of the prewar kingdom, and they looked at Croat attempts to preserve a measure of autonomy as antiquated and unnecessary. "Interwar Serbian domination," writes Gale Stokes, "proved that Yugoslavia would remain unstable unless the issue of equity was squarely faced."[17]

Many Yugoslav politicians and cultural figures of all the component nationalities struggled to find a formula, a way of thinking, that would defuse the ongoing national confrontations weakening the state and threatening its future.[18] The failure of this experiment became evident in the explosion of nationalist resentments during World War II. Croat Ustasha genocidal massacres of Serbs, Serb Chetnik collaboration with Nazis, Bosnian Muslim units in the SS, and Kosovar Albanian attacks on former Serb colonists all reflect the failures of the Yugoslav state to satisfy the needs of its component nationalities between the world wars. The very intensity with which the Yugoslavist communist Partisans attacked and eliminated "bourgeois nationalist" opponents of all stripes— Chetnik, Ustasha, Muslim—both during and after the Second World War also demonstrates the extent to which the first Yugoslavia not only failed to bridge the different visions of its component nations but in fact deepened the fatal abyss between them.[19]

Tito's solution was to grant each nation its own territorial unit and governmental apparatus. On the Soviet model, these units would be "national in form and socialist in content," meaning that the Communist Party, representing the socialist future, would ensure unity through its Leninist principle of democratic centralism. The "sword and shield" of the party, the secret police, would hold the nationalist deviations in check. The Yugoslav People's Army, heavily imbued with the Partisan ethos of Yugoslav patriotism, also served as an important counterweight to separatist tendencies. Especially after the break with the Soviet Union in 1948, Tito was in firm control of this powerful Yugoslav communist triad of party, police, and army. Tito and his friends, writes Ivo Banac, held the state together "by the skillful use of fear." "Without communism," he says, "there would have been no postwar Yugoslav state."[20] Nevertheless, the new postwar communist cultural elite made considerable progress developing a "supranational Yugoslav culture," one that found some support in the works of the writers Ivo Andric and Miroslav Krleza and the sculptor Ivan Mestrovic, among others.[21] Numerous challenges to this Yugoslavist ideology arose even before Tito died in 1981. But after his death, tensions between the component nations resurfaced to threaten the integrity of the state, and the supranational Yugoslav culture was increasingly challenged by particularist critics.

Two models are commonly used to describe the emergence of nationalist struggles in Yugoslavia after Tito's death. The first, which might be called the "freezer model," implicitly praises Tito's dictatorship for holding separatist strivings in check and for forcing Serbs, Croats, Slovenes, and others to be Yugoslavs. The proponents of this model argue that once the constraints imposed by Tito's rule dissolved, nationalism reared its ugly head and resumed its destructive force, picking up where the World War II interethnic fighting left off. The second model, which might be called the "incubator model," looks much more critically at Tito's contribution to postwar nationalism in Yugoslavia. Here, Tito's penchant for maintaining a balance between the nationalities by giving to one and taking from the other, depending on the time and circumstances, ended up antagonizing all of them eventually and exacerbating resentments among them. His support for satisfying national interests "up to a point" in Croatia and Slovenia built up expectations for autonomy and wound up alienating local nationalists, who were unwilling to accept limitations on their activities, especially in the cultural realm. At the same time, this policy provoked Serb unitarists, who already thought of themselves as exploited and maligned by ungrateful Croats and Slovenes. The crushing of Croat attempts to develop complete cultural autonomy in 1971 turned out to be a harbinger of what was to come.

Much as in the Soviet Union, the policies that promoted nationalist "form" and socialist "content" by the 1970s and 1980s actually produced the opposite: republics that looked and acted as though they were socialist but were increasingly nationalist in their essentials.[22] However justifiable, Tito's recognition of Bosnian Muslims as a nationality in 1968 had much the same effect as his granting of legal autonomy to Kosovo and the Kosovar Albanians in the constitution of 1974.[23] It promoted the Muslims' own demands for greater status within the Yugoslav federation, while worrying and angering Serbian leaders in Belgrade, not to mention Serbs who lived in both areas. The "brotherhood of nations" fostered and developed by the Tito regime, especially in the 1960s, backfired on Yugoslavia. Each brother nation paid more attention to its own needs that those of the brotherhood itself.[24]

Like most dictators, Tito made sure that no logical successors were around to step into his shoes when he died in 1980. Instead, he set up a rotating presidency to lead the state—institutionalizing the dysfunctional bargaining between nations at the very pinnacle of the federal government. The devolution of power to the republics and the paralysis at the federal executive and legislative levels became even more pronounced, and trends toward separatism and nationalism intensified as a result. The two largest nations of Yugoslavia, the Serbs and Croats, increasingly attempted to manipulate the federal system in order to forward their own narrow national interests.[25] Economic problems in the 1980s, including severe inflation and high rates of unemployment, were compounded by pressure from the country's creditors. This economic crisis prompted the richer republics, Croatia and Slovenia, to cut loose from the ballast of the poorer ones, including Serbia.[26] Meanwhile, the Serbs felt they also had been dealt a bad hand by Tito and now sought to redress the balance by asserting their dominance within the federation in general and within Serbian lands in particular, especially Kosovo. Meanwhile, a sea change was occurring in the impending collapse of communism in Eastern Europe and the Soviet Union. At the time, it was hard to see that Yugoslavia would be its most bloodied victim.

The Nationalist Frenzy of the 1980s

The acceleration of national antagonisms that drove Yugoslavia into war and ethnic cleansing from the summer of 1991 onward has a number of important reference points during the previous decade. Although few could have predicted what was to come from these events individually or collectively, no one doubted that conflict was in the air and that political leadership would have to be exerted to avoid bloodshed. Kosovo was one of these reference points, where overwhelming Serbian domination of a substantial Albanian majority—by the end of the 1980s some 90 percent of the population—could not continue indefinitely. Every attempt by the Kosovar Albanians to increase control over their own affairs met with more violent Serbian countermeasures and brutality. Student protest demonstrations in the spring of 1981 led to the declaration of a state of emergency in Kosovo and further Serbian repression against the Albanian community, which continued in one form or another throughout the decade.[27]

The second reference point was the ongoing hostility in the Yugoslav Federation between the Serbs on the one hand and the Croats and Slovenes on the other. In 1985 and 1986 the Slovene government took unilateral steps toward assuming complete control over their own budgetary and judicial affairs. Meanwhile, the nonconformist Slovene youth magazine *Mladina* doggedly attacked and ridiculed the Yugoslav federal parliament and the armed forces.[28] By the mid-1980s, the Croats also sought to introduce a genuinely confederal arrangement by which they could control more of the revenues of their profitable industries, including the booming Dalmatian tourist business. But control of the Croatian party by political conservatives and periodic repressive measures against manifestations of nationalism kept Croat dissent below the surface for most of the decade.[29]

The third reference point, less noticed but equally important to the development of interethnic antagonisms, was the growing national consciousness of the Bosnian Muslims. The Muslim elite looked to deepen its influence on the republic's policies and institutions, and alienated both Serbs and Croats in the process. In 1983, thirteen Muslim intellectuals, led by Alija Izetbegovic, later president of Bosnia-Herzegovina, were brought to trial on charges of "hostile and counter-revolutionary acts derived from Muslim nationalism."[30] The primary evidence used against Izetbegovic was his authorship of the so-called Islamic Declaration of 1970. Noel Malcolm writes: "Izetbegovic pointed out that the text said nothing about making Bosnia ethnically pure, and indeed that it contained no reference to Bosnia at all; but such details did not detain the court, which sentenced him to fourteen years imprisonment, reduced on appeal to eleven years."[31] Like other Muslims in Yugoslavia as a whole, the Bosnians were deeply aware of their second-class status in the communist state and were determined to express their nationality as distinct from their Serb and Croat Slavic cousins.

Developments in Kosovo, Croatia, and Bosnia were tied to nationalist rumblings in Belgrade, the fourth and most important reference point. Serbs felt a growing sense of hostility and isolation from their neighbors. Like the Russians in the Soviet Union, the Serbs understood their role as the preservers and defenders of Yugoslav unity and integrity. Also mirroring Russian attitudes about Soviet policies, the Serbs felt that their own interests had been sacrificed in the Yugoslav system. They were the ones who should complain, not the Croats, Slovenes, or Bosnian Muslims. From their point of view, they had fought two world wars on behalf of the other nations of the federation; they had lost countless sons on the battlefield; and now they were faced with criticism and accusations of hegemony. The Croats and Slovenes lived much better than they, yet both republics sought to control more of their resources. Even more galling to the Serbs was the sense that the growing nationalism of the other peoples of Yugoslavia jeopardized the life and property of Serbs who lived outside of Serbia proper. In the Croatian borderlands, in Kosovo, and in Bosnia-Herzegovina, Serbs perceived that their nation was on the defensive and in trouble.

Only slightly overstating his case, Warren Zimmermann, former U.S. ambassador to Yugoslavia, writes: "In the Balkans, intellectuals tend to be the standard bearers of nationalism; in Serbia, this is carried to fetishistic lengths."[32] Therefore it was fitting that the first important open manifestation of Serb nationalist rhetoric came with the release of the now infamous "Memorandum of the Serbian Academy of Sciences" in September 1986.[33] The memorandum was more important for what it represented than for what it actually said. Leading Serb writers and scholars, with Dobrica Cosic and Antonije Isakovic at their head, gave notice of a public turn in the ideology of the Serb intelligentsia. The memorandum signaled the shift from the promotion of Yugoslavism, colored with a tinge of Serbian patriotism, to outright Serbian nationalism and even pan-Serbism.

For some Serb intellectuals, like Mihailo Markovic and Svetozar Stojanovic, adherence to the memorandum indicated their abandonment of the humanistic Marxism of the heady days of *Praxis,* the world-famous democratic Marxist journal, and their new allegiance to the exclusive interests of the Serbian nation.[34] Many leading Serb intellectuals felt profound disappointment in the Yugoslav experiment and resentment at having been taken advantage of by the other nations of the federation. "Not all the national groups were equal" in Yugoslavia, the memorandum stated. "The Serbian nation, for instance, was not given the right to have its own state. The large sections of the Serbian people who live in other republics, unlike the national minorities, do not have the right to use their own language and script; they do not have the right to set up their own political or cultural organizations or to foster the common cultural traditions of their nation together with their co-nationals."[35]

The memorandum expressed particular resentment against the situation of the Serbs in Kosovo, who, it claims, were the subject of "genocide." Kosovo is the symbol of the Serbs' "historical defeat" in Yugoslavia. "In the spring of 1981," the memorandum asserts, "open and total war was declared on the Serbian people." "Unless things change radically, in less than ten years' time there will no longer be any Serbs left in Kosovo, and an 'ethnically pure' Kosovo, that unambiguouisly stated goal of the Greater Albanian racists, already outlined in the programmes and actions of the Prizren League of 1878–1881, will be achieved."[36]

The memorandum captured the mood of the Belgrade nationalist intelligentsia in the mid-1980s. It also was eerily accurate in predicting a sanguinary future. For example, it identified the potentially explosive mood of the Serbs, while in some ways also contributing to it: "The present state of depression of the Serbian people, against a background of chauvinism and Serbophobia which are gaining in intensity in some milieux, provides fertile soil for an ever more drastic manifestation of the national sensibilities of the Serbian nation and reactions which might be inflammatory and dangerous."[37] It accurately focused on Kosovo as the critical test case of Yugoslav unity. Indeed, the Croats, Slovenes, Bosnians, and others were watching carefully as the Serbs tried to deal with the Kosovo situation.

Unfortunately, the memorandum called for extreme actions. Serbia could not allow the other republics to determine its policies to bring "to heel" "aggressive Albanian nationalism in Kosovo." Thus, both Vojvodina and Kosovo "should become genuinely integral parts of the Republic of Serbia, while receiving that degree of autonomy which does not disrupt the integrity of the Republic and which will be able to satisfy the general interests of the community at large."[38] In short, the memorandum recommended removing Kosovo's autonomy and subordinating the interests of the Kosovar Albanians to those of the Serbs. Milosevic would take this fateful path in 1989, which would lead to the Serbian ethnic cleansing of Kosovo and NATO bombing of Serbia in the spring of 1999.

Just as the "Memorandum of the Serbian Academy of Sciences" encapsulated the transformation of Serb intellectuals into nationalist propagandists, the career of Slobodan Milosevic represented the marked shift of Serbian politics in a nationalist direction. Milosevic was a former law student and banker, a member and by the mid-1980s leader of the Serbian branch of the Yugoslav Socialist Party, and an ambitious and attractive politician. Some biographers attribute his drive for power to a psychosis derived from two desperately unhappy parents, both of whom committed suicide. Some emphasize the important influence of his wife, Mirjana Markovic, to whom he had been close since school days in Pozarevac and who has been his life-long political partner.[39] Markovic is the head of her own "communist" political party, the Yugoslav United Left. When Milosevic visited the town of Kosovo Polje in April 1987, no one imagined that the visit would "change the course of history."[40] Milosevic encouraged the ultranationalist Kosovar Serbs to take their fate in their own hands. In saying to the assembled crowd, "From now on, no one has the right to beat you!" he let the Kosovar Serbs, as well as the Serbs back in Belgrade, know that the force of the Yugoslav state would be used to maintain Serbian control of Kosovo. The crowd shouted back "Slobo, Slobo," and Milosevic understood immediately the intoxicating power of nationalist rhetoric. Milosevic's exaltation was captured on a film clip included in the BBC documentary, "Yugoslavia: Death of a Nation."[41]

In a subsequent meeting with Kosovar Serbs, Milosevic raised the ante even higher, calling for active struggle against the Albanians. "This is your land, here are your houses, fields and gardens, your memories. You are not going to leave your land just because life has become difficult, because you are suffering from injustice and humiliation. It was never in the spirit of the Serb and Montenegrin people to withdraw in face of difficulties, to demobilize itself when it should fight, to become demoralized when the situation is hard. You should stay here because of your ancestors and your heirs."[42]

Shortly after his visit to Kosovo, Milosevic seized control of the Serbian government and party apparatus, deposing his former mentor, Ivan Stambolic, and purging opponents of his nationalist course. Milosevic then sought to abrogate those provisions of the Serbian constitution that allowed Kosovo (and Vojvodina) autonomous status within Serbia and therefore within the Yugoslav entity as a whole. By his actions, Milosevic intended to withdraw the rights of Kosovar Albanians that they had held in the province since 1974, when they effectively were given republican status by Tito and the new Yugoslav constitution. The Kosovar Albanians protested moves to limit their autonomy, calling strikes and mass meetings around the country. That was all that Milosevic needed to send in the army and proclaim a state of emergency. By the end of March 1989, Milosevic had what he wanted. "Kosovo's 'autonomy,'" writes Noel Malcolm, "was now reduced to a mere token."[43]

But this was only the beginning of the Kosovars' problems. Continuing clashes with police led to the arrest of large numbers of Kosovar Albanian activists. Albanian-language schools were closed down. Albanians were persecuted on the street and in their homes. Many lost their jobs. Serbs were openly favored in economic policies, Albanians clearly discriminated against. Many young and talented Kosovar Albanians left to find work and practice their occupations in Western Europe. The situation was bleak; Kosovo was effectively under martial law.

Meanwhile, Milosevic continued to ride the wave of nationalism, using it to oust his political opponents and consolidate his power. He seemed as gifted at isolating and eliminating potential centers of political opposition as he was at finding support among Serb nationalists.[44] On June 28, 1989, the 600th Anniversary of the Battle of Kosovo, Milosevic called a mass rally on Kosovo Field, and a million Serbs showed up. Like Hitler descending through the clouds by airplane to attend the Nuremberg rally portrayed in Leni Riefenstahl's "Triumph of the Will," Milosevic arrived by helicopter amidst a throng of excited supporters to deliver a warning of war and sacrifice: "Serbs in their history have never conquered or exploited others. Through two world wars, they have liberated themselves and, when they could, they also helped others to liberate themselves . . . The Kosovo heroism does not allow us to forget that, at one time, we were brave and dignified and one of the few who went into battle undefeated . . . Six centuries later, again we are in battles and quarrels. They are not armed battles, though such things should not be excluded yet."[45] Surrounded by Serbian Orthodox priests, Milosevic repeated the refrain that Serbia had suffered too much to allow Yugoslavia's component parts to fall away through autonomy or separation. Wherever Serb bones lie buried in the soil, Milosevic insisted, that was Serbian territory. Wherever Serb blood was shed, that was the Serbian patrimony.

Much like the "Memorandum of the Serbian Academy of Sciences," Milosevic's speeches at rallies in Kosovo in 1987 and 1989 were nationalistic but hardly Hitlerian in content. Nor was there any of the nasty racism or exaltation of violence that was to characterize the wars of the 1990s. But the turn to nationalism was as apparent in Serb political life as it was in Serb intellectual circles. Milosevic's major rivals on the Serbian political scene, Vuk Draskovic of the Serbian Renewal Movement and Vojislav Seselj of the Serbian Radical Party, propounded ultranationalist programs. In typical rhetoric, the back cover of the Radicals' program proclaimed:

> Serb, brother, never forget!
> These are Serbian lands!
> Rivers of blood have been spilt for them
> And that is why they must be in a Serbian state.[46]

The Serbian National Renewal claimed that the "Bolshevik-Titoist" conspiracy that brought glorious Serbdom to a state of "civilizational penury and the very brink of biological extinction."[47] The Serbian countryside also fed the upsurge of nationalist sentiment. Religious intolerance and resentment of the cosmopolitan city resonated in the villages with Milosevic's "anti-bureaucratic revolution." The unity of the folk, religion, and nation had broad appeal.[48] Socialism and Yugoslavism belonged to the past; the failure of one meant the collapse of the other.[49] The future would have to be negotiated with an armed and dangerous Serbia.

These changes in the thinking of Serbian politicians and intellectuals at the end of the 1980s were part of a rapid—even revolutionary—paradigm shift in both Yugoslavia and the former communist bloc. Socialism had failed as an economic and political system. People in the region had understood this fact for a long time; what now became apparent was that something could be done about it. One after another, the communist regimes in Eastern Europe were deposed in 1989 and replaced by ostensibly democratic ones. Finally, the Soviet Union itself broke apart in 1991, and in its successor states socialism gave way to "capitalism" and "democracy," at least in the minds of the new leaders. But the absence of historical experience with the marketplace or with parliamentary democracy undermined programs for a rapid transition. Even with decently functioning institutions, it was hard to change peoples' habits and thinking. Corruption flourished; the open market turned into robber capitalism; the *nomenklatura* found ways to control natural resources and industries. As political parties proliferated and the excessive privileges among political leaders fostered suspicion, common citizens gave in to cynicism and withdrew from politics and voting. Democratization came to mean little more than freedom of movement and freedom of speech, and even these were sometimes imperiled.

Multiethnic civil societies had little hope of flourishing without a functioning democracy and market economy. Instead, nationalism reigned supreme. It had served a positive function in opposing communism and providing the peoples of the region with a sense of purpose and belonging during the long and hard domination of authoritarian parties and secret police. Deprived of familiar institutions and a feeling of security after 1989, the peoples of the region found solace in ideas of national solidarity and patriotism. Poverty, unemployment, and disappointed expectations led many to support nationalist parties. With nationalism's major enemy—Soviet-inspired communism—defeated and everywhere in retreat, nationalist ideologues naturally sought out other enemies, usually "other" nations, whether minorities within one's own nation or one's neighbors. More than any other factor, nationalism prompted the demise of the multinational states of Czechoslovakia, the Soviet Union, and Yugoslavia. But breaking up these federations did not resolve the problems of nationalism. The Estonians simply turned on the Russians, the Georgians on Abkhazians, Armenians on Azeris, Slovaks on Hungarians, and Czechs on gypsies.

With their constitutions weak and their political institutions underdeveloped, with democracy and the market economy beyond their immediate reach, Yugoslavia and many of its sister socialist countries were dry kindling for the flames of nationalism. This was only somewhat less the case for Slovenia and Macedonia than it was for Serbia and Croatia. Given the problematic relations between the Croats and Serbs over the course of the century, Croatian nationalism seemed destined to come into conflict with the Serbs. In the late 1960s, Croats were already seeking greater cultural and political autonomy within Yugoslavia. The Croatian cultural organization Matica Hrvatska called for recognition of an independent Croatian culture and language. In 1971 Tito moved against the increasingly liberal League of Communists of Croatia in an attempt to stem the tide of Croatian nationalism inside the party and out. But the Pandora's box of nationalism was opened; by the late 1980s, Croat intellectuals were convinced that there would have to be either a genuine confederation in Yugoslavia or no Yugoslav state at all. Full independence was on the mind of many, who felt increasingly alienated from Belgrade and the Serbs.

Among this group was the historian and former Partisan fighter, later general, Franjo Tudjman. Tudjman was a Croat nationalist and the author in 1989 of *Absurdities of Historical Reality,* which rejected Serb accusations that the Ustashas had engaged in genocide against Serbs during the war and tried to whitewash Ustasha crimes against the Jews.[50] Although Tudjman backed off of his denials about the Holocaust in Croatia, he continued to insist that the wartime Croatian state was an honored predecessor of future Croatia. Tudjman's party, the Croatian Democratic Union (HDZ), held its first meetings in the summer of 1989 and was legalized in December. During the election campaign of 1990, Tudjman hammered unremittingly on the anvil of nationalism, gaining support at home and abroad among the wealthy and influential Croat émigré community. Despite attempts by the Serbian military and political leadership to bully the Croats, Tudjman intimated that nothing short of independence would satisfy the country.

On May 30, 1990, amid a profusion of Croat nationalist symbolism, Tudjman was inaugurated as president of Croatia. Silber and Little describe the scene and the inherent tensions behind it. "He [Tudjman] wore a red-white-and-blue sash. The *sahovnica* [the red and white checkered traditional coat-of-arms of Croatia, also used by the Ustashas] was displayed in the background, the communist star abandoned. The Croatian President had not yet, however, accomplished what he wanted. Just out of reach was his dream of a Croatian state. There was one problem—the Serbs."[51]

Milosevic was both very much like Tudjman and very different. The Serbian leader never quite abandoned his communist roots.[52] After 1990 his party, the Socialist Party of Serbia, blended neo-Yugoslavism with Serb nationalism, partisan traditions with those of the Chetniks, bellicosity and aggressiveness with the pathos of victimization.[53] He dominated the Serbian state apparatus, yet appealed to populist slogans and antigovernment sentiments among the peasants.[54] His mix of Serbian chauvinism and Yugoslav integralism meant that non-Serb nationalisms were interpreted as reactionary and separatist. For Tudjman, the problem was the Serbs; for Milosevic, every nationality of former Yugoslavia—Croats, Slovenes, Bosnian Muslims, and Kosovar Albanians—stood in the way of his ambitions.

The War in Yugoslavia

On June 25, 1991, Slovenia declared its independence; hours later, Croatia did the same. Both were outraged by Serbia's actions in Kosovo and anxious to jump from the sinking ship of Yugoslavia while they still had a chance. Both were encouraged by hopeful signs from the European community, and especially from the Germans, that their new states would be protected by ties with Europe. They were wrong. Forces of the Yugoslav Peoples' Army (JNA) moved to secure the borders and control vital transportation links. The Slovenes decided to fight, but fortunately casualties were minimal. In a short ten-day war, Milosevic and his Belgrade supporters made it clear they were not interested in a bloody clash with the Slovenes. Very few Serbs lived in the republic; the two nations had no common boundaries; and Milosevic himself indicated that he was prepared to let Slovenia secede.

Not so, however, with Croatia. Backed by the JNA, Serb militia forces began to seize control of Serb-inhabited territory inside Croatia, setting up the Republic of Serb Krajina, "cleansing" the region of Croats, and erecting armed barriers on roads to Zagreb and the coast. Former Chetnik strongholds during World War II, Knin among them, served as the most radical centers of Serbian aggression.[55] Thousands of Croats fled from the Krajina for the coast, looking for relief from vengeful Serb militiamen. A Croat village located in the Krajina, Kijevo, was the first to be cleansed of its inhabitants in a process that became integral to the wars of Yugoslav succession. In this case, it was called "cleansing of the ground" *(ciscenje terena)*.[56] Like the later cases of ethnic cleansing in Croatia, Bosnia, and Kosovo, the expulsion of the Croats and the destruction of the village of Kijevo was planned and coordinated by the Serbian forces.

Outmanned and fearful of an outright war with the JNA, the Croats initially hesitated to fight. But facing a similar Serbian attack on Vukovar in eastern Slavonia in late August 1991, they had no choice but to organize their forces to resist the Serb militias and the JNA. If Slovenia had fought a brief war with Yugoslavia and its armed forces for the right to secede, Croatia was at war with the Serbs for control of Serb-inhabited territory in Croatia claimed by Milosevic and the Croatian Serb nationalist leadership. The Serbs claimed they needed "living space" for their people, and they intended to secure it in Croatia.[57] The JNA itself had become an almost exclusively Serb army; members from the other nationalities either deserted or fell in line with the goals of the Serb-dominated high command.

Vukovar fell to the Serbs on November 20 after three months of bombardment and bitter fighting. Vukovar, writes Nebojsa Popov, was "the Hiroshima of our days."[58] Panic set in at nearby Osijek, and Serbian officers confidently predicted the fall of Zagreb.[59] However, the Croats had succeeded in forming an army and offering up enough resistance to force Milosevic to accede to international pressure for placing peacekeepers between his forces and those of the Croats. Behind the lines, however, Milosevic proceeded with his plans to absorb the occupied Croatian territories into a newly constituted, Serb-dominated Yugoslavia. Zeljko Raznatovic, known as Arkan, and his paramilitary forces, the Tigers, wreaked havoc among Croatian civilians, robbing, threatening, and killing. Not only did the Serbs do everything they could to drive the Croats out of territory they claimed as their own, but they destroyed private homes, businesses, and cultural monuments as a way to make sure the Croats would never come back.

If Kijevo set a pattern for ethnic cleansing that was to repeat itself throughout the 1990s, the taking of Vukovar and occupation of eastern Slavonia introduced the element of genocide into campaigns of ethnic cleansing. On November 19, 1991, JNA soldiers and Serb paramilitary forces entered a local hospital in Vukovar. Most of the sick and the wounded were evacuated to a "detention center" located at a nearby warehouse, where the prisoners were robbed and beaten. A number of the wounded soldiers were then transferred to a prison in Sremska Mitrovica (in Vojvodina). The next morning, according to the International Tribunal in the Hague, JNA officers separated the women and children from the remaining men, many still on stretchers, and transported them from the detention center. Many of the men, both civilians and soldiers, were tortured and beaten senseless, two of them so badly that they died. Dennis Miller, a Hague tribunal investigator, later described a regular "orgy of beatings" in Vukovar.[60] Two hundred prisoners were then taken to the Ovcara farm outside of Vukovar, massacred, and buried in a mass grave.[61] It was the first, though certainly not the last, time in the war that ethnic cleansing was accompanied by acts of genocide.

Both the Serbs and the Croats raised the stakes in their six-month-long war by conjuring up images of World War II. The Serbs in Krajina mobilized around the threat of a new Jasenovac, the Ustasha camp where tens of thousands of Serbs, Jews, and other opponents of the fascist regime died. "For the second time in half a century," the Serbs claimed, "Croatian government organs and their paramilitary and rebel outlaw formations have committed the crime of genocide against the Serb people in Croatia."[62] The Serbs wildly exaggerated the number of their co-nationals killed at Jasenovac, some claiming more than half a million, others more than a million victims, when the number is likely somewhat less than 100,000.[63] Meanwhile, the Croats focused on the Titoist massacres of Croat troops in 1945, whose numbers were also wildly exaggerated. This "verbal civil war"—reinforced by the almost complete control of the media by Tudjman and Milosevic—was reenacted by the militias on the ground.[64] Traumatic memories of war and extermination that had been repressed in individuals and suppressed and distorted by the Titoist regime became instruments of political struggle and fratricidal war.[65]

The bitterness of the fighting reached into the everyday life of towns and villages in the war zone. Serbs and Croats blew up one another's houses, businesses, wells, and cisterns, and poisoned one another's cattle. They destroyed graveyards, churches, and monuments. Mart Boax describes the Croat destruction of a monument to victims of fascism: "We silently climbed the partly ravaged staircase; sixty-eight steps, I remember. It stopped at a plateau with the remains of a monument. 'Comrades blew up this blasted Chetnik thing,' Franjo [the host] informed me with a torrent of curses. And in his school-English he added emotionally: 'We killed the dead because they kept them alive.' An ultimate form of ethnic cleansing, I thought. He spit with contempt on the remains and turned away."[66] Tudjman eventually planned to convert Jasenovac itself into a memorial to "all war victims," including victims of the Partisans and those who fell in the wars of the 1990s.[67] Predictably, this enraged the Serbs. Meanwhile, wanton Serbian attacks on the beautifully preserved medieval city of Dubrovnik and the destruction of Croat monuments in Krajina added even more fuel to the fire.

The conflagration, it is worth adding, had little to do with the particular characteristics of the "Dinaric type," highlander Serbs, Croats, and Montenegrins, who have been described as being more blood-thirsty than the Serb farmers of the Sumadija or Croats from the Pannonian plain. In Fernand Braudel's classic studies of Mediterranean civilization in the sixteenth century, the fighters of the Dinaric mountain clans played an important role. Hand-to-hand combat, blood feuds, and long memories are certainly part of the history of warfare in the region. Nor can the traditions and habits of the uskoks (pirates) and the hajduks (bandits) in the borderlands between the Ottoman Empire and Europe be forgotten. Still, the brutal and uncompromising nature of the struggle in Croatia and later in Bosnia and Kosovo in the 1990s had much more to do with the history of the region since 1940 and the urban social groups that fostered Serbian paramilitaries than it did with the inheritance of the distant past.

Bosnia

By the beginning of 1992, it became clear that Bosnia was the next crisis point on the Yugoslav agenda. Milosevic and the Serbs had arranged for the JNA units in Bosnia-Herzegovina to be manned by Bosnian Serbs, so that when formal withdrawal of the JNA took place in May, the Bosnian Serbs could legitimately stay behind, with their ordnance and men in place. The Bosnian Serbs, under the aggressive nationalist Radovan Karadzic, set up a Bosnian Serb Republic in January 1992 as a way to preempt the separation of Bosnia-Herzegovina from Yugoslavia and recognition by the European Union. If Bosnia-Herzegovina declared its independence, Karadzic warned, it would not last a single day.[68] Alija Izetbegovic, president of Bosnia-Herzegovina and leader of the Bosnian Muslim party, nevertheless steered a reluctant course toward independence. He was determined to maintain the integrity of the republic and was uninterested in sharing power with the militant Serb minority (31 percent) and the equally nationalist Croat minority (17 percent). Talks had been held between Milosevic and Tudjman on March 25, 1991, in which the two ostensibly antagonistic leaders agreed to the partition of Bosnia, leaving the Muslims only a small enclave around Sarajevo. At the beginning of April, open warfare began, first in Zvornik in the north and then inside Sarajevo itself. For three-and-a-half years, Bosnia was to be the scene of the worst fighting and massacres in Europe since the Second World War.

Especially at the outset, the Serbs had by far the better of the war. Bosnian Muslim police units were no match for the Serbs and their JNA-armed and led forces. Even more than the war in Croatia, the Serb attacks were accompanied by horrendous campaigns of ethnic cleansing, which quickly became the term to describe the forcible expulsion of Bosnian Muslims from towns, cities, and villages claimed by the Serbs. This nasty work of creating ethnically homogeneous Serb territory was carried out primarily by paramilitary soldiers, who systematically beat, robbed, brutalized, and expelled the Muslim population, killing and raping as they moved from region to region. The paramilitaries were joined by local recruits, who operated close to their own towns and villages.[69] This made the violence up-close and personal, as old scores were settled. Serbs who tried to help their Bosnian neighbors were isolated and attacked.[70] The idea was to instill terror in the local Muslim population and to get them to run for their lives.

It worked. By the end of 1992, two million Bosnians, the vast majority of whom were Muslims, had fled from their homes. If the Serb attacks were not enough, the Bosnian Croats got in the act toward the end of the summer of 1992. They, too, attacked Bosnian Muslims and drove them out of their towns and villages in acts of ethnic cleansing. Mate Boban, president of what became called Herceg-Bosna (Croatian Bosnia), met with Ed Vulliamy, a writer for *The Wall Street Journal,* and told him that "spiritually, culturally, and economically, Herceg-Bosna is part of Croatia . . . [It is] historically Croatian living space."[71] In the name of Serb and Croat *Lebensraum,* Bosnian Muslims were attacked, beaten, raped, murdered, and expelled.

The genocidal treatment of the Muslim population in the first months of the war was particularly focused in a series of makeshift detention facilities and prisons set up by the Bosnian Serbs for their victims. Ethnic cleansing is not just about attack, violence, and expulsion; in almost every case it also includes punishment. Those who are driven off are punished for their existence, for the very need to expel them. Non-Serbs in the Prijedor region were isolated and forced to wear white armbands, which left them vulnerable to abuse and attacks by local Serbs. More than 47,000 homes belonging to non-Serbs were destroyed. Women were removed to the Trnopolje camp, while some 6,000 people, mostly men, were incarcerated at Omarska.[72] In this terrifying camp, whose horrors first came to light in the journalistic accounts of Roy Gutman, Bosnian Muslims endured all the tortures of hell.[73] Between May and August of 1992, according to the Hague Tribunal, guards "regularly and openly killed, raped, tortured, beat and otherwise subjected prisoners to conditions of constant humiliation, degradation and fear of death."[74] Zeljko Mejakic, the commander of the camp in Omarska, was the first person indicted by the Tribunal for genocide; he remains at large.

In many ways even worse than the Omarska camp was the camp at Keraterm, outside of Prijedor. According to the Tribunal indictment, between late May and the beginning of September 1992, some 3,000 Bosnian Muslims and Bosnian Croats from the Prijedor district were interned in this former ceramics factory and storage complex. Here, as elsewhere, Serb guards and overseers seemed to derive pleasure from regularly beating, bloodying, and humiliating their prisoners. They hit and bludgeoned them with every imaginable implement: "wooden batons, metal rods, baseball bats, lengths of thick industrial cable that had metal balls affixed at their end, rifle butts, and knives." Night after night, the beatings would take place; young, old, men, women, boys, and girls were the victims. The beatings were sometimes so severe that those who endured them were injured for life. Many died as a result; some were simply killed. The worst case of murder at Keraterm took place in late July 1992, when 140 men from Brdo near Prijedor were confined to one of the rooms in the complex. The officer on duty gave orders that the room be surrounded by guards and soldiers with machine guns. At night, they opened fire, continuing to shoot into the room on and off over a period of several hours. If there were reasons for the shootings, they remain unknown. A couple of people survived to tell the tale.[75]

The most severe damage to life and limb in the former Yugoslavia was done by paramilitary groups based in Serbia proper. Many of them had been initially armed and trained by the Serbian Ministry of Interior. Their officers were subordinate to the "military line" *(vojna linija)*, a small group of ranking secret police officials who reported directly to Milosevic.[76] Some paramilitary soldiers wore uniforms of the Bosnian Serb Army; others wore uniforms with no insignia at all. They came from varied backgrounds: there were JNA soldiers who simply changed uniform; amnestied convicts looking for adventure; and nationalist thugs who, under other circumstances, would be skinheads persecuting minorities, fighting as gangs, or committing minor felonies. They sometimes operated in conjunction with the JNA and sometimes on their own.

The paramilitary group commanded by the indicted criminal Zeljko Raznatovic (Arkan) was notorious for its violent actions. His "soldiers" were mostly young toughs who had earlier been members of his group of soccer hoodlums, the Warriors, which followed the Belgrade club Red Star.[77] Now they dressed in black and khakis and wore headbands with their hair short or shaven in the style of European neo-Nazis. Their insignia read "Serbian volunteers" on the outside and had a tiger in the middle.[78] These Arkanovci or Tigers committed an unending string of atrocities in Croatia, Bosnia, and Kosovo. In an interview, Arkan rejected the notion that he acted on his own: "Let us understand each other. We are not just talking about paramilitary units. Every member of those units must, first of all, be responsible to the Serbian people and must respect the parliament and the president of the Republic."[79] In short, the crimes committed by his group were state-initiated and state-supported.

One woman from the Sanski Most region reported that the Tigers beat up a group of Muslim men so badly that "they were barely breathing and the only thing left in them was their souls, that was all." The body of her husband, who was thought to be in the Bosnian Army, was mutilated beyond recognition after being dragged by rope behind a car.[80] One fifteen-year-old Muslim boy from Bosanska Gradiska described systematic beatings at the hands of Serb paramilitary soldiers that he and others endured. The technique very much resembles the "bastinado" torture used by the Turks against the Armenians (and by the Spanish during the Inquisition): "Most of the beatings were on our bare feet. We had to kneel on the floor with our hands behind our heads and put our heads on the floor while they beat our feet; if you screamed you got twenty or thirty more hits. There were three or four of us that were beaten with the rubber hose . . . There were approximately twenty men, and they would beat you five at a time, and they took turns beating us." The Serbs routinized the agony. The men were released, sent home to recover, and then summoned to the police station again, sometimes on a daily basis, to be beaten.[81]

Arkan's Tigers went through the town of Sanski Most from house to house. Typically a neighboring Serb would identify where the Muslims lived and then show up together with a couple of Arkan's soldiers. One eyewitness describes the following scene, which was repeated many thousands of times in slightly different variations around Bosnia. It was September 1995 when Arkan's people arrived. "On a Thursday, around 11:00 A.M., while we were drinking coffee, three men entered the house. They asked for identification cards. They were looking for weapons and money. They proceeded to beat me. I was hit on the head. But my husband got it worse. He was covered in blood. They were beating my husband with three pistols. I gave them my money and they stopped. They counted the money and left the house."[82] In many cases, the Serbs came back and beat the inhabitants until there was no more money and then drove them from their home, either burning it or leaving it standing for Serb refugee use.

The Muslims had to pay exorbitant rates to get access to the buses that would transport them out of Serb-controlled territory. Before boarding the buses, they had to wait for days or weeks in ghettos—temporary housing in schools or community centers, where they were open season for more robbery and beatings. One group of Muslims was forced to run a gauntlet to get to their temporary housing. In Sehovici, where some 3,000 non-Serbs waited for transportation, the Serbs came at night, threatening violence to the children unless they got more money. Once they got on the buses, they were beaten again until they handed over money, jewelry, and other valuables. In the case of the thirteen or so checkpoints between Prijedor and the border, the buses were stopped, boarded by young thugs, who invariably checked papers, abused women, and threatened the lives of children unless the hapless Muslims came up with even more money. In the same way that the Turks stole ceaselessly from the "rich" Armenians and the Germans from the "wealthy" Jews, the Serbs also seemed to think that the Muslims were endlessly wealthy, and they stole from them until there was no more to take.

The last stage of ethnic cleansing was in some ways the most trying. During the trip, men of military age were removed from the buses and trucks. Especially toward the end, very few families could come up with cash or valuables to save their sons and husbands. Muslim men were moved to prisons and recruited to labor battalions. Some unlucky ones were killed outright. Younger Croats were inducted in the Bosnian Serb army; few dared to refuse. The rest of the busloads of refugees were dumped in fields several kilometers from the border, robbed, abused, and beaten again, and left to make their way through the woods and across rivers to Bosnian Muslim territory. "People were bloodied," wrote one woman. "I saw some women lying dead . . . When someone died, they wouldn't let the corpses remain on 'their' land; we had to carry them to the Bosnian side."[83] The British diplomat David Owen recounted the report of a U.N. refugee official, who watched Muslim refugees cross through the "no-man's land": "As they walked, weighed down by bags containing the few possessions that they had been able to gather up, the Serbs started to fire small arms over their heads and a few fell wounded or dying. Then, as they moved out of range, shell fire started and he watched as they struggled on stumbling and running as shells landed around them. Some were hit."[84]

This particular circle of violence—beating, stealing, humiliating, beating, stealing, and humiliating again, then expelling—was hardly peculiar to Arkan and the Serbs. But somehow, in contrast to their Nazi, Polish, or Turkish predecessors, who also beat and robbed their victims, the Serb paramilitaries seem to have had regular routines. They beat young men more than the old, men more than women. They had lists of names, ostensibly of Bosnian Army soldiers, government agents, spies, and their families, whom they beat more viciously than others. Serb paramilitaries also engaged in outright murder. All over Bosnia, young Muslim men were shot in groups and buried in common graves.

The most devastating case of mass shootings took place in Srebrenica in July 1995. Enough evidence has been collected by journalists, human rights activists, and the international tribunal in the Hague to reconstruct the terrible story of ethnic cleansing turned to genocide.[85] Srebrenica was a U.N. designated "safe area," protected, in theory, by a small contingent of Dutch soldiers. On July 6 General Ratko Mladic, the swashbuckling commander of the Bosnian Serb army, led an assault on the area that ended ten days later in the capture of Srebrenica. Muslim forces in the area, commanded by the notorious Bosnian fighter Naser Oric, had abandoned Srebrenica to its fate. The Dutch U.N. peacekeepers essentially stood aside as the Bosnian Serbs advanced. Some have argued that they even helped to turn over the area (and its Muslim population) to the Serbs.[86] The final U.N. report on the Srebrenica massacre confirms accusations of inaction in face of Mladic's determination to seize the area: "The Bosnian Serb forces ignored the Security Council, pushed aside the UNPROFOR troops, and assessed correctly that air power would not be used to stop them. They overran the safe area of Srebrenica with ease, and then proceeded to depopulate the territory within 48 hours. Their leaders then engaged in high-level negotiations with representatives of the international community while their forces on the ground executed and buried thousands of men and boys within a matter of days."[87]

Thousands of Muslims from the region of Srebrenica—men, women, children, and old people—fled through the woods and mountains for Tuzla in Bosnian Muslim territory. Most made it; hundreds, maybe a thousand, did not. They succumbed to Serb attacks, exhaustion, and sickness. In Srebrenica itself, the Bosnian Serb forces, army and paramilitary, seized men of supposed fighting age, meaning from 16 to 65, and confined them at the soccer stadium in town. Within a period of a week to ten days, they were taken to a variety of sites, killed, and buried in mass graves. During the process, they were beaten, marched about at double-pace, and forced down on their knees and told to pray to Allah.[88] Some simply had their throats cut on the spot, as described by Drazen Erdemovic, a convicted war criminal.[89] Busloads of men, blindfolded with their arms tied behind their backs, were transported to killing fields. There, they were executed by firing squads and buried in mass graves. Erdemovic described the process: "Another bus arrived. Each one held approximately sixty men. As the morning passed, the execution squad kept having to move to new positions. Rows of dead bodies were slowly filling up the field."[90] They buried the corpses with bulldozers. Erdemovic estimated that 1,000–1,200 were killed at his site in one day. No one will ever know exactly; roughly six to eight thousand were killed altogether.[91] The U.N. accepted responsibility for badly misreading the situation: "Through error, misjudgement and an inability to recognize the scope of evil confronting us, we failed to do our part to help save the people of Srebrenica from the Serb campaign of mass murder."[92]

Srebrenica was the site of the most serious genocidal massacre that accompanied the ethnic cleansing of Bosnia and Herzegovina. "These are truly scenes from hell, written on the darkest pages of human history," stated Judge Riad of the Hague Tribunal.[93] But the terror of ethnic cleansing was felt throughout the territories controlled or even threatened by the Bosnian Serbs. Sarajevo faced its own peculiarly terrifying fate, as Serbian artillery lobbed shells into the city below from the heights of Mt. Igman. Designated a U.N. "safe area" like Srebrenica, Sarajevo was hit by an average of one thousand artillery shells per day, aimed primarily at civilian targets.[94] Karadzic, in particular, was determined both to destroy the city as a home of Bosnian Muslims and to remake it as a Serb entity. "The attacks were not intended merely to hammer Sarajevo, 'to kill the city in it', and to punish it for its former spirit of tolerance and cosmopolitanism," writes Sreten Vujovic, "but also to cleanse it ethnically and regenerate it nationally."[95] Sometimes completely isolated and cut off from the world, with the bare minimum of food, water, and power, Sarajevo and its citizens suffered severely during the war and are still recovering from its traumatic effects.

Banja Luka, the second biggest city in Bosnia, was turned into the "Heart of Darkness," in the words of the U.N. High Commissioner on Refugees, the "worst place in Bosnia in terms of human rights abuses."[96] From the beginning of 1992 on, Muslims and Croats in Banja Luka were intimidated, attacked, fired from their jobs, and sometimes tortured and murdered. In the city and its surrounding towns and villages, Serbian police and soldiers roused families in the middle of the night, hauled off the men to camps and labor battalions, stole from the population, and confiscated their property.

The bureaucratic persecution faced by the Bosnian Muslims who sought to leave Banja Luka reminds one of Victor Klemperer's descriptions of the financial exploitation of Jews who wanted to leave Germany at the end of the 1930s. The governments—Nazi and Bosnian Serb—insisted that their hated minorities leave as quickly as possible. Yet they punished, persecuted, and exploited the ready emigrants, making it harder and more intimidating to exit the country. Diana Paul, a human rights worker in Banja Luka, described the situation: "Those who wanted to leave had to visit numerous municipal offices and pay fees at each one during certain periods. The fees and the rules and regulations changed all the time, and here again, I'm talking about the finality of evil. It was necessary to go to numerous municipal offices for telephones, electricity, to the bank to certify that you didn't owe them anything each time you went and obtain a receipt so that you would be permitted to be ethnically cleansed."[97] Just as in the situation of the Nazi persecution of the Jews at the end of the 1930s, the Muslims' properties were systematically registered by the Banja Luka authorities and then taken away.

By the spring of 1995, fewer than 10 percent of the Muslims and 15 percent of the Croats still remained in the Banja Luka region itself. After the expulsion of some 200,000 Krajina Serbs by the Croats in August and September 1995 and the arrival of many of these and other refugees in Banja Luka, the pressure on the remaining Muslims and Croats grew even more pronounced. By October 1995 fewer than 15,000 non-Serbs resided in a region that had a prewar non-Serbian population of over 500,000. Of Banja Luka's 60,000 or so non-Serbs, all but a few thousand had left. Radoslav Brcanin, then director of Banja Luka television, openly advocated ethnic cleansing. No more than 2,000 or so elderly Muslims should remain in Banja Luka, he is reported to have said, "Only enough to clean our streets and clean our shoes."[98]

Brcko was strategically located at the top of the horseshoe of Bosnian Serbian territory, linking western Bosnia, with Banja Luka as its chief city, and eastern Herzegovina, with Pale as its political center and newly designated capital of the Bosnian Serb Republic. As a result, at the outset of the war in Bosnia, in May 1992, Serbs attacked resident Muslims and Croats, driving them into internment camps. Some 2,000 people were killed outright; over 90 percent of the non-Serb population was expelled from the city. Those who were unlucky enough to be interned ended up in the camp at Luka, commanded by Goran Jelisic, the self-described "Serbian Adolf."[99] Jelisic forced prisoners to sing patriotic Serb songs, and if they missed a verse or got the words wrong, they were beaten and sometimes executed. Jelisic openly advocated creating "a clean territory for the Serbian people" and eliminating those Muslims who refused to leave. The result was that he was allegedly responsible for the "extermination" of at least a hundred Muslim men. Although Muslim women were raped in Luka, as they were in nearly all the internment camps in Bosnia, he claimed to have no part in it, saying that "Muslim women were dirty." But his murderousness was so extreme, according to the prosecutors in the Hague, that even the Bosnian Serb authorities got nervous about his activities and replaced him as head of the camp.[100] On October 19, 1999, Jelisic was found guilty of 31 counts of war crimes and sentenced to 40 years in prison.[101]

Rape

Rape and the sexual abuse of women has been associated with cases of ethnic cleansing throughout this century. But in none of the other cases that we have examined has rape appeared to be so central to the purposes of punishing and driving out the "other" as in Bosnia. All the major parties to the war—Serbs, Croats, and Muslims—have been guilty of rape and vicious attacks on women. Although many of the women felt too shamed to report their experiences, enough have been interviewed by human rights activists to allow one to generalize about their treatment. Clearly, the victims were primarily Muslim women and the perpetrators primarily Serb army and paramilitary soldiers. The Helsinki report on Bosnia, which relied on interviews with many rape victims, states: "Soldiers attacking villages have raped women and girls in their homes, in front of family members and in the village square. Women have been arrested and raped during interrogation. In some villages and towns, women and girls have been gathered together and taken to holding centers—often schools or community sports halls—where they are raped, gang-raped and abused repeatedly, sometimes for days or even weeks at a time. Other women have been taken seemingly at random from their communities or out of a group of refugees with which they are traveling and raped by soldiers." The report goes on to state that there was a political purpose behind the rapes, multiple rapes, and gang rapes of women—"to intimidate, humiliate and degrade her and others affected by her suffering." In other words, the rapes were intended to induce families to flee and never come back, not just for their lives but for the honor of their women. Yet the Helsinki report also makes clear that, as in the case of the beatings, Muslim women were also being punished for their very existence. The interviewed women described "how they were gang raped, taunted with ethnic slurs and cursed by rapists who stated their intention forcibly to impregnate women as a haunting reminder of the rape and an intensification of the trauma it inflicts."[102] The forcible impregnation of Muslim women and, in some cases, the incarceration of pregnant women in order to compel them to carry the pregnancy to term was part of the torture to which they were subjected. All this so that the women would bear "little Chetniks."

As part of the ethnic cleansing of the Banja Luka region, in camps, such as those in Trnopolje and the sawmill at Kotor Varos, female internees were assaulted sexually, sexually tortured, and sadistically abused. Rape and gang rape was only part of the horrors these women and girls were forced to endure. According to the Hague Tribunal, "'Visitors' would come to the camp especially to enjoy the brutality."[103] The rape "regime" was especially highly developed in Foca. Between April 1992 and February 1993, Muslim women were interned throughout the city in "rape houses"—brothels of sorts—where Serb soldiers and paramilitary fighters beat and assaulted the women as part of an evening's entertainment. They would shave the women's heads, tattoo their bodies with their persecutors' first names, and force them to submit to their alcohol- and drug-induced sexual-sadistic fantasies. According to the June 1996 Foca indictment, some of the girls involved were no older than twelve, and the terrible circumstances in which they were kept compounded the incessant abuse.[104]

Mladen Vuksanovic records in his Pale diary a conversation with a Serb soldier who tried to convince him that killing a person was sexually exciting.[105] The torture and abuse of Muslim women seemed to arouse and entertain Serb soldiers in a similar way. Catherine MacKinnon talks about the way war and ethnic strife provides potential rapists the opportunity to play out their misogynist and pornographic fantasies.[106] But the problem may be even more psychologically complex than that, relating to deep-seated attraction to and repulsion from women and even men of the persecuted minority.[107] Such factors clearly played a role in German attitudes toward Jewish women and Turkish attitudes toward Armenian women. This psychosexual aggression was repeated in the treatment of Bosnian women by Serb soldiers.

One of the complicated issues related to rape in Bosnia—as well as to the killings, beatings, and burning of houses and property—was that it occurred among former neighbors from the same villages and towns. It seemed that from the Serbs' point of view old scores were settled, old slights were repayed, and "uppity" Muslims were brought down a peg or two by these sexual assaults on neighbors. When the Serb rapists came from the outside, then the motives were different—to demoralize the Muslim fighters, who, after all, were not professional soldiers but "fathers, sons, and brothers from the region."[108] In the rape camps,

Muslim women often recognized Serbs from their home villages and begged for mercy; and sometimes, in fact, they were helped and protected.[109] But usually the rapists prevailed, whether they knew the women or not. Sometimes they claimed they had been ordered to carry out the rape; sometimes they said nothing. One 38-year-old Muslim woman reported that her 19-year-old neighbor raped her. "So often he had sat at our place, drank coffee with us. He even worked for me," she noted.[110]

In some cases, Serb women tried to protect their Muslim friends, by hiding them from rampaging paramilitaries. But just as often they ignored their plight. One Serb woman claimed that the problem was that Muslim women were promiscuous. One stated: "They lie to the world about how our modest young men raped so many Muslim women, while the latter give birth to black babies in European hospitals, having become pregnant from UNPROFOR personnel."[111] Denial was and remains the overwhelming Serb response to the indictment of rape. General Mladic, for example, categorically stated that his men never raped Muslim women. "We Serbs," he sneered to a reporter, "are too picky" to do such things.[112]

Beverly Allen's *Rape Warfare* is a scathing indictment of the Serb use of rape against Bosnian Muslims. She maintains that "tens of thousands" of rapes took place, primarily with the intention of impregnating Muslim women.[113] The Serbs felt that the Bosnian Muslims were originally Serbs who had been forced to convert to Islam. Thus, the babies would be savable for the Serb nation, while their Muslim mothers and their families would be devastated by the experience. The larger purpose of the rapes, Allen claims, was to destroy the Muslim nation. In other words, rape was not simply an instrument of ethnic cleansing but a form of genocide.

The European Union estimates that some 20,000 rapes took place; the Bosnian government claims that the number is closer to 50,000.[114] Whatever the numbers, it is apparent that rape in Bosnia was not simply another example of the excesses of men at war or even a byproduct of ethnic cleansing as it has taken place in the course of the century.[115] We know, for example, that Serb soldiers reported having been ordered to rape. Even the victims felt certain about that. One Muslim woman from Doboj states: "These orders, they all came from Serbia; they were Serbian directives . . . I know some who had to do it, who were forced to do it and weren't doing it for their own enjoyment."[116] Rape camps received logistical and financial support from branches of the Bosnian

Serb government. Rape was organized and directed from above for a two-fold purpose. First, because traditional Muslims, in particular, would consider the crime a blight on their family honor; the very threat of rape would drive Muslims from what the Serbs thought was their land. Thus, ethnic cleansing would be accelerated by rape. Second, the forced impregnation of Bosnian women and the attempt to force the women to give birth to the "Chetnik" babies indicated a policy that combined humiliation of the Muslim women and their families with attention to the growth of the Serbian population.

Croats and Muslims

The ethnic cleansing carried out by the Serbs against the Bosnian Muslims was unmatched anywhere in the Balkans in its extent and intensity. Pointing out that Croats also engaged in ethnic cleansing against Muslims (and Serbs) or that Muslims committed violence against Serb and Croat civilians does not in any way diminish the criminality of the Serbs. We are not dealing with equally destructive phenomena. Still, Croat attacks contributed markedly to the devastation of the region and its peoples. Together, the Serbs and Croats shared the "counter-historical" and "anti-traditional" program of ethnic cleansing in Bosnia.[117] Both Milosevic and Tudjman felt that ethnically pure states would contribute to building their political power and solidifying their rule.[118] Muslim violence, much more limited in scale, was directed against alleged secessionists and traitors to Bosnia-Herzegovina.

Franjo Tudjman's views of the Bosnian Muslims were similar to those of his ostensible antagonist, Slobodan Milosevic. "In a strange way the two men were bound together," write Dusko Doder and Louise Branson, "they were like Siamese twins who had one heart. And that heart was Bosnia."[119] If Serb nationalists claimed that Bosnians were really Serbs who had been forced to convert to Islam, Tudjman insisted that most Bosnians were converted Croats. Like the Serbs, Tudjman and his Croat underlings claimed a good part of Bosnia for their own. On March 25, 1991, at Karadjordjevo, Tudjman and Milosevic met in secret and talked about the partition of Bosnia between them. Both leaders agreed that the Bosnian state could not be sustained as an independent entity.[120] Ambassador Zimmermann recalls a meeting with Tudjman in the summer of 1991 in which the Croatian leader "erupted into a diatribe against Izetbegovic and the Muslims of Bosnia," claiming that they were "dangerous fundamentalists" and threatened all "civilized nations." "Bosnia has never had any real existence," he stated. "It should be divided between Serbia and Croatia."[121]

Like Milosevic, Tudjman talked about the natural historical order of the resettlement of peoples. This could be done peaceably and humanely, but it was the only way to deal with peoples who otherwise have "no chances for their survival."[122] Like Churchill and Benes, Tudjman talked about the successful "transfer" of the Greek population by the Treaty of Lausanne, according to which "Turkey gained the preconditions for its development as a national state."[123] Serb leaders talked much the same. Karadzic spoke of "ethnic shifting" as a perfectly normal phenomenon in international affairs, necessary to keep peoples from fighting like "cats and dogs." When accused of being the "ethniccleanser in chief," Mladic responded that it was his obligation to defend his people: "It's a holy duty."[124]

Talk of the partition of Bosnia continued during the war. The first president of the Bosnian HDZ and member of the presidency of Bosnia-Herzegovina from 1992 to 1993, Stjepan Klujic, testified that he had a conversation with Tudjman at the beginning of 1993 in which the Croatian president reiterated his intention to divide Bosnia, as a country created by Turkish "colonial" conquest.[125] Even as late as May 1995, at a formal London celebration commemorating the fiftieth anniversary of VE Day, Tudjman told his dinner partner, Paddy Ashdown, leader of the British Liberal Democratic Party, that Bosnia would have to be partitioned. Tudjman apparently drew a map of Bosnia on a menu card and divided it into Croat and Serb parts. According to Ashdown, Tudjman said: "There will be no Muslim part," but that Muslims would be "an unimportant part" of the Croatian state. Tudjman then repeated his idea that the Muslims were "only Serbs and Croats who could not stand up to the Turks during the days of the Ottoman Empire." Ashdown was apparently shocked by Tudjman's racist attitude toward Bosnian Muslim leader Alija Izetbegovic, whom Tudjman called "a fundamentalist, Algerian, and wog."[126] Ivan Zvonimir Cicak, president of the Croatian Helsinki Committee, also noted that Tudjman frequently made references to the Muslims as "dirty stinking Asians," while speaking of the Serbs as "our Christian brothers."[127]

Tudjman's position in Croatia's Bosnian parastate, Herceg Bosna, was consolidated in the winter of 1992 by the takeover of the Bosnian HDZ by Mate Boban, an extreme Croat nationalist from Herzegovina. The Vance-Owen plan of March 1993, which, if implemented, would have assigned three of the Bosnian "cantons" to Croatia, gave Boban and his compatriots the impetus to take over "their" Bosnia.[128] Backed by Zagreb, the Bosnian Croat army, the HVO (Croat Defense Council), demanded that the Bosnian government in Sarajevo withdraw its forces from the areas to be controlled by the Croats according to Vance-Owen.[129] When Izetbegovic refused, the HVO launched its own campaign of occupation and ethnic cleansing. The strategically located Lasva Valley was the Croats' primary target. On April 16, 1993, the HVO attacked Vitez, the largest town in the region, and laid siege to its Muslim quarter, Stari Vitez. The Croats opened fire with artillery pieces, mortars, cannon, and howitzers, destroying large sections of the town. At one point, they used a truck bomb to demolish the center of the Muslim quarter. The HVO also attacked Muslim areas with about a thousand "fire babies"—fire extinguishers packed with explosives and metal objects. Then ground forces attacked, burning down Muslim houses and deporting Muslim civilians.

In Stari Vitez and throughout the Lasva Valley, the Croats brutally expelled the Muslims. As in the Serbian case, military units were supported by paramilitary groups, which were often little more than gangs of thugs. The Knights from Croat Vitez did great damage, as did the Jokers unit, which dressed in black and wore the insignia of the Ustasha movement. "We were witnessing something [we] had never seen before and we were distressed and shocked" by "the level of destruction and violence," testified British Colonel Geoffrey Thomas.[130] The most extreme violence took place in the undefended village of Ahmici, which was attacked by the HVO in mid-April 1993. In a familiar pattern, Muslim houses were identified by local Croats and burned to the ground. At least a hundred Muslim inhabitants were killed outright or burned to death in their homes.[131] According to one witness, Sahib Ahmic, two Croat soldiers broke into his house, shot and wounded his son, poured petroleum on the furniture, and set his house on fire. He himself suffered multiple burns before escaping; his sister-in-law was burned alive.[132]

The Lasva Valley had its own detention camps for Muslims, where the inmates were tortured and beaten. One of the worst was in Kaonik, where prisoners were used to dig trenches, repair roads, and sometimes serve as human shields against potential Bosnian Muslim counterattacks. Just as in the Serb camps, the Croat warders sought money from the inmates and beat them regularly to get them to turn over their last valuables. Kaonik was also known for its overcrowded cells; sometimes there were up to twenty inmates in a two-by-three-meter room. Even honest and decent warders could do little about the "night calls," when drunken or drugged HVO soldiers would stop by in the middle of the night for brutal entertainments, especially with the female internees.[133] The Croats also sometimes raped and abused Muslim women. The prosecutor in the Hague Tribunal told of the sadistic handling of one woman by interrogators from the Jokers unit. While the chief interrogator, Goran Jelisic, asked questions, his deputy, called Cicko, "grabbed the victim by the hair, forced her to take her clothes off, and then began to stroke her naked body with a knife and threatened to insert it in her vagina if she did not tell the truth. And then he commenced raping her by vaginal, oral, and anal penetration." Meanwhile, Jelisic continued his questions. Every time she answered unsatisfactorily, or so it seemed to her, she was sexually attacked by Cicko. With her in detention was a Bosnian Croat who had been accused of helping her and her family. While she was being abused, he was beaten to a pulp.[134] The Tribunal found Jelisic of thirty-one counts of war crimes and crimes against humanity. He was sentenced to thirty years in prison.[135]

The Herzegovinian town of Mostar, with its graceful and beautiful Turkish bridge, was the scene of brutal ethnic cleansing on the part of the HVO. Here a special unit, known as the Convicts Battalion, did much of the dirty work. Between May 1993 and January 1994, the Croats attacked thousands of Muslims, expelling them from their homes on the west bank of the Neretva and plundering their possessions. Thousands of men were taken away to the infamous detention camp of Dretelj. Part of the assault included the destruction of the Turkish bridge on November 9, 1993, a purposeful act of cultural vandalism, in that sense very similar to the Serbs' shelling of Dubrovnik. The Croats' intention was clear: to partition the town, creating a purely Croat West Mostar.[136]

Croat ethnic cleansing reached its pinnacle much later in the war, when it was directed against the Serbs in the Krajina. In two highly successful military operations—Flash, in western Slavonia in May, and Storm, launched at the beginning of August 1995—the Croatian forces uprooted some 180,000 to 200,000 Serbs. Investigators from the Hague came to the conclusion that the Croatian army itself was involved in the expulsion of Serb villagers and townspeople. Croat regulars "carried out executions, indiscriminate killing of civilian populations, and 'ethnic cleansing.'"[137]

Ethnic cleansing was an integral part of the Serb and Croat strategies for securing those parts of Bosnia they saw as their own. If they could not partition Bosnia outright, as Milosevic and Tudjman would have liked, then they would do it by violent acts on the ground. This was the main thrust of their war against the Muslims, the main reason for the attacks, the burning, the killing, the robbing, the beating, and the rape. The journalist Ed Vulliamy correctly states that the war was more about the opponents' civilian population than it was about their armies. "Very little [of] what happened in Bosnia can be described as war between armies. We like to use [the] term refugees, meaning a side-effect of war between armies, but in this conflict the refugees were the raw material, its raison d'etre, that was the whole point: the removal of the population was what the war was all about."[138] Yet unlike genocide, ethnic cleansing is as much about securing control of the land as it is attacking a group for its own sake.[139]

Strictly speaking, the Bosnian Muslims did not engage in ethnic cleansing. Their goal was to maintain the integrity of the territory of Bosnia-Herzegovina. Any kind of partition or cantonization countered their interests as the dominant nationality in the country as a whole. They recruited Serbs and Croats to their armed forces and government apparatus and tried to maintain the ideal, backed by their NATO Allies, that Bosnia-Herzegovina could remain a multinational country. This did not mean that the Muslims did not attack Croat and Serb civilians or that they did not perpetrate war crimes, though the U.S. State Department estimates that only a handful of the documented atrocities, some 8 percent of the total number reported, were carried about by the Muslims.[140]

Reports about the actions of the 7th Muslim Brigade, which engaged the Croat troops in the Lasva Valley and elsewhere in the region, indicated that the Muslims periodically murdered civilians and burned down their homes.[141] At the Hague Tribunal, one female Croat witness described how her husband was impaled and sawed in two by Bosnian Muslim soldiers; another Croat witness described the murder of her three sons.[142] In particular, the Tribunal cited war crimes carried out at the Celebici prison camp, where Serbs from the Konjic region were interned under the supervision of two sadistic wardens, Hazim Delic and Esad Landzo. One former inmate testified that he was taken with a group of villagers to the camp, "placed against the wall and heavily beaten for several hours." Then fifteen or so people were pushed into "tunnel nine," which measured one by twenty meters. The inmates were savagely beaten with baseball bats and tortured with electric devices. Sometimes, the Serb detainees simply vanished, after having been murdered during the course of "the interrogation of Chetniks." Landzo regularly tortured prisoners by pouring petroleum on them, burning them on the legs and arms—always, he testified, because he was ordered to do so. The prosecutors charged that he would also carve crosses into the palms of prisoners "with a white-hot knife." Landzo confessed to a series of sadistic acts, ranging from forcing two brothers to perform oral sex on each other to tying slow-burning fuses to prisoners genitals and lighting them.[143]

Kosovo

The ethnic cleansing that took place in Kosovo in 1998 and 1999 resembled that in Bosnia in important ways. In a systematic campaign undertaken by the Serb military, paramilitary, and police forces, Serbs attacked Albanian villages, killing, raping, and burning down homes with the purpose of forcing the Kosovar Albanians to leave. In bigger cities, like Pristina and Prizren, the Serbian authorities—like those in Banja Luka or Brcko in Bosnia—made life so unpleasant for the local Albanians that they escaped, like their cousins in the countryside, to Macedonia, Albania, and Montenegro. Forcible expulsion led to general flight, as Kosovar Albanians sought relief from Serb repression.[144] As in the case of Bosnia, no one was exempt; the intelligentsia and educated classes were driven out along with peasants and artisans, young people along with the elderly. The NATO bombing that commenced on March 24, 1999, in a vain attempt to stop the Serb action dramatically accelerated ethnic cleansing. Hundreds of thousands of Kosovar Albanians left their homeland or sought refuge from Serb violence (and the bombing) by fleeing into the hills.

On June 10, 1999, after 78 days of bombing, Milosevic conceded defeat and NATO took control of Kosovo. The pattern of ethnic cleansing was now reversed, though hardly on the gargantuan scale that took place under Serbian leadership. The relatively small Serb community in Kosovo, roughly 8 percent of the total population, at the beginning of the 1990s was itself attacked and driven off by returning Albanians. In some places, notably north of the divided city of Mitrovica, small Serb communities remain. Milosevic's intention to expel the bulk of the Albanian population from Kosovo ended up condemning the small Serb population of the region to ghettoization and isolation.

If some structural aspects of ethnic cleansing in Kosovo resemble that of Bosnia, the two experiences were also different in profound ways. Although Bosnia had been the site of fratricidal warfare between Serbs, Croats, and Muslims during World War II, for the most part the region had evolved over the centuries into a multiethnic society that tolerated cultural and religious diversity.[145] Although professing different religions, all three groups were Slavs; they looked pretty much alike and spoke the same dialect of Serbo-Croatian. This was not the case with Kosovo, which for at least a century had been the focus of national tension between Albanians and Serbs, two very distinct peoples who speak completely different languages. As a province of the Ottoman Empire, Kosovo had been more welcoming to the Muslim Albanians than to the Orthodox Serbs, who claimed the region as the original cultural home of their people. The Serbs seized Kosovo from the Turks in the Balkan Wars, while the creation of an independent Albania in 1912–13 did not include Kosovo inside its borders. Especially after Kosovo became part of the Kingdom of Serbs, Croats, and Slovenes (later Yugoslavia), the Serbs began an intense campaign of colonization from Serbia proper, with the intention of depriving the Kosovar Albanians of their land and discriminating against their culture, institutions, and language. During World War II, the Italian occupation of Albania and western Kosovo reversed Serbian fortunes. Now the Albanians gained the upper hand over the Serbs, expelling large numbers of colonists and other Serbs and seizing their property and landholdings.[146]

The struggle between Serbs and Albanians over Kosovo continued into the communist period. Initially, Tito's Yugoslavia favored Serbian control of Kosovo, including a renewed campaign of colonization. But Tito's policies changed in the late 1960s, when he gave in to the growing economic, intellectual, and demographic influence of the Kosovar Albanians by recognizing their rights as a nationality in the province. The constitution of 1974 completed the process; the province was given autonomy within Serbia and a formal place within the Yugoslav commonwealth of nations. Again, the tables were turned, and Serbs complained of discrimination by the Albanians and of "ethnic cleansing"—the use of violence, rape, and job discrimination to chase Serbs from the province. The nationalist "Memorandum of the Serbian Academy of Sciences" was in good measure a response to the perceived attack on Serbs by Kosovar Albanians. As we know, Milosevic used the issue to build his political base among former communists.

For the Kosovar Albanians, Milosevic's rise to power was a nightmare from the very beginning. As early as the spring of 1987, he led the Serbian nationalist charge to deprive Kosovo of its independent voice in

Yugoslav affairs and sharply cut back on the autonomy granted by Tito and the Yugoslav Constitution of 1974. On March 8, 1989, Milosevic formally revoked the autonomy of Kosovo (and of Vojvodina), sparking six days of rioting in Pristina during which some 100 Albanians were killed and another 900 arrested. On July 5, 1990, Kosovo's regional police force, still in the hands of Albanians, was disbanded and a state of emergency declared. Pristina University was closed, and Albanian language schools were severely restricted. The Serbs controlled the Albanian media and shut down Albanian political, cultural, and sports associations.[147] Relations between Serbs and Albanians in Kosovo were so tense that they walked on different sides of the street in Pristina, the capital, and in other towns and cities.[148]

The Serbian authorities singled out the leaders of the Kosovar independence movement for arrest, imprisonment, and physical abuse. Discriminated against in society and systematically deprived of their jobs and livelihoods, thousands of Kosovar Albanians left their homeland to seek work in Western Europe. In March of 1991 the Albanians organized huge demonstrations on the streets of Pristina to protest against the revocation of their rights. But the demonstrations were brutally suppressed by Serbian police; thousands of demonstrators were arrested and perhaps hundreds were killed.[149] The other republics of Yugoslavia were shocked and dismayed by these repressive actions. With the Serb showing so little respect for Kosovar claims to autonomy, the Slovenes, Croats, and Bosnians, among others, worried that the Serbs might try to limit their own. The result, as we know, was a series of declarations of independence and sovereignty at the beginning of the 1990s that triggered Serbian military intervention. In this sense, the wars of Yugoslav succession began in Kosovo and ended in Kosovo.

By the early 1990s the Kosovar Albanians seethed with resentment at Serbian domination and virtual martial law. Led by the "Gandhian" pacifist Ibrahim Rugova, the Albanians set up a shadow state and withdrew any cooperation with the Serbs. Like the Solidarity underground in martial-law Poland, the Albanians constructed their own schools and university, held their own cultural events, published their own newspapers and books, and carried on their own foreign policy. Unfortunately, Rugova's movement was unable to attract much attention from the world community during the Bosnian war. Only the Serbian police seemed to notice; they periodically raided the makeshift Albanian schools and cultural institutions, assaulted and arrested teachers and Albanian human rights activists, and imprisoned and tortured at will.[150]

From 1981 to 1988, official Yugoslav statistics confirm the incarceration of more than 7,000 Kosovar Albanians. Some 586,000 Kosovars—more than a quarter of the population—were stopped on the street by police, interrogated, threatened, hauled into police stations, arrested, jailed, and so on in this period.[151]

The end of the Bosnian war and the convening of the Dayton talks in November 1995 gave the Kosovar Albanians some hope that their cause would be taken up by the United States and NATO. But the Allies were too intent on concluding the mess they had helped create in Bosnia to complicate the Dayton accords with the increasingly dangerous situation in Kosovo; Milosevic was too important to the successful implementation of the agreement. Especially the younger generation of Kosovar Albanian activists, who had known only Serbian oppression and discrimination, came to the conclusion that Rugova's nonviolent approach accomplished nothing. Dayton reinforced the inclination of these young people to take up arms against the Serbs and force the West to pay attention. Not only that, Dayton had the effect of strengthening Milosevic's hand, both in the international community and in Kosovo.[152] Although Albanian radicals established the kernal of the Kosovo Liberation Army in 1993, only in 1996, after Dayton, did it become a genuinely "pro-active intifada-type protest movement" to organize armed resistance against the Serbs.[153] The KLA's cause was helped considerably in the spring of 1997, when civil strife in Albania resulted in the "liberation" of hundreds of thousands of small arms weapons from armories and weapons depots around the country.

The first phase of the war in Kosovo began on February 28, 1998, when KLA fighters ambushed and killed four Serbian policemen on a deserted road between Pristina and Podujevo. The Serbs retaliated in force, engaging KLA bands in the Drenica region with 20 helicopter gunships and 30 armored personnel carriers. From March 4 to 7 the Serbian forces attacked two Drenica villages, killing entire families and clans allegedly involved in the KLA attack. In what became known as the Drenica Massacre, some 85 Albanians were killed, including 25 women and children.[154] The escalation of violence was almost inevitable. Repression of the Kosovar Albanians got worse, and more and more young men, many of them jobless and hungry, took up arms against the Serbs under the banner of the KLA. With funds from their increasingly radicalized co-nationals in Europe and America, the KLA quickly grew into a well-armed opponent of Serbian domination. Although its political organization was weak and its ranks divided into numerous factions, the KLA nevertheless was able to control almost 30 percent of the territory of Kosovo by the middle of 1998.[155]

The Serbian response to the growth of the KLA insurgency and to increasing violence in Kosovo was predictably savage and brutal. Moreover, beginning in February 1998, Serbian military, paramilitary, and police forces began a systematic campaign of ethnic cleansing, designed, or so it seemed at the time, to secure strategic areas and force hundreds of thousands of Albanians to leave Kosovo. The Serbs appeared to engage in selective ethnic cleansing as a tactic of "counter-insurgency," intended at least in part to deprive the KLA of their infrastructure of support.[156] Milosevic told Christoper Hill, U.S. Ambassador to Macedonia, that the Serbs could drive out all the Albanians if they wished, but they wouldn't. "We're not Nazis," he said.[157] Instead, the Serbs claimed they wanted to expel only those who migrated recently to the area from Albania or who moved from abroad. But this statement was camouflage for Milosevic's policies to redress the population balance of Serbs to Albanians in Kosovo by driving out hundreds of thousands of Albanians and moving Serbs—both refugees from the Croatian war and others from Serbia proper—into Kosovo. However, a Human Rights Watch report estimates that only 16,000 Serbs were moved into Kosovo, and most of them lived in abysmal conditions.[158]

Complicating the picture on the ground was the introduction into Kosovo of the first contingents of OSCE monitors in October 1998, as the consequence of Richard Holbrooke's negotiations with Milosevic about the fate of the region.[159] Yet even with some 1,300 monitors present, the Serbs attacked and cleansed Kosovar Albanians, while the KLA continued to strike a variety of targets: Serbian policemen, government installations, and alleged Albanian collaborators. A brief OSCE-negotiated ceasefire at the end of December 1998 was broken on January 8 when the KLA seized eight Yugoslav army soldiers who had mistakenly driven their truck into KLA-controlled territory. Although the OSCE managed to get them released, the Serbs again retaliated with extreme force, attacking the "guilty" village of Racak and murdering 45 Albanian civilians.[160] Eyewitnesses reported that they had seen the "hooded men dressed in black" who had carried out the execution-style killings.[161]

Racak had an instantly mobilizing effect on the Allies as a consequence of their chastening experience with the Srebrenica massacre in Bosnia. NATO leaders attempted to force the Serbs and Kosovar Albanians to sign an agreement at Rambouillet (February 6–23, 1999) that gave NATO the right to control Kosovo militarily, while ensuring the Albanians that after three years they would be able to vote in a referendum for independence. Neither side was initially willing to accept the ultimatum. The Serbs refused to surrender sovereign control over their own airspace, not to mention Kosovo. The Albanians were not interested in waiting to gain their independence.[162] In the end, the Albanians were convinced by the Allies to sign the agreement on March 18, and after the withdrawal of the OSCE Kosovo Verification Mission on March 19 the stage was set for the NATO bombing of Serbia and Kosovo, which proceeded on March 24.

Contrary to the expectations of Western policymakers, the Serbs did not give in and instead accelerated their campaign of ethnic cleansing during the 78 days of bombing. There was no more pretense that their goal was to hunt down KLA members and expel their supporters. Now the Serbs seemed intent on reversing the population percentages in Kosovo: what was once 90 percent Albanian and 10 percent Serbian would now be 90 percent Serbian and 10 percent Albanian. Milosevic also hoped to destabilize neighboring Albania, Macedonia, and Montenegro with a stream of refugees.[163] Serbian motivations and goals in what was supposedly called Operation Horseshoe remain poorly documented and understood.[164] What is apparent is that 800,000 to 900,000 Kosovar Albanians were expelled in this period, leaving roughly 600,000 still inside the borders, many of them in hiding, and another 400,000 abroad. "Surely Milosevic can't ethnically cleanse 1.8 million people?" Timothy Garton Ash had said to Milan Kucan, president of Slovenia, six months earlier. Kucan answered: "You don't know Milosevic."[165]

Ethnic cleansing in Kosovo took on many of the patterns already established in Bosnia. Local Serbs (and gypsies) identified Kosovar Albanian homes; paramilitaries broke in, beating up the inhabitants, and forcing them to hand over their money and valuables before leaving. Houses were often burned to the ground, sometimes with families still in them.[166] Serbs also forced Kosovar Albanians to leave their apartments in the cities. Serbian forces spread out over Pristina, shouting through bullhorns and distributing pamphlets, threatening the Albanians who remained with injury and death. Tens of thousands were detained in the Pristina Sports Complex before being moved to the trains, buses, and trucks that were to transfer them to the Macedonian border. In these cases, as in Bosnia, the Albanians were forced to pay extravagant prices for tickets and ended up in dangerously overcrowded railway cars and vehicles. In Kosovo, Serbian forces were particularly intent on confiscating the Albanians' documents. At checkpoints inside the country and at refugee camps near the border, the Serbs seized both the money and personal documents of Albanians. The idea was to deprive them of any legal claim to citizenship or property. They would be treated like Albanians from Albania, who the Serbs claimed had illegally infiltrated the country. Even license plates, voter registration records, and civil registries were destroyed in the campaign of ethnic cleansing in Kosovo.[167]

Just as in Bosnia, Serbs raped women and girls both to punish the Albanians and to accelerate the Albanians' departure. The U.S. State Department report on ethnic cleansing in Kosovo notes that "Ethnic Albanian women are reportedly being raped in increasing numbers; according to refugees, Serbian forces have raped women in an organized and systematic fashion in Djakovica and Pec. Rape victims were reportedly separated from their families and sent to an army camp near Djakovica where Serbian soldiers repeatedly rape them. In Pec, refugees alleged that Serbian forces rounded up young Albanian women and took them to the Hotel Karagac, where they were raped repeatedly. The commander of the local base reportedly uses a roster of soldiers' names to allow all of his troops an evening in the hotel. In addition to these specific accounts, refugees claim that during Serbian forces' raids on their villages, young women have been gang raped in homes and on the sides of roads."[168]

It is difficult to know the true dimensions of the problem, even after the conclusion of the war, because of the highly traditional culture of a significant portion of the Kosovar Albanian population. No woman likes to talk about being raped, and reporting the crime under any circumstances is a humiliating and psychologically painful act. But in the more traditional regions of Bosnia and particularly in Kosovo, Muslim women were very hesitant to state what happened to them.

Abduction, internment, torture, rape, beating, and murder took place in Kosovo as they had in Bosnia, but it is too soon to know how many of the missing are dead or are still living in the hills or somewhere abroad. With so much of the housing stock burned, destroyed, and bombed and so many people displaced, it is not easy to determine who is still alive. According to the German expert Stefan Troebst, between December 1998 and May 1999, 30,000 Albanians were killed in

Kosovo, 960,000 Kosovar Albanians became refugees, and 550,000 people were internally dislocated. Troebst adds that NATO bombing operations killed some 1,000 Serbs, including 114 policemen and 462 soldiers.[169] However, as of November 11, 1999, Hague Tribunal investigators had found only 2,108 bodies, far short of the number estimated to have been murdered and buried in mass graves in Kosovo.[170] A major problem in assessing the number of casualties is the fact that the Serbs tampered with the mass graves. We know a great deal about the brutality of the Serb paramilitaries and police in Kosovo; still, the final story remains to be told.

Just as ethnic cleansing did not end in Bosnia with the signing of the Dayton Treaty, ethnic cleansing in Kosovo continues after the NATO bombing and ceasefire agreement in Kosovo. The return of the Kosovar refugees puts tremendous pressure on the already very limited housing stock, much of which had been destroyed either by the Serbs or by NATO bombing. The stance of the KFOR troops has not been sufficiently militant to prevent Kosovar Albanians from attacking Serbs, as well as gypsies, Turks, and Goranis accused of collaborating with the Serbs. In some cases, the Albanians have taken over the Serbs' property and forced them to leave Kosovo. In others, the Albanians have beaten up and killed Serbs, causing the noted Kosovar Albanian journalist Veton Surroi to lament the brutalization of his people and wonder about their future and that of the Kosovar Serbs, who are now "the victims of victims."[171]

At a bridge over the river dividing Kosovska Mitrovica, French troops stand guard to keep Albanians to the south from attacking the Serbs to the north. Periodically, the crowds of Albanians pelt the soldiers with rocks and try to break through their lines. Among other contingents, American troops in full battle regalia cross into the Serbian-controlled north to look for weapons and munitions. The de facto partition of Kosovo—Serbs to the north of the line, Albanians to the south—seems to have become permanent. Albanians continue to threaten, beat, and sometimes kill Serbs if they resist leaving. Meanwhile, in the north, Serbs periodically oust Albanians from their homes. The atmosphere is tense and bitter on both sides. In Kosovo, as in Bosnia, NATO forces and U.N. governing bodies state their commitment to multinational entities; in both regions, the divisions between nations wrought by the war remain starkly evident. Ethnically pure enclaves are under construction, separated from their former neighbors by walls, barbed wire, and heavily armed NATO forces.

Conclusions

Ethnic cleansing in the former Yugoslavia has cast a pall over the end of this century. The West has been forced to face the deeply depressing fact that once again millions of Europeans—in this case Bosnians, Kosovar Albanians, Serbs, and Croats—have been chased from their homes, robbed, brutalized, raped, and killed. Once again, dominant ethno-national groups have committed crimes against humanity in their determination to rid what they consider their territory of the "other"—minorities who are culturally different and ostensibly alien. Once again, state programs of ethnic cleansing have easily accommodated genocidal actions. Hundreds of thousands have died, mostly at the hands of Serb soldiers and paramilitary, and many are buried in mass graves.[172] Once again, rape and attacks on women have become commonplace. Serbian paramilitaries have left a trail of victims among Muslim women, who will carry these crimes and a sense of violation with them for the rest of their lives.

The states and parastates that have been formed as a consequence of the breakup of Yugoslavia seek social cohesion and political stability through ethnic homogenization. The policies of ethnic cleansing during the war have been continued in the peace. National exclusivism dominates political programs almost everywhere in the region. This is as true today for the Kosovar Albanians and Bosnian Muslims as it has been since the start of the war for the Serbs, Croats, and Slovenes.[173] Politicians employ the state-controlled media to disseminate the message of the organic unity of their respective peoples. History is rewritten to exclude the role of minorities in the past and future. The lingering bitterness of the recent fighting provides little hope for multiethnic solutions to the region's immediate problems.

Yet the successor states to Yugoslavia seek entry into European forums and eventually into the European Union and NATO. Each in its own way wants to rebuild, modernize, and join the contemporary community of nations. Whether these states can do so as democracies or not will depend on constructive leadership at home and the political will of the West. Tito sought to eliminate backwardness and ethnic strife by employing the high modernist techniques propounded by Marxist-Leninist ideology. The experiment failed miserably. Now small states based on modern nationalist and democratic ideologies seek to mobilize their populations for economic and political advancement. Slovenia and, most recently, Croatia have made important gains in this direction.

It remains to be seen whether Serbia (and, with or without it, Montenegro and Kosovo) can do the same. Macedonia and Bosnia-Herzegovina still struggle with multinational democratic solutions.

The Bosnian and Kosovo cases reiterate the incapacity of the international community to do much about ethnic cleansing in this century. NATO dropped bombs to get the Serbs to sign the Dayton agreement, but only after three and a half wrenching years of ethnic cleansing that displaced over two million people. Because NATO could not muster a credible ground threat, the NATO bombing in Kosovo actually accelerated the Serbian campaign of ethnic cleansing, which concluded with nearly a million Kosovar Albanians uprooted. Perhaps the most depressing part of ethnic cleansing in the Balkans is the apparent permanence of the results. Two distinct national entities—one Serb, another Croat-Muslim—will likely survive into the twenty-first century in Bosnia. Kosovo is even more of a foregone conclusion. Western lip service to the return of the Serbs is laughable. But the laugh is ironic and bitter. The Armenians and Greeks are gone from Turkey forever, making that country poorer in every way as a result. Although some Jews have returned to Germany—and Soviet and Russian Jews find it a haven—the Germany that could produce an Albert Einstein or Walter Benjamin is a phantom of the past. Czechs and Poles have not yet come to the point where they regret the expulsion of their German minorities, but that time is not far away. They lost a lot as a consequence. And the sad reverberations of the deportations of the Chechens-Ingush and Crimean Tatars can be felt in a fierce and unremitting war in the Caucasus. The peoples of former Yugoslavia, too, will look back with regret and sadness at the decade of the 1990s. Even after they recover from the loss of relatives and friends and recoup economically, they will feel poorer as a consequence of ethnic cleansing.

Conclusion

The character of mass violence in Europe changed dramatically over the course of the twentieth century. The world wars of 1914–1918 and 1939–1945 gave way to civil wars, wars of "national liberation," and ethnic wars. Ethnic cleansing, on the other hand, has remained remarkably consistent over the past hundred years. From the Balkan Wars, through the two world wars, up to the present, political elites of modern (and modernizing) states have espoused the cause of integral nationalism and have attacked and expelled minority peoples. Ethnic cleansing continues in the Balkans, its force far from spent. It threatens to break out in other regions, as well, from the new postcommunist states in the Caucasus and Central Asia to a crescent of modernizing nations running from Turkey in the west through South Asia, Pakistan, Afghanistan, and Indonesia in the east. In the longer term, no state is free of its potential dangers. Ethnic cleansing will probably happen again, and the community of nations should be prepared for the next round. Toward that end, in this Conclusion I will attempt to summarize the characteristics of ethnic cleansing and examine the way it works in concrete cases, in the hope that we may perhaps find ways to prevent future episodes, or at least stop them earlier in their fearsome trajectories toward genocide.

Violence

Ethnic cleansing always involves violence. People do not leave their homes willingly. They must be forced out, sometimes in the most brutal fashion. But whereas war generally matches armed men against armed men in a contest of will, machines, and numbers, ethnic cleansing usually involves an armed perpetrator and an unarmed victim—more often than not, an armed man and an unarmed woman, child, or elderly person. The violence occurs up close, and it is vicious. Very little about ethnic cleansing is impersonal. Arnold Toynbee used the metaphors of the hunter and the hunted, the cat and the mouse, to try to capture the peculiar evil that was involved in the Greco-Turkish war of 1921–22 and the expulsion of the Greeks from Anatolia. From the Armenian genocide through Kosovo, men, women, and children have been massacred and then tossed into mass graves and haphazardly buried. Some have been buried alive, and a few of those have survived to tell about it. The level of torture, physical abuse, fearsome beatings, and maiming suggests that the victims are being forced to pay for their crime of being different. In some sense, almost all violence against human beings is gratuitous, but in cases of ethnic cleansing all the explanations in the world cannot account for the sheer horror inflicted on the victims by their persecutors—the chopped off ears and fingers, the brandings, the mutilated genitals, the brains of babies splattered against walls; the gauntlets that victims are forced to run, the sexual assaults. The litany of abuses is unending, and it repeats itself from case to case throughout the century.

Ethnic cleansing almost always takes a substantial toll in human life. Sometimes the killing is intentional, as when the Nazis killed nearly six million Jews. The Young Turk government appeared ready to see the Armenian nation die in large numbers, and as a result, some 800,000 Armenians did not survive the expulsion from Anatolia. But even when there is no intent to kill, disease, hunger, and the perils of displacement take a staggering toll in lives lost. Of the 300,000 Anatolian Greeks who died, a very large number succumbed from typhus, tuberculosis, exposure, and hunger during transport and after arriving in Greece and the islands, despite heroic relief efforts. The relatively well-organized and premeditated removal of Chechens-Ingush and Crimean Tatars also wiped out tens of thousands of deportees. The lack of sanitation, food, water, and ventilation on the freight and cattle cars caused thousands to die en route. When they got to their destinations in Central Asia, no food, shelter, or medical care was available. The result was catastrophe.

Freight cars packed with thirsty, starving, suffocating, refugees—the bodies of people already dead crumpled in pools of excrement on the floor—could be the central image of twentieth-century atrocities. From the Armenians transported on newly completed stretches of the Berlin-to-Baghdad railroad to the transport of Muslims out of Bosnia and Kosovo, these horrible railway cars spelled disease and death to their passengers. In the Greek case, thousands died in the packed holds of ships. The nominal killers in ethnic cleansing are typhus, dysentery, dehydration, exhaustion, and starvation, but the real murderers are the political leaders, guards, and soldiers who drive these populations from their homes.

The expulsion of Germans from Poland and Czechoslovakia is often divided into a "wild" phase, before Potsdam, and an orderly "transfer" phase afterward. The wild phase saw much random killing of Germans, periodic massacres, and collective suicides among the terrified German population. In the so-called orderly phase, Germans were marched into labor camps, deprived of food, and brutalized by guards. It is hard to know how many Germans died at what stage of the forced deportation. (Some died under the harsh conditions of the displaced persons camps in Germany.) But the estimate of 30,000 Germans from Sudetenland and 500,000 from Poland does not strike me as excessively high. The death toll for the war in Bosnia-Herzegovina has been placed at 250,000. Here it is particularly hard to separate war dead from the victims of ethnic cleansing, because the war was *about* ethnic cleansing. There is some controversy about the number of victims in Kosovo. Nearly 2,000 bodies have been found, but the U.S. State Department gives its best estimate, as of December 9, 1999, at 10,000.[1]

War

Ethnic cleansing is very often closely related to war. The cases examined in this book all have taken place during war or during the chaotic transition from war to peace. War provides cover for rulers to carry out projects of ethnic cleansing that would be more closely scrutinized and even condemned by their own public or by the international community during peacetime. War provides the opportunity to deal with a troublesome minority by suspending civil law in the name of military exigency. Journalism is highly restricted, and military censorship prevents the investigation of reported atrocities. The minds of nations and of the international community are on other issues in time of war. The Young Turks decided to deal with the Armenian "problem" during the war, just as the Nazis dealt with the Jewish "question" after the attack on Russia. Both the Young Turks and the Nazis sought to conceal the extent of their actions. It is unclear what would have happened in peacetime in both cases. The Greeks were expelled as a direct consequence of the Greco-Turkish war. Stalin and Beria dealt with the Chechens-Ingush and Crimean Tatars during the war, and the Poles and Czechs began the expulsion of Germans even before the war ended and continued it afterward. Ethnic cleansing in Bosnia accompanied and followed upon warfare. The case of Kosovo is particularly instructive in this regard. Milosevic began the ethnic cleansing of Kosovo in conjunction with the struggle against the KLA in the winter of 1998–99. But when NATO bombing starting on March 24, 1999, much to the surprise of the West, Milosevic intensified the ethnic cleansing campaign. It was clear that he hoped that he could accomplish the long-held aim of ridding Kosovo of the Albanians under the cover of war. Just as the Young Turks, the Nazis, and Stalin had to divert important resources and manpower needed to fight the war to the tasks of ethnic cleansing, Milosevic seemed willing to expend important resources and suffer severe bombing damage to the Serbian infrastructure in order to expel the Albanians from Kosovo.

War habituates its participants to killing and to obeying orders. No one ever totally acclimates to bloodshed and rotting corpses, but the soldier adapts more readily than others. Regular armies are almost always involved in ethnic cleansing, whether the Turkish Army, the Wehrmacht, the Red Army, the newly constituted postwar Polish and Czechoslovak armies, or the JNA. But war also breeds paramilitary groups that more often than not do most of the damage in ethnic cleansing. Asocial types and criminals are often attracted to these paramilitaries, whether it was the Turkish and Greek chettes or Arkan's "Tigers." In totalitarian societies such as the Soviet Union and Nazi Germany, the paramilitaries, the NKVD special troops and the SS, served as organized branches of state power. They, too, were the primary perpetrators of ethnic cleansing. Although these paramilitaries are often responsible for the "excesses" associated with ethnic cleansing, it is important to reiterate that the forced deportations are initiated and supervised by the political leadership of the state. Despite their sometimes chaotic appearance and random actions (or, in the case of the NKVD and SS, despite their seeming autonomy), the paramilitaries are instruments of the state and ultimately receive their instructions from political leaders.

War provides governments and politicians with strategic arguments for ethnic cleansing. The Young Turks accused the Armenians of collab-

oration with the Russian enemy at the onset of the First World War. Located in their ancient homeland in eastern Anatolia, not far from the
Russian front, the Armenians, or so the Turks asserted, had to be
moved to the south and southwest of the Ottoman Empire so they
could not aid the enemy. Similarly, the Turkish government of Mustafa
Kemal claimed that the Anatolian Greeks on the Aegean and Pontic
coasts supported the invading Hellenic Greek armies and their British
sponsors. Unless they were expelled from that territory, the argument
went, the Anatolian Greeks would continue to serve as indigenous resources for enemies of the Turkish Republic. The Nazi argument about
the role of the Jews in supporting the enemies of the Third Reich—
Bolshevism and world capitalism—derived not from any geographical
concentration of Jews in a specific territory but rather from Nazi anti-
Semitic ideology. Nevertheless, the Nazis took seriously the accusation
that world Jewry conspired in their overthrow; thus Hitler's vow in his
infamous Reichstag speech of January 1939 that if the Jews started a
new world war, they would pay with their obliteration. Hitler, Goebbels, and others liked to recall that vow during the course of the war.

Strategic interests were cited by both the Czechs and the Poles for expelling their respective German minorities. In this case, they both could
point to recent history in which the German minorities were easily manipulated by Hitler to undermine the integrity of their states. They both
argued that the rebuilding of a secure East Central Europe demanded
the elimination of the Germans as a factor; talk of a Polish-Czechoslo-
vak confederation—which in the end did not get very far because of ri-
valry over the Teschen region—also included a strong anti-German
component. Stalin and Beria did not articulate their geostrategic reasons for the deportation of the Chechens-Ingush and Crimean Tatars.
They claimed rather that these peoples—along with the Balkars,
Karachaevtsy, Kalmyks, and others—had collaborated with the Nazis.
Nevertheless, strategic concerns were certainly part of the overall rationale. Chechen-Ingush territory in the northern Caucasus could serve as
a critical gateway north and south between Russian and Georgian territory, and east and west between the Caspian and Black seas. Moreover,
Chechnya had oil and gas fields, important to the war effort and to
postwar rebuilding. The strategic argument about the Crimean Tatars
was even more powerful and persuasive. Because the Crimean Tatars
had been traditional allies of the Turks, their location on the Black Sea
left the Soviet Union vulnerable to purported Tatar treachery. Even in
the nineteenth century, Russians had sought a Crimea without Tatars;

tens of thousands were deported in the aftermath of the Crimean War. World War II was Moscow's chance to finish the job.

Strategic arguments, both overt and secret, influenced the campaign of ethnic cleansing during the Bosnian War. The Bosnian Serbs (and Bosnian Croats) sought to carve out ethnically pure territories inside the borders of Bosnia-Herzegovina, both as a way to create a *fait accompli* in case of international negotiation but also to secure military supply lines and communications between their Bosnian governments in Pale and Mostar and their home supporters in Belgrade and Zagreb. Ethnic cleansing was often justified on these bases. The Croatian expulsion of Serbs from Krajina was accompanied by statements, not unlike those of the Czechs and Poles after the war, that the Krajina Serbs had betrayed the Croatian state and were a clear security threat to Croatia's survival. The Serbs asserted that the growth of the Albanian population in Kosovo, which they claimed derived primarily from illegal immigration from Albania, threatened the security of Serbs and Serbian-run Yugoslavia. Serb attacks of ethnic cleansing in the winter of 1998–99 were carried out ostensibly as campaigns of "counter-insurgency" against KLA rebels. Taken as a whole, Serbian ethnic cleansing aimed toward securing the region militarily and protecting supply lines and communications.

Totality

One aspect of ethnic cleansing that links it to "high modernism" and the ambitions of the modern state and its leaders is its totalistic quality. In the European cases examined here, the goal is to remove every member of the targeted nation; very few exceptions to ethnic cleansing are allowed. In premodern cases of assaults of one people on another, those attacked could give up, change sides, convert, pay tribute, or join the attackers. Ethnic cleansing, driven by the ideology of integral nationalism and the military and technological power of the modern state, rarely forgives, makes exceptions, or allows people to slip through the cracks. There is also an internal logic which asserts that any members of the nationality who were allowed to remain would become even more resolutely opposed to the dominant power and hence a more potent threat; for this reason, no one must be allowed to remain.

The Soviet cases are the most notable in this regard, where every single member of the Chechen-Ingush and Crimean Tatar nations, as registered in their internal passports, were forced into internal exile, whether they were high party officials, heroes of the Soviet Union, or champion athletes. Those few who managed to find their way back to their homeland in the late 1940s were removed again. Similarly, during the course of the war the Nazis attempted to deport and later to kill every single Jew, as defined by the Nuremberg Laws, whom they could their hands on—converted or not, married to a Christian or not, necessary to military industry or not. The attacks on the Armenians and Greeks by the Ottoman Turks and the Kemalists, respectively, did allow for some exceptions. Armenian women and girls, for example, were sometimes given the opportunity to convert and join Muslim households in order to save themselves. The Armenians of Smyrna and Constantinople, under the watchful eyes of foreign consuls, sometimes survived the genocide. After the Greco-Turkish war, the Greeks of Constantinople were able to remain in place, though large numbers were deported at the end of the 1920s and the rest in 1955.

In the Polish and Czech cases, some Germans were officially allowed to stay behind to work in critical industries and, in Poland, in the mines. But the idea was to expel them once a sufficient number of Polish and Czech workers were trained to take on the skilled positions. Especially in the first year and a half of ethnic cleansing, armed gangs, paramilitaries, and communist action groups expelled Germans, and legalities were seldom respected. Later on, courts were involved in the process of determining who was a German and who was not. Racial criteria were applied, and those classified as Germans were forced to leave. In Czechoslovakia, there were provisions for German spouses of Czechs to remain; in Poland, a large number of so-called autochtons (Silesians, Mazurians, Kashubians, and others) were allowed to claim Polish nationality. In both cases, however, in principle, all Germans were deprived of citizenship and forced to leave the country. Ethnic cleansing in Yugoslavia had a similarly totalistic quality to it. Everyone was compelled to leave, even the elderly who could not possibly do harm to the dominant Serbs (in the case of Bosnia) or the Croats (in the case of Serbs in the Krajina). Whether Milosevic intended to reverse the percentages of Serbs to Albanians, from 10–90 percent to 90–10 percent, which is sometimes asserted, or whether he meant to expel the entire Kosovar Albanian nation is unclear. At this point, the Kosovar Albanians certainly seem intent on expelling all the Serbs from Kosovo, without exception.

Monuments and Memory

Ethnic cleansing involves not only the forced deportation of entire nations but the eradication of the memory of their presence. The physical remnants of the nation are the first to be destroyed. In Anatolia, the Ottoman Turks blew up, destroyed, and defaced Armenian churches and other architectural monuments. In the mutual ethnic cleansing that took place as a consequence of the Greco-Turkish War, Greeks attacked and defiled mosques; Turks did the same to Orthodox churches. Many of the Greek Orthodox churches were rapidly transformed into mosques. Armenian and Greek houses were burned down; in Smyrna, the Armenian and Greek quarters were burned to the ground. The Nazis' destruction of Jewish synagogues in Germany began on Kristallnacht, November 9, 1938, and during their occupation of Eastern Europe the Germans systematically burned wooden synagogues and holy books. Göring was interested in collecting materials for a Jewish museum in Berlin. But the impulse to destroy any trace of Jewish life in Germany or Eastern Europe was overwhelming. The Soviets bulldozed Chechen-Ingush graveyards, the central architectural heritage of the people, and used the gravestones to line streets or pave roadways, just as the Nazis did with Jewish gravestones. Poles and Czechs destroyed German monuments and chiseled German writing off of churches and graveyards. The houses were far too valuable to burn, but they too were rapidly altered, as it was illegal to have German sayings etched into the portals of homes or on their moldings. In Banja Luka alone, fourteen mosques were blown up, two of them dating from the seventeenth century. In the town of Trebinje, a graceful Turkish manor was burned to the ground. Everywhere, traces of the "other" have been torched, blown up, or taken apart. Especially in Yugoslavia, the homes of Serbs, Croats, and Muslims have been destroyed by one or the other of their persecutors. Especially the Serb torching of Albanian homes in Kosovo has left that region with a severe housing crisis.

In addition to leveling churches, houses, and graveyards, ethnic cleansers burn books, encyclopedias, and dictionaries. No remnant of the language and culture of the ethnically cleansed people should be left behind. In the formerly German parts of Poland and Czechoslovakia, local archives were set aflame, just to be sure no one could make any claims about coming back. Town names and street names were changed in both Poland and Czechoslovakia; German storefront names were changed to Polish or Czech. In Kosovo, local citizens' registries were burned for the same reasons. Perhaps nowhere was the memory of peoples attacked as completely as in the former Soviet Union. The Chechen-Ingush Autonomous Republic was abolished, and all Chechen names and markings were erased. The same occurred in the Crimea, where all Tatar city, town, school, and street names were changed. In neither case was anyone allowed to talk about the fact that the respective peoples had been deported. It was as if they had vanished into thin air, never really having existed in the first place. All that was left was talk of their treachery. History books were changed to diminish the role of the Tatars in the Crimea, and the Chechens-Ingush disappeared from books altogether.

Both nationalist Serbs and nationalist Croats claimed that the Bosnians were not a separate nationality at all but were rather Serbs and Croats who had been forcibly converted by the Ottoman Turks to Islam. In fact, had the partition plans of Milosevic and Tudjman come to fruition, the idea that such a people as "the Bosnian Muslims" had ever existed would likely have been expunged. The rewriting of history has been part and parcel of the war in the Yugoslavia from its beginning to its most recent phase in Kosovo. According to the Serbs, Albanians came to the region only after the Serbs had established their presence there. Most Kosovar Albanians, in the official Serbian cant, are not Kosovars at all but illegal immigrants from Albania or their descendents. The Nazis wrote the history of the Jews and of Germans of Jewish origin out of their books, too, burning the rest in infamous fires at the beginning of Hitler's regime. Book-burning and the destruction of churches, synagogues, mosques, and graveyards are as much a part of ethnic cleansing as the forced removal of peoples.

Property

There is nothing "clean" about ethnic cleansing. It is shot through with violence and brutality in the most extreme form. But ethnic cleansing is also associated with crimes against property as well as people—that is, stealing and theft, both on the part of the state and of individuals. Although the motivations for the expulsions were primarily political and ideological, not economic, nevertheless the idea was prevalent in every case—Greeks and Armenians, Jews, Chechens-Ingush and Crimean Tatars, Germans, Bosnians, and Kosovar Albanians—that the victims were rich, and indeed had become rich by exploiting their dominant neighbors. Therefore they deserved to be expropriated and robbed. Armenian property was seized by local Ottoman officials and placed in warehouses, ostensibly to be returned to the Armenians after their exile ended. But this property, often quite substantial, was quickly divided among the state, local officials, and rapacious individuals. The robbery did not stop with confiscation of property. Armenians were bilked by local cart and carriage drivers to provide transportation to the south. In a pattern repeated over and over again, the drivers would take the money, provide transportation out of town, and then dump the hapless Armenians on the road. Guards along the treks took money for everything from a crust of bread to a drink of water from a river. By the end, the Armenians were robbed of everything, even of money that frantic relatives managed to get to their families through the auspices of local missionaries. Greeks, desperately trying to leave the Pontic coast or the area around Smyrna, paid exorbitant fees to Turkish boatmen. But once they were away from land, in some cases the Greeks were reportedly pushed overboard, and the Turks returned for another boatload. Others continued to rob the Greeks once they boarded their ships. There was a great deal of talk at Lausanne about compensating the Greeks for the property they lost as a result of ethnic cleansing and the final exchange of populations. This never happened; everything was taken by the Turkish government and individual Turks. Turkish holdings in Greece, especially substantial in and around Salonika, were also never compensated by the Greek government.

A similar process affected the Jews, who had to pay and keep paying, first to avoid deportation, then to avoid the ghettos, and then to survive in the ghettos. German Jews paid endless sums just to stay in Germany under increasingly restrictive conditions. Jewish property had long been seized by the state, Aryanized, or destroyed when guards and SS overseers continued to rob the Jews and violently collect their valuables on the way to the concentration camps. In both Poland and Czechoslovakia, the Germans were stolen blind. Even toward the end of the deportations, when groups of Germans were moved to occupied Germany by Allied-authorized railway transports, Polish and Czech customs officials boarded the trains and stole the Germans' property. If anyone raised a fuss, they were beaten and sometimes detained. Although there is no evidence of theft during the deportation of the Crimean Tatars and Chechens-Ingush, they—like all the other deportees—were allowed to take only the minimal of property with them. As soon as they were taken away, gangs of "treasure-seekers" made their way through their homes, stealing what they could. The Chechens-Ingush knew this would happen and concealed as much of their property as possible in the walls of their homes and cottages, not understanding they would not return for at least a dozen years.

Where deportation orders were issued prior to the cleansing, hordes of bargain hunters came to the doors of the expellees in search of cheap goods. The Armenians, in particular, were plagued by Turkish neighbors, looking to buy cheaply or steal Armenian goods and furniture. But the same happened to Jews who were forced to leave Germany or were deported from sections of Poland incorporated in the Reich. After the war, Poles and Czechs simply walked in the doors of German houses and took what they wanted, unceremoniously expelling the inhabitants in the process. In former Yugoslavia, Bosnian Muslims were beaten and robbed repeatedly on their way out of their villages and towns. The Serbs also searched Albanian homes for gold, coins, and German marks, the preferred currency of the Serbian ethnic cleansers. Today, Albanians steal from Serbs. Serb property has been ransacked in much the same way that the Albanians' property was at the outset of open hostilities there.

Gender

Ethnic cleansing is inherently misogynistic. Whereas war sets men against men, ethnic cleansing more often than not entails men attacking women. The ideology of integral nationalism identifies women as the carriers, quite literally, of the next generation of the nation. Not only do women constitute the biological core of nationality, but they are often charged with the task of passing on the cultural and spiritual values of nationhood to their children. The result is that ethnic cleansing often targets women.

But part of the reason that so many women are victims is also circumstance. When trouble is imminent, men usually emigrate first, hoping to send for their families afterward. Thus many Armenian, Greek, and Jewish men left their families behind. Men are also the first to take up arms, go to the hills, seek to resist, or join a foreign brigade, if that is a possibility. Once again, the women and children are left behind and in harm's way. This was the case with some Armenians and Greeks, as well as Chechens-Ingush, Kosovar Albanians, and Bosnian Muslims. Some men also become involved directly in war. Many Greek men had fought and died in the campaigns against the Turks; German men died or were missing in great numbers in Eastern Europe, leaving mostly women, children, and old people behind in the new Poland and Czechoslovakia. Chechen-Ingush and Crimean Tatar men were often away fighting in the Red Army, or were already among the casualties, when ethnic cleansing came to their towns and villages in 1944.

Sometimes, men of military age are shot right off. This happened to the Armenians in February 1915, when the men were transferred to labor battalions and massacred or taken away from the towns and killed. In the case of the Greeks, men 16 to 60 were deported to the interior, where many of them died. Jewish men, too, were the first to be shot in large numbers by the Einsatzgruppen in June and July 1941, though the murder of women and children soon followed. In the worst case of mass murder in the war in Bosnia—some 6,700 men of military age in Srebrenica were taken off in groups, massacred, and buried in mass graves.

Once any remaining men are dealt with, ethnic cleansing turns on the women, who are its main victims. Women and girls are harassed, humiliated, and raped individually, serially, and by gangs. Women are stripped and forced to submit sexually to the sexual-sadistic fantasies of their persecutors, warders, and guards. This happened repeatedly in the case of the Armenians and Greeks. Armenian women in particular sought refuge from the constant attacks by voluntarily entering Turkish harems, converting themselves and their daughters to Islam in order to survive. Turkish women, in their turn, suffered at the hands of the Greek army and chettes during the Greek occupation and offensive. Jewish women were forced to dance and run the gauntlet naked and defenseless, sometimes to their deaths. German men seldom raped Jewish women—that would have been a "racial crime"—but they stood by and were greatly amused as Ukrainians, Lithuanians, and Poles committed rape. Jewish women were subject to forced sterilization and, in the camps, to German surgical experiments to make sterilization quicker, cheaper, and more efficient.

After the war, German women and girls were raped by Poles and Czechs as well as by the Soviet soldiers who were supposed to guard them in the Polish and Czech labor and internment camps. As far as we know, rape and sexual molestation were not part of the Soviet ethnic cleansing of Chechens-Ingush and Crimean Tatars, but women were clearly the primary victims of the forced deportation. Most of the men were at the front, and, in the case of the Chechens, many had fled to the mountains. The women were yanked from their homes and transported in box cars to Kazakhstan and Uzbekistan. Especially for traditional

Muslim women, the humiliation of the long journey, confined together with members of the opposite sex, was very hard to endure.

The abuse of women in the war in former Yugoslavia follows the patterns of earlier cases of ethnic cleansing. The Bosnian Muslim men had joined Muslim units or had emigrated to Western Europe to find work. Serb army and paramilitary units sometimes interned Muslim men of military age; sometimes—Srebrenica was the worst example—they simply took them out and shot them. This left the women, children, and old people to fend for themselves against the Serb soldiers. A similar process occurred in Kosovo, where the men left home to find work abroad or, eventually, to fight in the KLA. In any case, the women were easy prey for Serb soldiers, who claimed, sometimes, that they were following orders to rape Muslim women. In Bosnia and Kosovo, rape was one of the tools of ethnic cleansing, a way to terrorize the Muslim population and make sure that they did not come back. Rape was also a form of punishment for the Muslims. By raping their women, the Serbs sought to wound the pride of their opponents and insult their nation. As we have seen, raped women in Bosnia were sometimes forced to carry the resulting pregnancies to term, giving birth to "little Chetniks." It is hard to know what happened to these women and children. Numerous instances have been reported of women simply leaving their babies in the hospitals. The number of rapes in Bosnia and especially in Kosovo is even harder to register, since traditional Muslim women would find it extremely hard to report the offenses. Still, it is clear that rape was integral to ethnic cleansing in Bosnia and Kosovo as carried out by Serbs, and to some extent by Croats; it became an emblem of the war and a shameful part of the history of the 1990s.

Many more women die during expulsion and transportation than men. It was mostly Armenian women and children who trudged across the deserts to Mesopotamia, dropping by the roadside and dying by the tens of thousands. It was mostly Greek women who lined the quay at Smyrna, desperately trying to leave the country, and it was mostly women who suffered the cleansing of the Turks and the mortal dangers of the refugee camps in Greece and the islands. More Jewish women suffered medical experiments and died in the gas chambers of the concentration camps than did Jewish men. German women died in greater numbers as the result of Czechoslovak and Polish persecution; Chechen-Ingush and Crimean Tatar women suffered in greater proportions the terrible fate of forced deportation and starvation in Central Asia. It is likely that more Bosnian and Kosovar men died than did women in the recent struggle, but in nowhere near the proportions of men to women that one encounters in "normal" warfare.

The Future

The history of ethnic cleansing in the twentieth century gives no reason to hope that it will not recur in the twenty-first. Modern and modernizing states that seek to homogenize their populations and eliminate the "other" come into being with regularity. Political elites continue to use the ideology of integral nationalism as a way to achieve power and maintain it against potential rivals. In the process, they exploit the popular media to create historical images of national humiliation and suffering on the one hand and pride and revenge on the other. Nationalism remains an incredibly powerful force for the mobilization of populations. This is true in the West, as we have seen in France and Austria, but it is even more prevalent in the former communist regions of Europe and Eurasia, which have been succeeded by countries with weak civil societies, fragile constitutional arrangements, struggling economies, and ideological confusion. These countries cannot be drawn into NATO and the European Union fast enough to avoid the perils of ethnic cleansing.

What is more, the international community remains impotent when faced with trying to prevent, inhibit, or stop ethnic cleansing. The Armenian horrors were plastered on the front pages of newspapers all over the Western world, yet nothing was done to stop them. The same with the Greek catastrophe. In both cases, the West was satisfied with providing relief and shelter for the survivors after the fact. World War II was not fought because of the persecution and murder of the Jews. That appallingly little was done to publicize and condemn the Nazi actions against the Jews, much less to take in refugees or bomb railway lines to the camps, remains a blight on the conscience of the entire world, the United States included. A few newspapers and isolated politicians and publicists complained about the brutal treatment of the Germans by the Poles and Czechs after the war; but except for the Germans themselves, very few showed any compassion for their plight. Even if people had known about the deportations of the Chechens-Ingush and Crimean Tatars, it is unlikely they would have done anything about it. Even today, the Russian pummeling of Grozny and the Chechens has not exactly roused the moral conscience of the world community.

Part of the problem is the strong commitment of the international community to the ideals of Westphalian sovereignty, which makes it hard to interfere in the internal affairs of another nation. In the case of Bosnia-Herzegovina, this reluctance was overcome by the claim that Bosnia was an independent and sovereign state attacked from the outside by the Serbs and Croats. Even at that, it took three and a half years of fearsome ethnic cleansing for the United States and NATO to act decisively against Milosevic and the Serb aggressors. The case of Kosovo was fundamentally different. Kosovo was clearly within the borders of Yugoslavia as internationally defined. The Serb attack on the Kosovar Albanians, like the present Russian attack on the Chechens, was an internal affair. Yet the international community acted much more quickly and decisively, demonstrating, perhaps, that international norms about intervening in cases of ethnic cleansing are changing. At least, NATO and the Americans made it clear that they were not willing to face the repeated campaigns of ethnic cleansing by the Serbs. But what will happen in the next case, especially if Milosevic is not involved. Does the international community have the will to act promptly and decisively? If not, the horrors recounted in this book will surely happen again.

Notes

Introduction

1. See Laura Silber and Alan Little, *Yugoslavia: Death of a Nation* (New York: TV Books, 1995), p. 244.
2. Veljko Vujacic, "Communism, Nationalism, and Democracy in Russia and Serbia: 1985–1993" (draft ms.), p. 149 n. 30. My thanks to the author for making it available to me.
3. See William Safire, "On Language," *New York Times Magazine,* March 14, 1993, p. 24.
4. See Robert M. Hayden, "Schindler's Fate: Genocide, Ethnic Cleansing, and Population Transfers," *Slavic Review,* 55, no. 4 (Winter 1996): 727–748.
5. For a description of the origins and meaning of the word "genocide," see Robert Melson, *Revolution and Genocide: On the Origins of the Armenian Genocide and the Holocaust* (Chicago: University of Chicago Press, 1992), pp. 22–24; and Leo Kuper, *Genocide: Its Political Use in the Twentieth Century* (New Haven: Yale University Press, 1981), pp. 52–56.
6. See Michael Burleigh and Wolfgang Wippermann, *The Nazi Racial State: Germany 1933–1945* (Cambridge: Cambridge University Press, 1991), pp. 28–37; and George L. Mosse, *Toward the Final Solution: A History of European Racism* (Madison: University of Wisconsin Press, 1985), pp. 215–222.
7. Frank Dikötter, "Race Culture: Recent Perspectives on the History of Eugenics," *American Historical Review,* 103, no. 2 (April 1998): 467.
8. Some Croat sources claim that the Serbs used the word "cleansing" as early as 1807 to describe the desired eviction of Turks, Jews, and some gypsies from Belgrade. "'Ethnic Cleansing'—since 1807," in *The "Liberation" of Sarajevo—Oslobodjenje,* 1st English ed. (1994), p. 14.

9. Götz Aly, *"Endlösung": Völkerverschiebung und der Mord an den Europäischen Juden* (Frankfurt am Main: S. Fischer Verlag, 1995), pp. 35–50.

10. Cited in Geoff Eley and Ronald Grigor Suny, "Introduction," *Becoming National: A Reader* (New York: Oxford University Press, 1996), p. 21.

11. Andrew Bell-Fialkoff, *Ethnic Cleansing* (New York: St. Martin's Press, 1996), p. 7.

12. The theories of Rene Girard are ably applied to the problems of ethnic conflict in Robert Hamerton-Kelly's provocative *The Gospel and the Sacred: Poetics of Violence in Mark* (Minneapolis: Fortress Press, 1993).

13. Bell-Fialkoff, *Ethnic Cleansing*, p. 21.

14. Daniel Jonah Goldhagen, *Hitler's Willing Executioners: Ordinary Germans and the Holocaust* (New York: Alfred A. Knopf, 1996), p. 23. Goldhagen writes: "These chapters demonstrate the development in Germany well before the Nazis came to power of a virulent and violent 'eliminationist' variant of antisemitism, which called for the elimination of Jewish influence or of Jews themselves from German society. When the Nazis did assume power, they found themselves the masters of a society already imbued with notions about Jews that were ready to be mobilized for the most extreme form of 'elimination' imaginable."

15. Daniel Chirot, "Herder's Multicultural Theory of Nationalism and Its Consequences," *East European Politics and Societies,* 10, no. 1 (Winter 1996): 11–13.

16. Helmut Bley, *Southwest Africa under German Rule, 1894–1914,* tr. Hugh Ridley (London: Heinemann, 1971), pp. 163–164. "The Herero nation must leave the country," states the German commanding general. "If it will not do so I shall compel it by force." Elsewhere, he writes: "I believe that the Herero must be destroyed as a nation."

17. Zygmunt Baumann, *Modernity and the Holocaust* (Ithaca: Cornell University Press, 1989), pp. 61–62.

18. See Peter F. Sugar, "Nationalism and Religion in the Balkans since the 19th Century," *The Donald W. Treadgold Papers,* University of Washington, 8 (July 1996): 35.

19. James C. Scott, *Seeing like a State: How Certain Schemes to Improve the Human Condition Have Failed* (New Haven: Yale University Press, 1998), pp. 4–6.

20. Peter Holquist, "Information Is the Alpha and Omega of Our Work: Bolshevik Surveillance in Its Pan-European Context," *Journal of Modern History,* 69 (September 1997): 415–450.

21. Bjorn Wittrock, "Social Theory and Intellectual History: Towards a Rethinking of the Formation of Modernity," in Fredrik Engelstad and Ragnvald Kalleberg, eds., *Social Time and Social Change: Perspectives on Sociology and History* (Oslo and Stockholm: Scandinavian University Press, 1999), pp. 195–198.

22. Daniel Chirot, "Modernism without Liberalism: The Ideological Roots of Modern Tyranny," *Contention*, 5, no. 1 (Fall 1995): 144–147.

23. Omer Bartov, *Murder in Our Midst: The Holocaust, Industrial Killing, and Representation* (New York: Oxford University Press, 1996), pp. 3–11; Elisabeth Domansky, "Militarization and Reproduction in World War I Germany," in Geoff Eley, ed., *Society, Culture, and the State in Germany, 1870–1930* (Ann Arbor: University of Michigan Press, 1996), pp. 427–463.

24. Arnold J. Toynbee, *The Western Question in Greece and Turkey: A Study in the Contact of Civilizations*, 2nd ed. (London: Constable and Company Ltd., 1923), p. 265.

25. Vahakn N. Dadrian, "The Role of Turkish Physicians in the World War I Genocide of Ottoman Armenians," *Holocaust and Genocide Studies*, 1, no. 2 (Autumn 1986): 169–192.

26. Robert J. Lifton, *The Nazi Doctors: Medical Killing and the Psychology of Genocide* (New York: Basic Books, 1986). See also Burleigh and Wippermann, *The Nazi Racial State*, pp. 136–197; and Götz Aly, Peter Chroust, and Christian Pross, *Cleansing the Fatherland: Nazi Medical and Racial Hygiene*, tr. Belinda Cooper (Baltimore: The Johns Hopkins University Press, 1994), pp. 22–99. For the role of "technocrats," see Christopher R. Browning, *The Path to Genocide: Essays on Launching the Final Solution* (Cambridge: Cambridge University Press, 1992), pp. 59–76; also for doctors, see ibid., pp. 145–168.

27. Ronald G. Suny, "Rethinking the Unthinkable: Toward an Understanding of the Armenian Genocide," in *Looking toward Ararat: Armenia in Modern History* (Bloomington: Indiana University Press, 1993), p. 114.

28. Christopher Browning, "Hitler and the Decisions for the Final Solution," Elsie B. Lipset Lecture, Stanford University, March 4, 1997. See also Browning, *The Path to Genocide*, pp. 125–144. Philippe Burrin, *Hitler and the Jews: The Genesis of the Holocaust*, tr. Patsy Southgate (London: Edward Arnold, 1994), pp. 120–129.

29. See Gerhard Ziemer, *Deutscher Exodus: Vertreibung und Eingliederung von 15 Millionen Ostdeutschen* (Stuttgart: Seewald Verlag, 1973), pp. 94, 227.

30. Gerhard Weinberg, *A World at Arms: A Global History of World War II* (Cambridge: Cambridge University Press, 1994), p. 895.

31. Detlef Brandes, *Grossbritannien und seine osteuropäischen Allierten 1939–1943* (Munich: R. Oldenbourg Verlag, 1988), pp. 230–231.

32. Rogers Brubaker, *Nationalism Reframed: Nationhood and the National Question in the New Europe* (Cambridge: Cambridge University Press, 1996), p. 10.

33. Christopher Browning makes this point in a superb essay that also criticizes the Germanocentric explanation of the Holocaust offered by Daniel Goldhagen. Christopher Browning, "Human Nature, Culture,

and the Holocaust," *Chronicle of Higher Education*, October 18, 1996, p. A72.

1. The Armenians and Greeks of Anatolia

1. *The Other Balkan Wars: A 1913 Carnegie Endowment Inquiry in Retrospect*, intro. by George F. Kennan (Washington, DC: Carnegie Endowment, 1993). Leon Trotsky wrote a similar set of reports; see *The Correspondence of Leon Trotsky: The Balkan Wars, 1912–13* (New York: Pathfinder, 1981).
2. Katrin Boeckh, *Von den Balkankriegen zum Ersten Weltkrieg* (Munich: Oldenbourg Verlag, 1996), p. 227.
3. George Montandon, *Frontières nationales: Détermination objective de la condition primordiale necéssaire à l'obtention d'une paix durable* (Lausanne, 1915), cited in Hans Lemberg, "'Ethnische Säuberung': Ein Mittel zur Lösung von Nationalitäten problemen?" *Aus Politik und Zeitgeschichte*, B 46/92 (November 6, 1992), pp. B 45–46. See also Joseph B. Schechtman, *Postwar Population Transfers in Europe, 1945–1955* (Philadelphia: University of Pennsylvania Press, 1962), p. 389.
4. See, for example, Nancy Reynolds, "Difference and Tolerance in the Ottoman Empire: Interview with Aron Rodrigue," *Stanford Humanities Review*, 5, no. 1 (1995): 81–93.
5. This is very much the tone of Vahakn N. Dadrian's extensive writing on the Armenian situation in the Ottoman Empire. See, for example, *The History of the Armenian Genocide: Ethnic Conflict from the Balkans to Anatolia to the Caucasus* (Providence: Berghahn Books, 1995), pp. xx–xxi. See also his discussion of the "religious dimensions" of the 1894–1896 massacres, pp. 147–151.
6. Ronald Grigor Suny, "When Genocide: Interpretations of the Causes and Timing of the Armenian Deportations and Massacres," (March 2000), ms. p. 20.
7. Vahakn Dadrian, *Warrant for Genocide: Key Elements of Turko-Armenian Conflict* (New Brunswick: Transaction Books, 1999), pp. 5–28.
8. Benjamin Braude and Bernard Lewis, eds., *Christians and Jews in the Ottoman Empire* (New York: Holmes and Meier Publishers, 1982), pp. 3–4.
9. Bernard Lewis, *The Emergence of Modern Turkey*, 2nd ed. (New York: Oxford University Press, 1968), pp. 34–35.
10. The Armenian Genocide in the U.S. Archives, 1915–1918. Chadwyck Healy, Inc., Microfilms. (Hereafter AGUSA.) Fiche 325, Treaty of Berlin, Article 61.
11. Ronald G. Suny, *Looking toward Ararat: Armenia in Modern History* (Bloomington: Indiana University Press, 1993), pp. 77–78.
12. See Suny, *Looking toward Ararat*, pp. 19, 74–75, 85–86. See also Rich-

ard G. Hovannisian, *Armenia on the Road to Independence, 1918* (Berkeley: University of California Press, 1967), pp. 15–18.

13. Braude and Lewis, eds., *Christians and Jews*, p. 7.

14. This argument is developed by Dadrian in *The History of the Armenian Genocide*, pp. 147–151.

15. Ibid., pp. 114–119.

16. Richard G. Hovannisian, "The Historical Dimensions of the Armenian Question, 1878–1923," in R. G. Hovannisian, ed., *The Armenian Genocide in Perspective* (New Brunswick: Transaction Books, 1986), pp. 25–26.

17. Trutz von Trotha, "Die deutschen Kolonialkriege: Vom begrenzten zum genozidalen 'Pazifizierungskrieg,'" lecture, Hamburg, HIS, June 11, 1999, pp. 1–7.

18. Ibid., p. 3.

19. Taner Aksam, *Armenien und der Völkermord: Die Istanbuler Prozesse und die türkische Nationalbewegung* (Hamburg: Hamburger Edition, 1999), p. 34.

20. Lewis, The Emergence of Modern Turkey, p. 215.

21. See Vahakn Dadrian, "The Circumstances Surrounding the 1909 Adana Holocaust," *Armenian Review*, 41, no. 4 (1988): 1–16. Dadrian analyzes here the connection between the unsuccessful counterrevolution against the Young Turks and their involvement in the Adana massacre.

22. Ernest Edmundson Ramsaur, Jr., *Prelude to the Revolution of 1908* (Beirut: Khayats, 1965), pp. 33–38.

23. Cited in Christopher Walker, *Armenia: The Survival of a Nation* (New York: St. Martin's Press, 1980), p. 198.

24. Ibid.

25. See Robert Melson, "Provocation or Nationalism: A Critical Inquiry into the Armenian Genocide of 1915," in Hovannisian, ed., *The Armenian Genocide in Perspective*, p. 77.

26. Jacob M. Landau, *Pan-Turkism: From Irredentism to Cooperation* (Bloomington: Indiana University Press, 1995), pp. 7–14, 46. See also Hugh Poulton, *Top Hat, Grey Wolf and Crescent: Turkish Nationalism and the Turkish Republic* (London: Hurst & Company, 1997), pp. 72–80.

27. Serif Mardin, "The Ottoman Empire," in Karen Barkey and Mark von Hagen, eds., *After Empire: Multiethnic Societies and Nation-Building* (Boulder: Westview Press, 1997), pp. 118–119.

28. Suny, "When Genocide: Interpretations of the Causes and Timing of the Armenian Deportations and Massacres," p. 20.

29. Djemal Pasha, *Memories of a Turkish Statesman, 1913–1919* (New York: George H. Doran Company, 1922), pp. 251–252.

30. Caglar Keyder, "The Ottoman Empire," in *After Empire*, p. 37.

31. A. L. Macfie, *The End of the Ottoman Empire, 1908–1923* (London: Longman, 1998), p. 61.

32. Hovannisian, "The Historical Dimensions of the Armenian Question," p. 27. Not surprising for students of nationalism is the fact that many of the Young Turk ultranationalist leaders were not of Turkish extraction themselves. Gökalp was a Kurd from Diyarbekir; Talat Pasha was a Bulgarian gypsy; and Enver Pasha was of Cherkess and Albanian origins. R. Hrair Dekmejian, "Determinants of Genocide: Armenians and Jews as Case Studies," in Hovannisian, ed., *The Armenian Genocide in Perspective,* p. 93.

33. Aksam, *Armenien und der Völkermord,* p. 59.

34. Richard Clogg, "The Greek *Millet* in the Ottoman Empire," in Braude and Lewis, eds., *Christians and Jews,* p. 200.

35. Aksam, *Armenien und der Völkermord,* p. 43. Joseph Schechtman cites much higher numbers of Greeks deported and killed in the operation; see *European Population Transfers 1939–1945* (New York: Oxford University Press, 1946), p. 12. Ambassador Morgenthau writes: "Just how many [Greeks] were scattered in this fashion is not definitely known, the estimates varying anywhere from 200,000 up to 1,000,000." Henry Morgenthau, *Ambassador Morgenthau's Story* (Garden City: Doubleday, Page & Company, 1918), p. 325.

36. Dekmejian, "Determinants of Genocide," p. 93.

37. Dadrian, *The History of the Armenian Genocide,* p. 194.

38. Aksam, *Armenien und der Völkermord,* p. 46.

39. Ibid., p. 49.

40. Translation of Talat's report to the party congress in *Hilal,* September 19 and 30, 1916, AGUSA, fiche 11, p. 10.

41. Walker, *Armenia: The Survival of a Nation,* p. 200.

42. William S. Dodd to Morgenthau, September 8, 1915, AGUSA, fiche 81, p. 4.

43. Johannes Lepsius, ed., *Deutschland und Armenien, 1914–1918: Sammlung Diplomatischen Aktienstücke* (Potsdam: Der Tempelverlag, 1919), p. 189. Aksam, *Armenien und der Völkermord,* p. 52.

44. Statement of Miss Alma Johanson, AGUSA, fiche 12, p. 7; Statement of Dr. Floyd O. Smith, AGUSA, fiche 346. Johanson, a Swedish nurse attached to the German mission in Mush, writes of the tortures: "Feet, hands, chests were nailed to a piece of wood, nails of fingers and toes were torn out; beards and eyebrows were pulled out; feet were hammered with nails, same as they do with horses; others were hung with their feet up and heads down over [water] closets."

45. "Inquiry Documents," Mrs. T. W. Atkinson, April 11, 1918, AGUSA, fiche 344, p. 10.

46. Rev. Henry H. Riggs, "Personal Experiences in Kharput 1915–1917," AGUSA, fiche 341, p. 66.

47. William S. Dodd, Konya, to Morgenthau, August 15, 1915, AGUSA, fiche 79.

48. Diary of John Clayton of *The Chicago Tribune,* AGUSA, fiche 106, p. 20.

49. Riggs, "Personal Experiences," AGUSA, fiche 342, p. 114.
50. "Inquiry Documents," Mrs. Cyril H. Haas, Adana, May 11, 1918, AGUSA, fiche 343, p. 2.
51. "Inquiry Documents," William S. Dodd, M.D., Konya, December 21, 1917, AGUSA, fiche 344, p. 2.
52. Ibid., p. 3.
53. Riggs, "Personal Experiences," AGUSA, fiche 342, p. 155.
54. "Inquiry Documents," Miss Isabelle Harvey, Kharput, April 15, 1918, AGUSA, fiche 344, p. 6.
55. "Inquiry Documents," Elisabeth S. Webb, June 1, 1919, AGUSA, fiche 346, p. 4.
56. Reports of Jesse B. Jackson, Aleppo, to Secretary of State, AGUSA, fiche 86, p. 5.
57. Leslie A. Davies to Morgenthau, Kharput, June 11, 1915, AGUSA, fiche 69.
58. Morgenthau to Secretary of State, September 25, 1915 (citing Dodd report), AGUSA, fiche 383; Riggs, "Personal Experiences," AGUSA, fiche 342, p. 162.
59. "Inquiry Documents," Miss Ruth A. Parmalee, Mezereh, June 21, 1918, AGUSA, fiche 344.
60. *Documents of the American Relief Administration: European Operations 1918–1922,* vol. 12 (Stanford: Stanford University, 1932), pp. 127–128.
61. "Inquiry Documents," Miss Myrtle O. Shane, Bitlis, April 10, 1918, AGUSA, fiche 344, p. 7. Here Shane describes the terrible sport of chase, catch, rape, escape, and so on, carried on during the trek.
62. "Morgenthau Papers," J. B. Jackson, Consul in Aleppo, to Morgenthau, September 29, 1915, AGUSA, fiche 183.
63. *Documents of the American Relief Administration,* vol. 12, p. 135.
64. President George E. White, Anatolian College, Marsovan, AGUSA, fiche 346, p. 9.
65. In Smyrna, for example, the vigorous intervention of American Ambassador Morgenthau stayed the executions of the Armenian leaders of the city and delayed indefinitely plans to exile the Armenian population. See Morgenthau, *Ambassador Morgenthau's Story,* pp. 352–353.
66. Marjorie Housepian, *The Smyrna Affair* (New York: Harcourt, Brace, Jovanovich, 1966), p. 26. AGUSA, fiche 346, p. 8.
67. Morgenthau to Secretary of State Lansing, November 18, 1915, AGUSA, fiche 12, p. 5.
68. Morgenthau to Secretary of State Lansing, November 4, 1915, AGUSA, fiche 12, p. 6.
69. Riggs, "Personal Experiences," AGUSA, fiche 341.
70. William S. Dodd to Morgenthau, August 15, 1915, "Morgenthau Papers," AGUSA, fiche 382, p. 5.
71. For a bibliography of the Armenian literature on the genocide, see Richard G. Hovannisian, *The Armenian Holocaust: A Bibliography Relating to*

the Deportations, Massacres, and Dispersion of the Armenian People, 1915–1923 (Cambridge, MA: Armenian Heritage Press, 1978).

72. For the Turkish point of view, see Mim Kemal Öke, *The Armenian Question 1914–1923* (Oxford: K. Rustem & Brother, 1988), pp. 126–136; Heath W. Lowry, *The Story behind Ambassador Morgenthau's Story* (Istanbul: The Isis Press, 1990); and Stanford Jay Shaw and Ezel Kural Shaw, *History of the Ottoman Empire and Modern Turkey,* vol. 2 (Cambridge: Cambridge University Press, 1976–77), p. 30.

73. See, for example, the problem of the involvement of the Turkish government and the Atatürk Chair in Turkish Studies at Princeton in discussion of the genocide. Roger W. Smith, Eric Markusen, and Robert J. Lifton, "Professional Ethics and the Denial of the Armenian Genocide," *Holocaust and Genocide Studies,* 9, no. 1 (Spring 1995): 1–22.

74. For the trial documents, see Aksam, *Armenien und der Völkermord,* pp. 230–359.

75. See, for example, Carol Edgarian, *Rise the Euphrates* (New York: Random House, 1994); Abraham Hartunian, *Neither to Laugh nor to Weep* (Boston: Beacon Press, 1968); George Horton, *The Blight in Asia* (Indianapolis: Bobbs-Merrill, 1926).

76. See, for example, in AGUSA: Jesse B. Jackson to Secretary of State, September 7, 1921, fiche 375; telegrams from Talat to governor of Aleppo, January 1916, fiche 375; Morgenthau to Secretary of State, May 14, 1915, fiche 10; American Consul, Aleppo to Secretary of State, April 20, 1915, pp. 3–7, fiche 9.

77. Undated diary entry, Papers of Henry Morgenthau, Sr., AGUSA, fiche 386.

78. Morgenthau to Doctor and Mrs. Wise, October 19, 1915, "The Papers of Henry Morgenthau, Sr.," AGUSA, fiche 380.

79. Cited in Leo Kuper, "The Turkish Genocide of Armenians," in Hovanissian, *The Armenian Genocide in Perspective,* p. 48.

80. Admiral Mark Bristol, War Diary, August 14, 1922, AGUSA, fiche 37, p. 7. Unlike Morgenthau, Bristol tended to be quite sympathetic to the Turks. He wrote that "the Armenian soldiers in the French Army behaved so badly that they had to be disbanded."

81. Report to American Embassy, December 18, 1919, AGUSA, fiche 22; J. Pierrepont Moffat, U.S. Embassy, "Turkish History, 1918–1923," AGUSA, fiche 52, pp. 12–13; U.S. Naval Intelligence Report, "Conditions in Cilicia, Syria, and Palestine," July 25 and June 25, 1920, AGUSA, fiche 324; Admiral Bristol to Barton, Near East Relief, April 5, 1920, AGUSA, fiche 331.

82. See the materials submitted to the Paris Peace Conference on the "Armenian atrocities," AGUSA, fiche 350, pp. 4–7. Here it is claimed that the Turks were "slaughtered like cattle" by the Armenians, that there was widespread rape of Muslim women, and that atrocities were systematically carried out on the Turkish population. Much of this material is sup-

posedly taken from the translated diaries of Russian officers fighting with the Armenians.

83. Dadrian, *The History of the Armenian Genocide*, p. 360.
84. Abraham Tulin to Herbert Hoover (copy), May 4, 1919, in Hoover Institution Archives (hereafter HIA), ARA, Paris Office Country File, box 46.
85. Howard Heinz to Herbert Hoover, May 6, 1919, ibid.
86. Ibid.
87. Barton to Vickery, Near East Relief, March 14, 1919, AGUSA, fiche 151.
88. ARA report, June 20, 1919, in HIA, ARA, Paris Office Countries File, Armenia. The report suggests that even more Armenians would die if food transportation through Georgia continued to be blocked.
89. Dadrian, *The History of the Armenian Genocide*, p. 356.
90. Hovannisian, "The Historical Dimensions of the Armenian Question," p. 37.
91. Robert Melson, "Provocative Nationalism: A Critical Inquiry into the Armenian Genocide of 1915," p. 65.
92. Lepsius, ed., *Deutschland und Armenien*, p. xxv.
93. Aksam, *Armenien und der Völkermord*, p. 76. Dadrian, *The History of the Armenian Genocide*, pp. 225, 233 n. 40.
94. Peter Balakian, *Black Dog of Fate: A Memoir* (New York: Broadway Books, 1997), p. 269.
95. Lt. J. N. Gregory, *U.S.S. Cole*, AGUSA, fiche 333, p. 25. American Committee for Relief in the Near East, notes, March 6, 1919, *Documents of the American Relief Administration*, vol. 12, p. 127.
96. Schechtman, *European Population Transfers*, p. 12.
97. "Conversations with Talat in Smyrna," Stanford University Green Library Special Collections, Papers of E. J. Dillon.
98. John O. Iatrides, ed., *Ambassador MacVeagh Reports: Greece 1933–1947* (Princeton: Princeton University Press, 1980), p. 11.
99. "Near Eastern Intelligence," December 31, 1918, AGUSA, fiche 15.
100. A senior U.S. Naval officer reported: "They [the Greeks] have behaved abomidably all through their occupation of Smyrna district and they should be removed completely. There is no reason to show them any consideration." Report, November 9, 1919, AGUSA, fiche 21, p. 2.
101. Admiral Mark Bristol to George Horton, May 4, 1920, AGUSA, fiche 336.
102. "Reports in the District of Yalova and Geremlek and in the Ismid Peninsula," presented to Parliament, no. 1 (1921), His Majesty's Stationary Office, AGUSA, fiche 325.
103. Toynbee, *The Western Question in Greece and Turkey*, p. 262.
104. War Diary of U.S. Naval Detachment, Report of Intelligence Officer Lt. A. S. Merrill, September 6, 1922, AGUSA, fiche 337.
105. Ibid., September 7, 1922, AGUSA, fiche 337.
106. Lt. Perry, *U.S.S. Edsall*, October 3, 1922, AGUSA, fiche 337.

107. Lt. Merrill, War Diary, September 10, 1922, AGUSA, fiche 337.

108. Ibid., September 12, 1922, AGUSA, fiche 337, p. 13.

109. Ibid., September 11, 1922, AGUSA, fiche 337; War Diary of U.S. Naval Detachment, Report of Chief of Staff Capt. A. J. Hepburn, *U.S.S. Scorpion,* AGUSA, fiche 159.

110. Capt. Hepburn, AGUSA, fiche 159, pp. 26–27, 29.

111. Lt. Merrill, War Diary, September 14, 1922, AGUSA, fiche 337, p. 1.

112. Lt. Merrill, message, September 15, 1922, AGUSA, fiche 337.

113. Capt. Hepburn, report, September 14, 1922, AGUSA, fiche 337.

114. Lt. Merrill, War Diary, September 16, 1922, AGUSA, fiche 337.

115. Ibid., September 15, 1922, AGUSA, fiche 337.

116. The former figure, suggested by Lysimachos Econominos, *The Martyrdom of Smyrna and Eastern Christendom* (London: George Allen & Unwin, 1922), p. 84, may well reflect Greek losses in the region of Smyrna from all causes: defeat by the Turks; ethnic cleansing in the region; killings in Smyrna and its environs; deaths in Smyrna itself due to disease, crowding, and violence; and fire-related deaths. The figure of 12,000 is given by Dmitri Pentzopoulos, *The Balkan Exchange of Minorities and Its Impact upon Greece* (Paris: Mouton & Co., 1962), p. 47.

117. See, for example, the report on the Smyrna fire by E. M. Yantis, Manager of the Gary Tobacco Co., Inc., AGUSA, fiche 159.

118. Clafton Davis to Admiral Bristol, November 8, 1922, AGUSA, fiche 160.

119. J. Pierrepont Moffat, "Turkish History, 1918–1923," U.S. Embassy, AGUSA, fiche 55, p. 33. Here Moffat states that 262,587 Greeks were evacuated from Smyrna, mostly under American supervision.

120. Pentzopoulos, *The Balkan Exchange of Minorities,* p. 47.

121. Cited in Macfie, *The End of the Ottoman Empire,* p. 198.

122. Lt. H. E. Gardner (Med. Corps), February 24, 1923, AGUSA, fiche 47.

123. Pentzopoulos, *The Balkan Exchange of Minorities,* p. 1, no. 79. According to Stephen Ladas, Lausanne oversaw the actual transfer of 189,916 Greeks to Greece (1924–26) and 355,635 Muslims to Turkey (1923–1924). More than one million Greeks had already fled Anatolia by the time of Lausanne. See Stephen Ladas, *The Exchange of Minorities: Bulgaria, Greece and Turkey* (New York: Macmillan, 1932), pp. 17, 441.

124. Cited in Macfie, *The End of the Ottoman Empire,* p. 210.

125. Lord Curzon in response to a speech by Izzet Pasha at Lausanne, AGUSA, fiche 119, p. 4.

126. Ladas, *The Exchange of Populations,* p. 724.

127. League of Nations, *Greek Refuge Settlement* (translation) (Geneva: Publications of League of Nations, 1926), p. 4. Red Cross Commissioner to the Prime Minister of Greece, March 9, 1921, HIA, American Red Cross, box 7. "Even a casual inspection," the commissioner writes, "discloses an almost unprecedented state of misery and distress."

128. Memorandum to British Ambassador, June 3, 1924, AGUSA, fiche 365.

129. See Renee Hirschon, *Heirs of the Greek Catastrophe: The Social Life of*

Asia Minor Refugees in Piraeus (Oxford: Clarendon Press, 1989), pp. 1–4, 11, and Michael Herzfeld, *A Place in History: Social and Monumental Time in a Cretan Town* (Princeton: Princeton University Press, 1991), pp. 64–66.

130. John Randolph, American Consul, Angora, "Economic and Political Information Re Turkey," March 12, 1924, AGUSA, fiche 51, p. 4.

2. The Nazi Attack on the Jews

1. "Aufzeichnung ohne Unterschrift," IMG Nürnberg 1014-PS, *Akten zur deutschen auswärtigen Politik, 1918–1945,* Serie D (1937–1945), vol. 7 (Baden-Baden: Imprimerie Nationale, 1956), p. 171. Here the Louis Lochner account of the speech is reprinted, along with the official Nazi account.

2. See Kevork B. Bardakjian, *Hitler and the Armenian Genocide* (Cambridge, MA: The Zoryan Institute, 1985), pp. 1–36.

3. See Vahakn N. Dadrian, *German Responsibility in the Armenian Genocide: A Review of the Historical Evidence of Complicity* (Watertown, MA: Blue Crane Books, 1996), pp. 116–137.

4. Bardakjian, *Hitler and the Armenian Genocide,* pp. 25–32.

5. Hans Jansen, *Der Madagaskar-Plan: Die beabsichtigte Deportation der Europäischen Juden nach Madagaskar,* tr. from the Dutch by Markus Jung, Ulrike Vogl, and Elisabeth Weissenböck (Munich: Herbig, 1997), p. 1.

6. Peter Novick, *The Holocaust in American Life* (Boston: Houghton Mifflin Company, 1999), p. 268.

7. Tony Judt, "The Morbid Truth," *New Republic,* July 19 and 26, 1999, p. 40.

8. Robert M. Hayden, "Schindler's Fate: Genocide, Ethnic Cleansing, and Population Transfers," *Slavic Review,* 55, no. 4 (Winter 1996): 727–749.

9. See *I Shall Bear Witness: The Diaries of Victor Klemperer, 1933–41,* abr. and tr. Martin Chalmers (London: Weidenfeld & Nicolson, 1998), p. 122.

10. Ian Kershaw, *Hitler, 1889–1936: Hubris* (New York: W. W. Norton, 1999), p. 152.

11. Elke Fröhlich, ed., *Die Tagebücher von Joseph Goebbels,* part 1, "Aufzeichnungen," vol. 7 (July 1939–March 1940) (Munich: K. G. Saur, 1998), p. 177. See also his entry for October 17, 1939, p. 163.

12. Klaus Theweleit's studies of the frightening psychosexual fantasies of Freikorps veterans is very suggestive in this regard. Klaus Theweleit, *Male Fantasies,* 2 vols., tr. Stephen Conway (Minneapolis: University of Minnesota Press, 1987).

13. Adolf Hitler, *Mein Kampf,* tr. Ralph Mannheim (Boston: Houghton Mifflin, 1999), p. 308.

14. Frank Dikötter, "Race Culture: Recent Perspectives on the History of Eugenics," *American Historical Review*, 103, no. 2 (April 1998): 467.

15. Uli Linke, *Blood and Nation: The European Aesthetics of Race* (Philadelphia: University of Pennsylvania Press, 1999), pp. 200–201.

16. See "The Posen Diaries of the Anatomist Hermann Voss," ann. Götz Aly, in Götz Aly, Peter Chroust, and Christian Pross, eds., *Cleansing the Fatherland: Nazi Medicine and Racial Hygiene*, tr. Belinda Cooper (Baltimore: The Johns Hopkins University Press, 1994, pp. 104–105.

17. John Weiss, *Ideology of Death: Why the Holocaust Happened in Germany* (Chicago: Ivan R. Dee, 1996), p. 326.

18. Michael Burleigh and Wolfgang Wippermann, *The Racial State: Germany 1933–1945* (Cambridge: Cambridge University Press, 1991), pp. 136–137.

19. Ibid., pp. 147–148.

20. Götz Aly says that some 30,000 people were killed in the euthanasia program up to the fall of 1941 for this purpose. Götz Aly, "'Judenumsiedlung': Überlegungen zur politischen Vorgeschichte des Holocaust," in Ulrich Herbert, ed., *Nationalsozialistische Vernichtungspolitik 1939–1945: Neue Forschungen und Kontroversen* (Frankfurt am Main: Fischer Taschenbuch Verlag, 1998), pp. 88–89.

21. See Aly, Chroust, and Pross, *Cleansing the Fatherland*, p. 23.

22. Aly, "'Judenumsiedlung,'" pp. 88–89; Burleigh and Wippermann, *The Nazi Racial State*, pp. 150–151.

23. Richard Breitman, *The Architect of Genocide: Himmler and the Final Solution* (Alfred A. Knopf: New York, 1991), p. 202.

24. George L. Mosse, *Toward the Final Solution: A History of European Racism* (New York: Howard Fertig, 1978), p. 233.

25. Jansen, *Der Madagaskar Plan*, p. 397.

26. Christopher Browning, "Nazi Resettlement Policy and the Search for a Solution to the Jewish Question, 1939–1941," *German Studies Review*, 9, no. 3 (1986): 519. Philippe Burrin, *Hitler and the Jews: The Genesis of the Holocaust*, tr. Patsy Southgate (London: Edward Arnold, 1994), p. 88.

27. Christian Gerlach, "The Wannsee Conference, the Fate of German Jews, and Hitler's Decision in Principle to Exterminate All European Jews," *Journal of Modern History*, 70 (December 1998), p. 777.

28. Kershaw, *Hitler, 1889–1936*, p. 573.

29. Jansen, *Der Madagaskar Plan*, p. 179.

30. Ibid., p. 180.

31. Hitler, *Mein Kampf*, p. 302.

32. Klemperer, *I Shall Bear Witness*, p. 9.

33. Ibid., p. 12.

34. Saul Friedländer, *Nazi Germany and the Jews: The Years of Persecution, 1933–1939*, vol. 1 (New York: HarperCollins, 1997), pp. 62–63.

35. Jansen, *Der Madagaskar Plan*, p. 199, uses the figure of 45,000 Jews. Friedländer, *Nazi Germany and the Jews*, p. 63, uses 60,000.

36. Friedländer, *Nazi Germany and the Jews,* p. 62.
37. Klemperer, *I Shall Bear Witness,* p. 122.
38. Cited in Jansen, *Der Madagaskar Plan,* p. 243.
39. *Die Tagebücher von Joseph Goebbels,* part 1, "Aufzeichnungen 1923–1941," vol. 6, pp. 33, 65.
40. Ibid., p. 143.
41. Friedländer, *Nazi Germany and the Jews,* vol. 1, pp. 281–283.
42. Ibid., p. 179.
43. Cited in Aly, "'Judenumsiedlung,'" p. 73.
44. Ibid., p. 182.
45. See Mosse, *Toward the Final Solution,* p. 204.
46. Hoover Institution Archives, Heinrich Himmler: box 14, folder 10 (Kreisleitertagung, November 28, 1940, p. 7); box 8, folder 307, notes of April 29, 1944, April 2, 1943, May 14, 1943, and "Stellungnahme zum Schreiben des Gauleiters und Reichsstatthalters Greiser vom 16 März 1943."
47. Friedländer, *Nazi Germany and the Jews,* vol. 1, p. 242.
48. Jansen, *Der Madagaskar Plan,* p. 231. Friedländer, *Nazi Germany and the Jews,* vol. 1, pp. 245–246.
49. Yehuda Bauer, *Jews for Sale: Nazi-Jewish Negotiations, 1933–1945* (New Haven: Yale University Press, 1994), p. 32.
50. Max Domanus, *Hitler: Reden und Proklamationen 1932–1945,* vol. 2 (Wiesbaden, 1963), p. 1058.
51. According to L. J. Hartog, the threat was repeated by Hitler six times, though he purposely misdated the original "prophecy" to September 1, 1939, the first day of the war. L. J. Hartog, *Der Befehl zum Judenmord: Hitler, America und die Juden* (Syndikat: Bodenheim, 1997), p. 15.
52. Hans Mommsen, "Hitler's Reichstag Speech," *History and Memory,* 9. nos. 1–2 (Fall 1997): 151. Friedländer essentially agrees, noting that a general Nazi diplomatic offensive was under way to get the Western powers to act on the Jewish question. Friedländer, *Nazi Germany and the Jews,* vol. 1, pp. 310–311. Hartog believes that the warning was particularly directed to the United States and its influential Jewish community. Hartog, *Der Befehl zum Judenmord,* p. 12.
53. Mommsen, "Hitler's Reichstag Speech," pp. 157–158.
54. Domanus, *Hitler: Reden und Proclamationen,* vol. 2, p. 1057.
55. *Völkischer Beobachter,* 40 (February 9, 1939).
56. Robert C. Tucker, *Stalin in Power: The Revolution from Above, 1928–1941* (New York, London: W. W. Norton, 1990), p. 602.
57. Gabriel Gorodetsky, *Grand Delusion: Stalin and the German Invasion of Russia* (New Haven: Yale University Press, 1999), pp. 44–45, 318–319.
58. Robert L. Koehl, *RKFDV: German Resettlement and Population Policy, 1939–1945* (Cambridge: Harvard University Press, 1957), pp. 129–130.
59. Browning, *The Path to Genocide,* pp. 40–42.
60. Breitman, *The Architect of Genocide,* p. 81.

61. See Dieter Pohl, "Die Ermordung der Juden im Generalgouvernement," in *Nationalsozialistische Vernichtungspolitik 1939–1945*, p. 100.
62. Burrin, *Hitler and the Jews*, pp. 75–76.
63. For Schacht's plan and his negotiations with Jewish and refugee organizations, see Jansen, *Der Madagaskar Plan*, pp. 268–276.
64. Ulrich Herbert, "Vernichtungspolitik: Neue Antworten und Fragen zur Geschichte des 'Holocausts,'" *Nationalsozialistische Vernichtungspolitik, 1939–1945*, p. 26.
65. Cited in Götz Aly, *"Endlösung": Völkerverschiebung und der Mord an den Europäischen Juden* (Frankfurt am Main: S. Fischer, 1995), p. 9.
66. Burrin, *Hitler and the Jews*, p. 77.
67. Ibid., pp. 341–348.
68. Browning, "Nazi Resettlement Policy," p. 511.
69. Aly, *"Endlösung,"* pp. 167–169.
70. Raul Hilberg, Stanislaw Staron, and Josef Kermisz, eds., *The Warsaw Diary of Adam Czerniakow: Prelude to Doom* (New York: Stein and Day, 1979), p. 169. Some of the building plans in the ghetto were also abandoned as the result of the Madagascar option. Ibid., p. 39.
71. *Die Tagebücher von Joseph Goebbels*, vol. 8, p. 206.
72. Aly, "'Judenumsiedlung,'" pp. 90–91.
73. *Die Tagebücher von Joseph Goebbels*, part 1, vol. 9 (June 16, 1941), p. 377.
74. Gorodetsky, *Grand Delusion*, p. 131.
75. Jansen, *Der Madagaskar Plan*, p. 390.
76. *Die Tagebücher von Joseph Goebbels*, "Diktate," part 2, vol. 1 (September 24, 1941), p. 480.
77. Peter Witte, Michael Wildt, et al., eds., *Der Dienstkalendar Heinrich Himmlers 1941/42* (Hamburg: Hans Christian Verlag, 1999), p. 353. Heydrich here also talked about sending the Czechs to the Siberian north. His estimate of 11 million Jews to be "disposed of" included all of the Jews in the European realm plus North African Jews in the French colonies. Aly, "'Judenumsiedlung,'" pp. 73–74.
78. Alfred Streim, *Die Behandlung sowjetischer Kriesgefangener im "Fall Barbarossa": Eine Dokumentation* (Heidelberg: C. F. Müller, 1982), pp. 35–36.
79. Hannes Heer, "Killing Fields: The Wehrmacht and the Holocaust in Belorussia, 1941–1942," tr. Carol Scherer, *Holocaust and Genocide Studies*, 7, no. 1 (Spring 1997): 79.
80. Herbert, "Vernichtungspolitik," p. 49.
81. Ibid., p. 53.
82. Omer Bartov, *Murder in Our Midst: The Holocaust, Industrial Killing, and Representation* (New York: Oxford University Press, 1996), p. 83.
83. Bartov, *Hitler's Army: Soldiers, Nazis, and War in the Third Reich* (New York: Oxford: Oxford University Press, 1992), p. 83–92. Hannes Heer, *Krieg ist ein Gesellschaftszustand: Reden zur Eröffnung der Ausstellung*

"Vernichtungskrieg: Verbrechen der Wehrmacht 1941 bis 1944" (Hamburg: Hamburger Edition, 1998), p. 107.

84. Hannes Heer, *Tote Zonen: Die deutsche Wehrmacht an der Ostfront* (Hamburg: Hamburger Edition, 1999), p. 21.

85. *Die Tagebücher von Joseph Goebbels,* part 2, vol. 2, p. 484.

86. Bartov, *Hitler's Army,* pp. 84–87.

87. They survived for the moment because the Reichskommissar and the army insisted that "they must not be shot."

88. "The commander of Security Police and Security Service, Kovno, December 1, 1941," in Raul Hilberg, ed., *Documents of Destruction: Germany and Jewry 1933–1945* (Chicago: Quadrangle Books, 1971), pp. 46–57.

89. Dieter Pohl, "Die Ermordung der Juden im Generalgouvernement," in *Nationalsozialistische Vernichtungspolitik,* p. 104.

90. Bernhard Chiari, *Alltag hiner der Front: Besatzung, Kollaboration und Widerstand in Weissrussland, 1941–1944* (Düsseldorf: Droste, 1998), p. 251.

91. Christian Gerlach, "Deutsche Wirtschaftsinteressen, Besatzungspolitik und der Mord an den Juden in Weissrussland 1941–1943," in *Nationalsozialistische Vernichtungspolitik 1939–1945,* pp. 279, 313–315. Chiara, *Alltag hinter der Front,* p. 263.

92. Herbert, "Vernichtungspolitik," p. 49.

93. Ibid., p. 50; Gerlach, "Deutsche Wirtschaftsinteressen," pp. 289, 313–315.

94. *The Warsaw Diary of Adam Czerniakow,* p. 305.

95. *Die Tagebücher von Joseph Goebbels,* part 1, vol. 8, p. 390.

96. Ibid., part 2, vol. 2 (November 2, 1941), p. 222.

97. Gerlach, "The Wannsee Conference, the Fate of German Jews, and Hitler's Decision," *Journal of Modern History,* 70, no. 4 (December 1998), p. 777.

98. Henry Friedlander, *The Origins of Nazi Genocide: From Euthanasia to the Final Solution* (Chapel Hill: University of North Carolina Press, 1995), p. 285.

99. Burleigh and Wippermann, *The Racial State,* p. 102. Gerlach, "Hitler's Decision to Exterminate European Jews," p. 763.

100. Martin Gilbert, *Atlas of the Holocaust* (New York: William Morrow and Co., 1988), p. 83.

101. Christopher Browning is convinced that it is Hitler's euphoria about victory rather than worries about the war in the winter that prompts his decision to eliminate the Jews. See his *The Path to Genocide,* p. 54.

102. *Die Tagebücher von Joseph Goebbels,* part 2, vol. 2, pp. 498–499.

103. Herbert, "Vernichtungspolitik," p. 62. Here, Herbert is discussing the views of Christian Gerlach.

104. Cited in Aly, "'Judenumsiedlung,'" p. 95; Gerlach, "Hitler's Decision to Exterminate European Jewry," p. 790.

105. Bogdan Musial, *Deutsche Zivilverwaltung und Judenverfolgung im Generalgouvernement: Eine Fallstudie zum Distrikt Lublin, 1939–1944* (Wiesbaden: Harrassowitz Verlag, 1999), p. 220.
106. Browning, *Path to Genocide*, pp. 120–121; Aly, *"Endlösung,"* pp. 358–362. Burrin traces the decision to late September 1941. *Hitler and the Jews*, pp. 120–127.
107. Gerlach, "Hitler's Decision to Exterminate European Jews," p. 760.
108. *Hitler's Secret Conversations, 1941–1944* (New York: Farrar, Straus and Young, 1953), p. 193.
109. Ibid., p. 212.
110. Ibid., p. 269.
111. For a sensible discussion of these schools of thought, see Browning "Beyond 'Intentionalism' and 'Functionalism': The Decision for the Final Solution Reconsidered," in his *The Path to Genocide*, pp. 86–121.
112. A somewhat different version of this argument is made in relation to the Holocaust in Arno J. Mayer, *Why Did the Heavens Not Darken? The "Final Solution" in History* (New York: Pantheon Books, 1988), p. 12.
113. Cited in Heer, *Tote Zonen*, p. 312.
114. Williamson Murray and Allan R. Millett, *A War To Be Won: Fighting the Second World War* (Cambridge: Harvard University Press, 2000), p. 554.
115. Hoover Institution Archives, Heinrich Himmler, box 332, file 13.
116. Mary Lowenthal Felstiner, *To Paint Her Life: Charlotte Salomon in the Nazi Era* (New York: HarperCollins, 1995), pp. 205–211.
117. Dalia Ofer and Lenore J. Weitzman, eds., *Women in the Holocaust* (New Haven: Yale University Press, 1998), pp. 12–13.
118. In an extended conversation with Goebbels at his Rastenburg headquarters (August 19, 1941), Hitler reiterated his prophecy that the Jews would be destroyed if they started a world war, and added: "Their [the Jews'] last sanctuary remains North America and there they will also have to pay in the long or short run." *Die Tagebücher von Josef Goebbels*, part 2, vol. 1, "Diktate," 1941–1945, p. 269.

3. Soviet Deportation of the Chechens-Ingush and the Crimean Tatars

1. For a good summary of Soviet nationality policy in the 1920s and 1930s, see Ronald Grigor Suny, *The Revenge of the Past: Nationalism, Revolution, and the Collapse of the Soviet Union* (Stanford: Stanford University Press, 1993), pp. 102–106. See also Yuri Slezkine, "The USSR as a Communal Apartment, or How a Socialist State Promoted Ethnic Particularism," *Slavic Review*, 53 (Summer 1994): 414–452.
2. Terry Martin, "An Affirmative Action Empire: Ethnicity and the Soviet State, 1923–1938," Ph.D. dissertation, University of Chicago, 1996. See also his "The Russification of the RSFSR," *Cahiers du Monde russe*, 39, nos. 1–2 (January–June 1998), p. 104.

3. Peter Holquist, "To Count, to Extract, to Exterminate: Population Statistics and Population Politics in Late Imperial Russia," in Terry Martin and Ronald G. Suny, eds., "A State of Nations: Empire and Nation-Making in the Soviet Union, 1917–1953," ms. pp. 3–9.

4. Eric Lohr, "Enemy Alien Politics within the Russian Empire During World War I," Ph.D. dissertation, Harvard University, 1998, pp. 65–66.

5. Francine Hirsch, "The Soviet Union as a Work-in-Progress: Ethnographers and the Category *Nationality* in the 1926, 1937, and 1939 Censuses," *Slavic Review,* 56, no. 2 (1997): 251–275.

6. James Scott talks about both terms in Scott, *Seeing Like a State,* p. 193. See Richard Stites, *Revolutionary Dreams: Utopian Vision and Experimental Life in the Russian Revolution* (New York: Oxford University Press, 1989), p. 19.

7. Stephen Kotkin, *Magnetic Mountain: Stalinism as a Civilization* (Berkeley: University of California Press, 1995), p. 34.

8. Hoover Institution Archives (HIA), Nicolaevsky, Series 227, box 294, V. Pozdniakov, "Passportnaia sistema Sovetskogo soiuza," pp. 274–291.

9. See Hiroaki Kuromiya, *Stalin's Industrial Revolution: Politics and Workers, 1928–1932* (Cambridge: Cambridge University Press, 1988); David Hoffmann, *Peasant Metropolis* (Ithaca: Cornell University Press, 1994).

10. Scott, *Seeing Like a State,* p. 6.

11. Berman to Iagoda, December 8, 1933, State Archives of the Russian Federation (hereafter GARF), f. 9421, op. 1, d. 300, l. 10.

12. Kuromiya, *Stalin's Industrial Revolution,* pp. 27–45.

13. See Amir Weiner, "Nurture, Nature and Memory in a Socialist Utopia: Delineating the Soviet Socio-Ethnic Body in the Age of Socialism," *American Historical Review,* 104, no. 4 (October 1999): 13–14 n. 30, 90.

14. Gerhard Simon, *Nationalism and Policy toward the Nationalities in the Soviet Union: From Totalitarian Dictatorship to Post-Stalinist Society,* tr. Karen Forster and Oswald Forster (Boulder: Westview Press, 1991), p. 149.

15. Terry Martin, "The Origins of Soviet Ethnic Cleansing," *Journal of Modern History,* 70, no. 4 (December 1998): 857.

16. On the deportations of Poles, Germans, Koreans, Iranians, and others, see N. F. Bugai, *L. Beriia—I. Stalinu: "Soglasno Vashemu ukazaniiu"* (Moscow: "AIRO-XX", 1995), pp. 8–27; Terry Martin, "The Origins of Soviet Ethnic Cleansing," pp. 852–856. See GARF, f. 5446, op. 57, d. 52, l. 29.

17. Michael Gelb, "The Western Finnic Minorities and the Origins of the Stalinist Nationalities Deportations," *Nationalities Papers,* 24, no. 2 (1996): 242–243. Gelb demonstrates here, however, that the deportations had a class as well as ethnic component to them.

18. GARF, f. 5446, op. 57, d. 52, l. 29.

19. Bugai, *"Soglasno Vashemu ukazaniiu,"* p. 26.

20. Pavel Polian, *Geografiia prinuditel'nykh migratsii v SSSR* (Moscow 1999), ms. ch. 3, p. 3.

21. Alfred Streim, *Die Behandlung sowjetischer Kreigsgefangener im 'Fall Barbarossa': Eine Dokumentation* (Heidelberg: C. F. Müller, 1982), p. 41.

22. See Jeffrey Brooks, *Thank You, Comrade Stalin! Soviet Public Culture from the Revolution to Cold War* (Princeton: Princeton University Press, 2000), p. 188.

23. Vladislav Zubok and Constantine Pleshakov, *Inside the Kremlin's Cold War: From Stalin to Khrushchev* (Cambridge: Harvard University Press, 1996), pp. 7, 16, 28.

24. Simon, *Nationalism and Policy towards the Nationalities,* pp. 180–182.

25. Yuri Slezkine, *Arctic Mirrors: Russia and the Small Peoples of the North* (Ithaca: Cornell University Press, 1994), p. 304.

26. Gorodetsky, *Grand Delusion,* p. 23.

27. Cited in Burrin, *Hitler and the Jews,* pp. 79–80.

28. H. R. Trevor-Roper, in *Hitler's Secret Conversations, 1941–1944* (New York: Farrar, Straus and Young, 1953), p. xx.

29. Tucker, *Stalin in Power,* p. 275.

30. Cited in ibid., p. 619.

31. Shimon Redlich, ed., *War, Holocaust and Stalinism: A Documented History of the Jewish Anti-Fascist Committee in the USSR* (Luxemburg: Harwood, 1995), p. 130.

32. Redlich, ed., *War, Holocaust and Stalinism,* pp. 155, 162. Arkady Vaksberg, *Stalin protiv evreev* (New York: Liberty Publishing House, 1995), pp. 273–354. Brooks, *Thank You, Comrade Stalin!,* p. 231.

33. Slezkine, *Arctic Mirrors,* p. 304.

34. This process already began before the war. See Tucker, *Stalin in Power,* pp. 568–572.

35. Joanna Nichols, "Who Are the Chechens?" Center for Slavic and East European Studies Newsletter (University of California, Berkeley: spring 1995). See also John B. Dunlop, *Russia Confronts Chechnya: Roots of a Separatist Conflict* (Cambridge: Cambridge University Press, 1998), pp. 1–2.

36. Dunlop, *Russia Confronts Chechnya,* p. 1.

37. Anatol Lieven, *Chechnya: Tombstone of Russian Power* (New Haven: Yale University Press, 1998), pp. 327–332.

38. Nikolai Fedorovich Bugai, "The Truth about the Deportation of the Chechen and Ingush Peoples," *Soviet Studies in History,* 30, no. 2 (Fall 1991): 68–69. This piece was translated from an article by Bugai in *Voprosy istorii,* no. 7 (1990).

39. Aleksandr M. Nekrich, *The Punished Peoples: The Deportation and Fate of Soviet Minorities at the End of the Second World War,* tr. George Saunders (New York: W. W. Norton, 1978), p. 43. Here, Nekrich reports that there were 69 "acts of terrorism," meaning 69 killings of NKVD, party, and army officials.

40. Dunlop, *Russia Confronts Chechnya*, pp. 42–45. See also Holquist, "To Count, To Extract, To Exterminate," p. 1.

41. "Chechnia: Vooruzhennaia bor'ba v 20–30e gody," *Voenno-istoricheskii arkhiv*, vyp. 2 (Moscow, 1997): 118–175.

42. Bugai, "The Truth About the Deportation," pp. 68, 72. See also Nekrich, *The Punished Peoples*, pp. 48–49.

43. N. F. Bugai and A. M. Gonov, *Kavkaz: Narody v eshelonakh* (Moscow: Insan, 1998), pp. 136–141.

44. A. Avtorkhanov, "Pochemu likvidirovana checheno-ingushskaia respublika," typed ms. in HIA, Dallin, box 2–8, p. 55. Nekrich, *The Punished Peoples*, p. 45.

45. Avtorkhanov, "Pochemu likvidirovana checheno-ingushskaia respublika," p. 56. Simon, *Nationalism and Policy towards the Nationalities*, p. 203. Bugai and Gonov, *Kavkaz*, p. 137.

46. Order of the Supreme Soviet of the USSR, March 7, 1944, GARF, f. 7523, op. 4, d. 208, l. 51.

47. Nekrich, *Punished Peoples*, pp. 57–58. William Flemming, "The Deportation of the Chechen and Ingush Peoples: A Critical Examination," in Ben Fowkes, ed., *Russia and Chechnia: Essays on Russo-Chechen Relations* (St. Martin's Press: New York, 1998), p. 66.

48. Dunlop, *Russia Confronts Chechnya*, pp. 58–61. See Robert Conquest, *The Nation Killers*, 2nd ed. (New York: Macmillan, 1970), p. 170.

49. Iu. A. Aidaev, ed., *Chechentsy: Istoriia i sovremennost'* (Moscow: Mir domu tvoemu, 1996), p. 276.

50. Aleksandr N. Iakovlev, *Po moshcham i elei* (Moscow: Izdatel'stvo "Evrasiia", 1995), pp. 120–122.

51. See Russian Center for the Preservation and Study of Documents of Contemporary History (RTsKhIDNI), f. 178, op. 43, d. 2437 and 2438, for Chechen-Ingush *obkom* discussions of problems with the Chechen population. RTsKhIDNI has been recently renamed RGASPI, Rossiiskii Gosudarstvennyi Arkhiv Sotsial'no-Politicheskoi Istorii.

52. RTsKhIDNI, f. 17, op. 88, d. 376, l. 5.

53. Nekrich, *Punished Peoples*, pp. 42–46.

54. Bugai and Gonov, *Kavkaz*, pp. 141–142.

55. Beria to Stalin, February 29, 1944, GARF, f. 9401, op. 2, d. 64, l. 161.

56. Beria to Stalin, February 24, 1944, GARF, f. 9401, op. 2, d. 64, l. 166.

57. William Flemming, "The Deportation of the Chechen and Ingush Peoples: A Critical Examination," in Fowkes, ed., *Russian and Chechnia*, p. 72.

58. Avtorkhanov, "Pochemu likvidirovana," p. 64.

59. See Nekrich, *The Punished Peoples*, pp. 58–59.

60. Beria to Stalin, February 23, 1944, in GARF, f. 9401, op. 2, d. 64, l. 165. See also J. Otto Pohl, *Ethnic Cleansing in the USSR, 1937–1949* (Westport, CT: Greenwood Press, 1999), p. 84.

61. See D. Khozhaev, "Genotsid: ocherk" and "Krovavyi pepel Khaibakha," in *Tak eto bylo: natsional'nye repressii v SSSR 1919–1952 gody*, vol. 2 (Mos-

cow: Rossiiskii Mezhdunarodnyi fond kul'tury, 1993), pp. 170, 175–
179. See Flemming, "The Deportations of 1944," in Aidaev, ed.,
Chechentsy: Istoriia i sovremennost', pp. 276–277.

62. Aidaev, ed., *Chechentsy: Istoriia i sovremennost'*, p. 277. The attempts by
specially trained mountain units to flush these Chechens out of their
hideouts were studied by military historians of the Chechen war of the
early 1990s. "Bandity stremilis . . . sokhranit fashistiskii poriadok,"
Voenno-istoricheskii zhurnal, 5 (September–October, 1996): 83–89.

63. Different numbers are used in official statistics, all in the range of
450,000–500,000. This number comes from Beria to Stalin, July 9,
1944, GARF, f. 9401, op. 2, d. 65, l. 311. NKVD reports use ridicu-
lously precise statistics to describe the numbers who were deported and
who died. This false precision, which also meant that all the columns in
population tables had to add up, indicates a mentality of total control that
consistently misrepresented reality.

64. Dunlop, *Russia Confronts Chechnya,* pp. 65–66.

65. "Genotsid," in *Tak eto bylo,* vol. 2, p. 171.

66. Kazakh NKVD reports to Chernyshev in Moscow NKVD, January 21,
1945, GARF, f. 9479, op. 1, d. 177, ll. 2–4. Bugai and Gonov believe
that losses—both before and during transport—were much fewer in
number. They claim that only 40 Chechens were killed in the operation
itself and that 1,272 died in transport. Bugai and Gonov, *Kavkaz,* p. 148.

67. A. Sokolov to Voroshilov, June 21, 1944, in GARF, f. 9479c, op. 1c, d.
152. l. 4.

68. Official data on births and deaths in exile are in the Main Archive of Contemporary Documentation (TsKhSD), f. 2, op. 1, d. 65, ll. 14, 17, 65.

69. Lynne Viola has documented the terrible conditions of the kulak
spetspereselentsy in two recent draft articles (January 2000): "The Other
Archipelago: Kulak Deportations to the North in 1930" and "'Little Kulaks': The Children of the *Spetspereselentsy* of the North."

70. The situation of the deportees is well described in local Kazakh and
Kirghiz NKVD reports. See GARF, f. 9479, op. 1, d. 153, ll. 14–20, 37,
42–43. See also ibid., d. 183, ll. 46–48, which describes attempts by the
Chechens to protest against their fate.

71. "O likvidatsii Checheno-Ingushinskoi ASSR i ob administrativnom
ustroistve ee territorii," March 7, 1944, GARF, f. 7523, op. 4, d. 208, l.
51. See also GARF, f. 9401, op. 2, d. 64, l. 161.

72. For Grozny *obkom* records, see RTsKhIDNI, f. 17, op. 45, d. 423, d.
424. For similar results from the Crimean *obkom* records, see, for example, RTsKhIDNI, f. 17, op. 44, d. 758.

73. Ukaz of July 16, 1956, GARF, f. 7523, op. 4, d. 629, l. 201.

74. Dunlop, *Russian Confronts Chechnya,* p. 76.

75. See TsK KPSS, "O territorii Checheno-Ingushskoi ASSR, December 25,
1956," TsKhSD, f. 5, op. 32, d. 56, ll. 103–104.

76. V. Churaev, TsK KPSS, June 4, 1957, in "'Natsionalisticheskie elementy

postoianno provotsirovali vystupleniia': Kak nakalialas' obstanovka v Checheno-Ingushetii," *Istochnik,* no. 4 (1997): 51–52.

77. "O vostanovlenii Checheno-Ingushkoi SSSR v sostave RSFSR," January 1957, GARF, f. 7523, op. 72, d. 701, l. 72.

78. Andropov, chief of the KGB, February 13, 1972, in ibid., pp. 62–63.

79. Nekrich, *The Punished Peoples,* pp. 13–14.

80. Alan W. Fisher, *Crimean Tatars* (Stanford: Hoover Institution Press, 1978), p. 89.

81. See Neal Ascherson, *Black Sea* (New York: Hill and Wang, 1995), pp. 29–30.

82. Fisher, *The Crimean Tatars,* p. 145.

83. Alexander Dallin, *German Rule in Russia 1941–1945: A Study of Occupation Policies,* 2nd ed. (Boulder: Westview Press, 1981), pp. 253–269.

84. The Jewish population was completely wiped out, so that on April 16, 1942—at the same time as the creation of the "self-defense" units— Berlin was informed by the SS: "the Crimea is purged of the Jews." Gilbert, *Atlas of the Holocaust,* p. 86. See Nekrich, *The Punished Peoples,* pp. 24–25; Dallin, *German Rule in Russia,* p. 258.

85. These memoirs are held in the Archives of the Institute of History of RAN (the Russian Academy of Sciences). See especially "Predatel'skaia rol' tatarskogo naseleniia v period okkupatsii Kryma," ll. 1–17.

86. The sharp conflict in the Tatar *obkom,* which met at that point in Sochi, is recorded in the protocols of the November 18, 1942, and July 21, 1943, meetings, RTsKhIDNI, op. 43, d. 1045, ll. 74–84, d. 1044, ll. 251–282.

87. Kamenev to Malenkov, May 11, 1944, RTsKhIDNI, f. 17, op. 123, d. 306, l. 7.

88. Beria already prepared an attack on Bulatov in March 1944. See Sergienko to Beria, March 31, 1944, GARF, f. 9401, op. 2, d. 64, l. 258.

89. For a defense of the Tatars, see Fischer, *The Crimean Tatars,* p. 159.

90. For lists of the leading Soviet personnel involved in the deportations of the Crimean Tatars and Chechens-Ingush, see Michael Parrish, *The Lesser Terror: Soviet State Security, 1939–1953* (Westport, CN: Praeger, 1996), pp. 101–105.

91. Beria to Stalin and Molotov, May 19, 1944, GARF, f. 9401, op. 2, d. 65, l. 115.

92. GARF, f. 9479, op. 1, d. 177, ll. 2–3.

93. Ayshe Seytmuratova, "The Elders of the New National Movement: Recollections," in Edward A. Allworth, ed., *The Tatars of Crimea: Return to the Homeland: Studies and Documents,* 2nd ed. (Durham: Duke University Press, 1998), p. 155.

94. "Ukaz Presidiuma verkhovnogo soveta SSSR, 26 Noiabr 1948 g.," reproduced in Allworth, ed., *The Tatars of Crimea,* p. 182.

95. Slepov to Malenkov, November 30, 1945, RTsKhIDNI, f. 17, op. 122, d. 122, l. 42.

96. GARF, f. 9479, op. 1, d. 183, l. 290; d. 153, l. 20.

97. Vasilii Subbotin, "Bor'ba s istoriei," *Literaturnaia gazeta*, January 30, 1991, in *Tak eto bylo*, vol. 3 (1993), p. 71. The Soviet dissident champion of the Crimean Tatars, Petro Grigorenko, cites the figure of 46 percent. See Petro G. Grigorenko, *Memoirs* (New York: W. W. Norton, 1982), p. 347.

98. The large number of homeless orphans were a special problem for the NKVD. Many were rounded up and placed in special NKVD orphanages. RTsKhIDNI, f. 17, op. 118, d. 512, l. 24. In August 1946, a full two-and-half years after the deportations, only 20 percent of school-aged Chechen and Ingush children attended schools. Flemming, "The Deportation of Chechen and Ingush Peoples," p. 81.

99. Edige Kirimal, "The Crimean Turks," *Genocide in the USSR* (New York: Scarecrow Press, 1958), p. 20. Nekrich, *Punished Peoples*, p. 106.

100. Beria to Stalin, July 9, 1944, GARF, f. 9401, op. 2, d. 65, l. 275.

101. GARF, f. 9479, op. 1, d. 401, l. 8.

102. On the issue of redeporting returned Tatars, see GARF, f. 9479, op. 1, d. 402, ll. 17–29, and A. Kalinin to Kruglov, September 17, 1948, in ibid., d. 401, ll. 2–6.

103. See the work of the well-known Soviet scholars B. D. Grekov and Iu. V. Bromlei, who rewrote the history of the Tatars, demonstrating their lack of interest in economic development and their tendencies toward banditry and pillage. Subbotin, "Bor'ba s istoriei," p. 85.

104. "O pereimenovanii raionov, raionnykh tsentrov, MTS i sovkhozov Kryma," RTsKhIDNI, f. 17, op. 122, d. 83, l. 55.

105. Andrew Wilson, "Politics in and around Crimea: A Difficult Homecoming," in Allworth, ed., *The Tatars of Crimea*, p. 281.

106. Edward A. Allworth, "Renewing Self-Awareness," in Allworth, ed., *The Tatars of Crimea*, p. 13.

107. Lieven, *Chechnya: Tombstone of Russian Power*, p. 321.

108. Sebastian Smith, *Allah's Mountains: Politics and War in the Russian Caucasus* (London: I. B. Tauris, 1998), p. 60.

109. "Pravitel'stvo rossiiskoi federatsii: Rasporiazhenie ot 1 Dekabria 1994 g., n. 1887-r, r." Also, "Plan meropriatii po obespecheniiu evaluatsii naseleniia Chechenskoi Respubliki." Thanks to the Davis Center, Harvard University, Cold War Project for sending me copies of these documents.

110. *Sevodnia*, no. 227 (October 8, 1999). See also John Dunlop, "Second Time Around May be Worse," *Los Angeles Times*, October 24, 1999.

111. Allworth, ed., *The Tatars of Crimea*, pp. 246, 269.

112. Ascherson, *Black Sea*, p. 33.

4. The Expulsion of Germans from Poland and Czechoslovakia

1. See Stephen P. Ladas, *The Exchange of Minorities: Bulgaria, Greece and Turkey* (New York: Macmillan, 1932), pp. 3 ff.

2. Detlef Brandes, *Grossbritannien und seine osteuropäischen Alliierten 1939–1943* (Munich: R. Oldenbourg Verlag, 1988), pp. 230–231.

3. Lebedev to Vyshinsky, November 10, 1945, in T. V. Volokotina, T. M. Islamov, et al., eds., *Vostochnaia Evropa v Dokumentakh rossiiskikh Arkhivov, 1944–1953*, vol. 1: 1944–1948 (Moscow: Sibirskii khonograf, 1997), p. 292 n. 2. Hereafter, *Vostochnaia Evropa*, vol. 1.

4. Aleksei Filitov, "Problems of Postwar Construction in Soviet Foreign Policy Conceptions during World War II," in Francesa Gori and Silvio Pons, eds., *The Soviet Union and Europe in the Cold War, 1943–53* (New York: St. Martin's Press, 1996), p. 9 (citing from a Maisky memorandum of January 11, 1944).

5. Record of conversations between Molotov and Benes, March 21, 1945, *Vostochnaia Evropa*, vol. 1, pp. 174–176.

6. Record of the conversation between Stalin and Fierlinger and Klementis, June 28, 1945, *Vostochnaia Evropa*, vol. 1, p. 232.

7. Gomulka's memorandum of a conversation with Stalin, third quarter of 1945, *Cold War International History Project Bulletin*, Winter 2000, p. 273. (Draft; hereafter, *CWIHP Bulletin*).

8. Eduard Benes, "Draft of Conversations between President Benes and Mr. Compton Mackenzie," interview by Compton Mackenzie, transcript, 1944, pp. 5–6, HIA, Taborsky Collection, box 4.

9. *Foreign Relations of the United States, Diplomatic Papers: The Conference of Berlin, 1945,* vol. 1 (Washington: U.S. Government Printing Office, 1960), pp. 643, 648, 649. Hereafter, FRUS, Potsdam.

10. Record of Meeting at the Kremlin, October 9, 1944 (Churchill, Stalin, Molotov, et al.), *CWHIP Bulletin* (Winter 2000), p. 36.

11. *Foreign Relations of the United States, Diplomatic Papers: The Conferences at Malta and Yalta, 1945* (Washington: United States Printing Office, 1955), p. 720.

12. Entry for February 23, 1945, concerning meeting of Churchill with junior ministers, *The Second World War Diary of Hugh Dalton, 1940–1945,* ed. Ben Pimlott, in *CWHIP Bulletin* (Winter 2000): 133.

13. Klaus-Dietmar Hencke, "Der Weg nach Potsdam—Die Allierten und die Vertreibung," in Wolfgang Benz, *Die Vertreibung der Deutschen aus dem Osten: Ursachen, Ereignisse, Folgen* (Frankfurt am Main: Deutschen Taschenbuch Verlag, 1985), pp. 50, 56.

14. Cited in Schechtman, *Postwar Population Transfers,* p. 186. See also Benz, *Die Vertreibung der Deutschen aus dem Osten,* p. 8.

15. *FRUS,* 1943, vol. 3, p. 15. Cited in Klaus-Dietmar Henke, "Der Weg nach Potsdam—Die Allierten und die Vertreibung," in Benz, *Die Vertreibung der Deutschen aus dem Osten,* p. 56.

16. *FRUS,* Potsdam, vol. 2, pp. 262, 389.

17. Ibid., pp. 218, 383–384, 388–391.

18. Ibid., p. 1495.

19. See Hencke, "Der Weg nach Potsdam," p. 66.

20. See Benes's speeches in Pilsen and Melnik during the summer 1945, in

Bundesministerium für Vertriebene, Flüchtlinge und Kriegsgeschädigte, *Dokumentation der Vertreibung der Deutschen aus Ost-Mitteleuropa IV. Die Vertreibung der Deutschen Bevölkerung aus der Tschechoslowakei,* Band 1 (rpt.) (Munich: Deutsche Taschenbuch Verlag, 1984), p. 114 fn. 1.

21. Cited in Heinz Nawratil, *Vertreibungs-Verbrechen an Deutschen* (Munich: Ullstein, 1987), p. 96.

22. Jaromir Smutny, *Svedectvi prezidentova kanclere* (Mlada Fronta: Prague, 1996), p. 274.

23. Smutny, *Svedectvi prezidentova kanclere,* pp. 279–281. Brandes, *Grossbritannien und seine osteuropäischen Alliierten,* pp. 396–397.

24. Record of conversations between Benes and Molotov, March 21, 1945, *Vostochnaia Evropa,* vol. 1, p. 177.

25. Gottwald Proclamation of May 11, 1945, in *Dokumentation der Vertreibung,* vol. 1, p. 75 fn. 4.

26. Gottwald's speech to party functionaries in Prague, July 5, 1945, cited in Bradley Abrams, *"The Struggle for the Soul of the Nation": Czech Culture and Socialism 1945–1948,* Ph.D. dissertation, Stanford University, 1998, p. 265.

27. Tomas Stanek, *Odsun Nemcu z Ceskoslovenska 1945–1947* (Prague: Academia Nase Vojsko, 1991), p. 127.

28. Record of meeting held at the Kremlin, October 17, 1944 (Churchill, Eden, Stalin, Molotov, et al.), *CWIHP Bulletin,* Winter 2000, p. 67.

29. See Hans Lemberg, "Die Entwicklung der Pläne für die Aussiedlung der Deutschen aus der Tschechoslowakei," in Detlef Brandes and Vaclav Kural, eds., *Der Weg in die Katastrophe: Deutsch-tchechoslowakische Beziehungen 1938–1947* (Essen: Klartext, 1994), pp. 80–82.

30. See Gottwald to Prochazka, November 21, 1944, and record of conversations between Molotov and Benes, March 21, 1945, *Vostochnaia Evropa,* vol. 1, pp. 100, 176–177.

31. Lemberg, "Die Entwicklung der Pläne," pp. 84–86.

32. Nawratil, *Vertreibungs-Verbrechen an Deutschen,* p. 95.

33. HIA, Taborsky, box 8, Edward Taborsky, "Minority Regimes and the Transfer of Populations in Central Europe after This War" (prepared for Benes, 1943–44), pp. 42–49.

34. Cited in G. P. Murashko and A. F. Noskova, "Natsional'no-territorial'nyi vopros v kontekste poslevoennykh realnostei vostochnoi evropy," *Natsionalnyi vopros v Vostochnoi Evrope* (Moscow: RAN, 1995), p. 231.

35. Alfred W. Klieforth to Foreign Minister, June 28, 1945, p. 288, in *FRUS,* Potsdam, vol. 1, p. 644.

36. Ibid., p. 644.

37. Ibid., p. 647.

38. Archives of the Herder Institute (AHI), *Pravo Lidu,* June 12, 1945; on Lidice, see also *Pravo Lidu,* June 10, 1945.

39. *Dokumenten zur Sudetenfrage: Veröffentlichung des Sudetendeutschen Archivs* (Munich: Fritz Peter Habel, Langen Mueller, 1984), p. 287.

40. *Dokumentation der Vertreibung,* vol. 2, p. 71 n. 2.

41. Derek Sawyer, *The Coasts of Bohemia: A Czech History* (Princeton: Princeton University Press, 1998), p. 240.

42. Quoted in Sawyer, *The Coasts of Bohemia,* pp. 239–240.

43. AHI, "Vertreibungsbericht von Frau Erna Pätzold," November 1945.

44. For Soviet reports on the Czechs' brutality toward the Germans, see "Ob otnoshenii chekhoslovatskogo naseleniia k nemtsam," May 18, 1945, RTsKhIDNI, f. 17, op. 128, d. 320, l. 161, and Serov to Beria, July 4, 1945, GARF, f. 9401, op. 2, d. 97, ll. 143–144. Stanek talks about a "pogrom atmosphere" during this period. Stanek, *Odsun Nemcu,* p. 378.

45. See *Dokumentation der Vertreibung,* vol. 2.

46. Stanek, *Odsun Nemcu,* pp. 76–77. Sawyer, *The Coasts of Bohemia,* p. 243.

47. AHI, "Vyridit kriminalni pripad palicu a vlkodlaku," *Mlada Fronta,* August 1, 1945.

48. *Dokumentation der Vertreibung,* vol. 2, p. 123.

49. Ibid., p. 72.

50. Ibid., pp. 71–72, 81, 122. Stanek, *Odsun Nemcu,* p. 77. Sawyer, *The Coasts of Bohemia,* p. 243.

51. *Dokumente zur Sudetenfrage: Veröffentlichung des Sudetendeutschen Archivs* (Munich: Fritz Peter Habel, Langen Mueller, 1984), pp. 71–72.

52. See Naimark, *The Russians in Germany,* pp. 69–121.

53. *Dokumentation der Vertreibung,* vol. 2, p. 277.

54. Ibid., p. 458.

55. See the evocative memoir by Erich Anton Helfert, *Valley of the Shadow: After the Turmoil My Heart Cries No More* (Berkeley: Creative Arts Book Company, 1997).

56. *Dokumentation der Vertreibung,* vol. 2, p. 86.

57. Serov to Beria, June 14, 1945, *Vostochnaia Evropa,* vol. 1, p. 223.

58. Based on admittedly incomplete data, Tomas Stanek claims that some 6000–7000 Germans died in the camps. Tomas Stanek, *Tabory v ceskych zemich 1945–1948* (Opava: Nakladatelstvi Tilia, 1996), p. 196.

59. Stanek, *Odsun Nemcu,* p. 378.

60. Murashko and Noskina, "Natsional'no-territorial'nyi vopros," p. 235.

61. Jaroslav Kucera, *Odsunove ztraty sudetonemeckeho obyvatelstva* (Prague: Federalni ministerstvo zahranicnich veci, 1992), p. 24.

62. AHI, R. R. Stokes, House of Commons, "Camps in Czechoslovakia," *Manchester Guardian,* October 10, 1946.

63. *Dokumentation der Vertreibung,* vol. 2, p. 271.

64. Alois Harasko, "Die Vertreibung der Sudetendeutschen: Sechs Erlebnisberichte," in Benz, *Die Vertreibung der Deutschen,* p. 108. See also Jeremy King, "Loyalty and Polity, Nation and State: A Town in Habsburg Central Europe," Ph.D. dissertation, Columbia University, 1998, pp. 156–157.

65. Harasko, "Die Vertreibung der Sudetendeutschen," p. 117.

66. *Dokumentation der Vertreibung,* vol. 2, p. 330.

67. Ibid., p. 34.

68. Harasko, "Die Vertreibung der Sudetendeutschen," p. 108; *Dokumenten der Vertreibung,* vol. 2, pp. 158, 202, 210, 330–331, and so on.
69. *Dokumentation der Vertreibung,* vol. 2, p. 195.
70. Ibid., p. 567.
71. Harasko, "Die Vertreibung der Sudetendeutschen," pp. 109–111; Alfred-Maurice de Zayas, *A Terrible Revenge: The Ethnic Cleansing of the East European Germans, 1944–1950,* tr. John A. Koehler (New York: St. Martin's, 1994), p. 86.
72. Nawratil, *Vertreibungsverbrechen an Deutschen,* p. 71. Some German sources put the number even higher, up to 500,000. Luza, *The Transfer of the Sudeten Germans,* p. 293.
73. *Konfliktni Spolecenstvi, Katastrofa, Uvolneni: Nacrt vykladu nemecko-ceskych dejin of 19.stoleti* (Prague: Spolecna nemecko-ceska komise historiku), p. 71.
74. Hans Lemberg, "Die Arbeit der deutsch-tschechischen Historikerkommission," *Zeitschrift zur politischen Bildung,* 34, no. 4 (1998): 94.
75. Philipp Ther, "A Century of Forced Migration: 'Ethnic Cleansing' in the 20th Century," in *Expulsion, Settlement, Integration, Transformation: The Consequences of Forced Migration for the Postwar History of Central and Eastern Europe* (forthcoming from Rowan and Littlefield, 2001), p. 35.
76. Luza, *The Transfer of the Sudeten Germans,* p. 131; Sawyer, *The Shores of Bohemia,* p. 243.
77. For a discussion of some statistical issues in the counting of Sudeten German mortality rates, see Luza, *The Transfer of the Sudeten Germans,* pp. 293–300, and Kucera, *Odsunove ztraty sudetonemeckeho obyvatelstva,* pp. 2–38. Luza does not offer a precise figure himself; Kucera arrives at 24,000.
78. On the expulsion of communists, see Rudolf Slansky, *Nedopustime pripravunoveho Mnichova* (Prague: Vydava Kulturni a propagacni, 1945), pp. 7–8.
79. Ibid., p. 34.
80. Luza, *The Transfer of the Sudeten Germans,* p. 129.
81. Ibid., p. 320.
82. Benjamin Frommer, "To Prosecute or to Expel? Czechoslovak Retribution and the 'Transfer' of the Sudeten Germans," in Ther, ed., *Expulsion, Settlement, Integration, Transformation,* ms. p. 1.
83. King, "Loyalty and Polity," p. 167.
84. *Dokumentation der Vertreibung,* vol. 2, p. 247.
85. Benjamin Frommer, "Unmixing Marriage in Postwar Czechoslovakia," ms., forthcoming in *East European Politics and Societies* (2000).
86. Sawyer, *The Coasts of Bohemia,* p. 241.
87. Ibid., p. 248.
88. Nawratil, *Vertreibungs-Verbrechen an Deutschen,* pp. 69, 96–97.
89. Brandes, *Grossbritannien und seine osteuropäischen Allierten,* p. 505.

Benes describes the expulsion here as a "political, economic, and social Five-Year Plan."

90. *New York Times,* December 5, 1945.

91. See King, "Loyality and Polity," p. 146. Vojtech Mastny, *The Czechs under Nazi Rule: The Failure of National Resistance, 1939–1942* (New York: Columbia University Press, 1971), pp. 206, 224.

92. HIA, Polish Foreign Ministry, "Granice zachodnie," 341. To Vice Minister of Military Affairs from Ministry of Preparatory Work Concerning the Peace Conference, August 21, 1942, pp. 1–2; Seyda to Mikolajczyk, June 28, 1943. See also Sarah Meiklejohn Terry, *Poland's Place in Europe: General Sikorski and the Origin of the Oder-Neisse Line, 1939–1943* (Princeton: Princeton University Press, 1983), p. 100, and Brandes, *Grossbritannien und seine osteuropäischen Alliierten,* p. 406.

93. HIA, "Postwar Borders Poland," Kierownictwo Marynarki Wojennej, "Potrzeba Polityczno-Militarna Szczecina," November 1943, pp. 7–8.

94. Detlef Brandes, "Vorgeschichte von Flucht und Vertreibung," *"Wach auf, mein Herz, und denke" Zur Geschichte der Beziehungen zwischen Schlesien und Berlin-Brandenburg von 1740 bis heute . . . "Przebudz sie, serce moje, i pomysl" Przyczynek do historii stosunkow miedzy Slaskiem a Berlinem-Brandenburgia od 1740 roku do dzis* (Berlin: Gesellschaft für interregionalen Kulturaustausch, Stowarzyszenie Instytut Slaski, 1995), p. 384.

95. Cited in Brandes, "Vorgeschichte von Flucht und Vertreibung," p. 385.

96. See "Projekt dekretu o likwidacji niemczyzny w Polsce," "Dekret o szczegolnych przypadkach straty obywatelstwa," and "Sprawa wysiedlen i wywlaszczen na przyszlych terytoriach," in HIA, Polish Foreign Ministry, box 78, folder 20.

97. HIA, Polish Foreign Ministry, Granice zachodnie, 341, notes, September 25, 1944.

98. HIA, Ministerstwo Prac Kongresowych, London, August 1944.

99. *Information Bulletin of the Home Army,* July 1944, cited in Brandes, "Vorgeschichte von Flucht und Vertreibung," p. 387.

100. HIA, Mikolajczyk, box 72, "Rezolucje Rady Naczelny P.S.L.," October 6–7, 1946, p. 6. See also HIA, "Postwar Borders," "Tezy w Sprawie Wysiedlenia Niemcow z Polski," August 1944.

101. Cited in Antony Polonsky and Boleslaw Drukier, eds., *The Beginnings of Communist Rule in Poland* (London: Routledge and Kegan Paul, 1980), p. 425.

102. Padraic Kenney, *Rebuilding Poland: Workers and Communists, 1945–1950* (Ithaca: Cornell University Press, 1997), p. 152.

103. See Chiodo, *Sterben und Vertreibung,* p. 220.

104. Andrzej Paczkowski, ed., *Dokumenty do dziejow PRL: Aparat bezpieczenstwa v latach 1944–1956,* part 1, 1945–1947 (Warsaw: Instytut Studiow Politycznych PAN, 1994), p. 109.

105. For the many stories of Germans who could not accept the loss of their

homes, see Bundesministerium für Vertriebene, Flüchtlinge und Kriegsgeschädigte, *Der Vertreibung der deutschen Bevölkerung aus den Gebieten östlich der Oder-Neisse,* Bände 1 and 2, rpt. (Munich: Weltbild Verlag, 1993).

106. Interview with Lothar Baar, 1995, in *"Wach auf, mein Herz, und Denke"* ... *"Przebudz sie, serce moje, i pomysl"* ... , p. 416.

107. Borodziej, Hajnicz, "Der Komplex der Vertreibung," p. 30.

108. Cited in Brandes, "Vorgeschichte von Flucht und Vertreibung," p. 389.

109. The Russian historian of the war, Elena Zubkova, writes that the brutality of war seeped into society as a whole and did not disappear with the declaration of peace. E. I. Zubkova, "Obshchestvo, vyshedshee iz voiny: russkie i nemtsy v 1945 godu," *Otechestvennaia istoriia,* no. 3 (1996): 97.

110. M. Sobkow, "Do innego kraju," in *"Wach auf, mein Herz, und Denke"* ... *"Przebudz sie, serce moje, i pomysl"* ... , p. 433.

111. Unlike the Czechoslovak case, it is hard to know how many Germans were expelled in the first place. According to early German figures, some 3 million Germans were driven from Silesia alone and 4.5 Germans from the new Poland as a whole. Stanislaw Senft, "Weryfikacja Narodowa i repolonizacja na slasku w latach 1945–1950," *"Wach auf, mein Herz, und Denke"* ... *"Przebudz sie, serce moje, i pomysl"* ... , p. 448. The German-Polish Historical Commission reluctantly uses the number of roughly 3.5 million Germans driven out of Polish territory administered by both Poland and the Soviet Union (meaning, primarily, north East Prussia). Of these, approximately 400,000 died of various causes. Wlodzimierz Borodziej and Artur Hajnicz, "Der Komplex der Vertreibung: Abschlüssbericht," Warsaw, December 7, 1996, p. 34. However, the number 3.5 million relates to those "transferred" after November 1945. Bernadetta Nitschke, *Wysiedlenie Ludnosci Niemieckiej z Polski w latach 1945–1949* (Zielona Gora: Wyzsza Szkola Pedagogiczna, 1999), p. 305. A recent statistical study uses the figure of 473,013 dead, of whom 58,256 were shot, 14,356 committed suicide, 80,522 died in camps, 93,283 died while in flight, and 63,876 died while being driven from their homes. Gert von Pistohlkors, "Informationen zur Klärung der Schicksale von Flüchtlingen aus der Vertreibungsgebieten östlich von Oder und Neisse: Die Arbeit der Heimatortskarteien (HOK)," in Rainer Schulze, Doris von der Brelie-Lewien, and Helga Grebing, eds., *Flüchtlinge und Vertriebene in der westdeutscher Nachkriegsgeschichte: Bilanzierung der Forschung und Perspektiven für die künftige Forschungsarbeit* (Hildesheim: Verlag August Lax: 1987), p. 5. According to Robert Trana, some two million Germans died in the process of Soviet occupation, Polish occupation, and forced deportation—most in the Western territories—of violence, hunger, and disease. Robert Trana, "Wysiedlenia Niemcow z Polski—refleksje na marginesie literatury najnowszej," in Elzbiety Traba and Roberta Traba, eds., *Tematy polsko-niemieckie* (Olsztyn: Wspolnota Kulturowa, 1997), pp. 28–29.

112. Madajczyk, *Przylaczenie Slaska Opolskiego do Polski*, p. 88.
113. Naimark, *The Russians in Germany*, pp. 71–76.
114. Ibid., pp. 146–150.
115. Rudolf von Thadden, "Die Gebiete östlich der Oder-Neisse in den Übergangsjahren 1945–1949: Eine Vorstudie," in *Flüchtlinge und Vertriebene in der westdeutschen Nachkriegseschichte*, pp. 119, 124.
116. From the report of the Political Section of the Northern Group of Forces, August 30, 1945, *Vostochnaia Evropa*, vol. 1, p. 260.
117. Ibid., p. 262.
118. Kenney, *Rebuilding Poland*, pp. 140–141.
119. Madajczyk, *Przylaczenie Slaska Opolskiego do Polski*, p. 222.
120. Ibid., p. 102.
121. *Dokumenty do dziejow PRL: Aparat bezpieczenstwa*, pp. 108–109.
122. From the report of the Political Section of the Northern Group of Forces, August 30, 1945, *Vostochnaia Evropa*, vol. 1, p. 261.
123. Edmund Nowak, *Cien Lambinowic* (Opole: Centralne Muzeum Jencow Wojennych w Lambinowicach, 1991), pp. 51, 55.
124. Naimark, *The Russians in Germany*, pp. 75–76.
125. Karol Jonca, Marek Maciejewski, et al., eds., *Wysiedlenia Niemcow i osadnictwo ludnosci polskiej na obszarze Krzyzowa-Swidnica (Kreisau-Schweidnitz) w latach 1945–1948: Wybor Dokumentow/ Die Aussiedlung der Deutschen und die Ansiedlung der polnischen Bevölkerung im Raum Krzyzowa-Swidnica (Kreisau-Schweidnitz) 1945–1948* (Wroclaw: Wydawnictwo Leopoldium, 1997), p. 88.
126. Madajczyk, *Przylaczenie Slaska Opolskiego do Polski*, p. 227.
127. Nitschke, *Wysiedlenie ludnosci niemieckiej*, p. 309.
128. AHI, *Freie Presse*, January 8, 1947.
129. Madajczyk, *Przylaczenie slaska opolskiego do Polski*, p. 220.
130. From the report of the Political Section of the Northern Group of Forces, *Vostochnaia Evropa*, vol. 1, p. 261.
131. Von Thadden, "Die Gebiete östlich der Oder-Neise," p. 121.
132. Nitschke, *Wysiedlenie ludnosci niemieckiej*, p. 306.
133. Ibid., p. 307.
134. Madajczyk, *Przylaczenie Slaska Opolskiego do Polski*, p. 220; Nowak, *Cien Lambinowic*, p. 73.
135. Helga Hirsch, *Die Rache der Opfer: Deutsche in polnischen Lagern 1944–1950* (Berlin: Rowohlt, 1998), p. 93.
136. Nitschke, *Wysiedlenie ludnosci niemieckiej*, p. 307.
137. Hirsch, *Die Rache der Opfer*, pp. 35–36, 39.
138. Zygmunt Wozniczka, "Oboz pracy w Swietochlowicach," *Dzieje Najnowsze, rocznik*, 31, no. 4 (1999): 29.
139. Madajczyk, *Przylacenie Slaska Opolskiego do Polski*, p. 220.
140. Nowak, *Cien Lambinowic*, p. 111.
141. Wozniczka, "Oboz pracy w Swietochlowicach," p. 18.
142. Senft, "Weryfikacja Narodowa i repolonizacja na Slasku w latach 1945–1949," pp. 452–453. Hirsch, *Die Rache der Opfer*, p. 200.

143. Nowak, *Cien Lambinowic,* p. 111.
144. Some Germans claim that up to 500 people were killed in the incident. Ibid.
145. Ibid., p. 73.
146. Borodziej, Hajnicz, "Der Komplex der Vertreibung," p. 34.
147. Nowak, *Cien Lambinowic,* p. 106.
148. See Hirsch, *Die Rache der Opfer,* pp. 187–191.
149. Ibid., p. 182; Von Thadden, "Die Gebiete östlich der Oder-Neisse," p. 118; Senft, "Weryfikacja narodowa i repolonizacja na slasku," p. 445.
150. See Naimark, *The Russians in Germany,* pp. 71–74.
151. See Chiodo, *Sterben und Vertreibung der Deutschen,* pp. 239–244.
152. Ministerial Circular of August 9, 1947, p. 46. Ministerial Circular of June 5, 1947, p. 387, in *Die Vertreibung der deutschen Bevölkerung aus den Gebieten östlich der Oder-Neisse: Polnische Gesetze und Verordnungen 1944–1955,* vol. 3.
153. Kenney, *Rebuilding Poland,* p. 153.
154. "Przemowienia Prezesa Polskiego Stronnictwa Ludowego Stanislawa MIKOLAJCZYKA wygloszone na posiedzeniu Rady Naczelnej," October 6, 1946, HIA, Mikolajczyk, box 76, p. 6.
155. See Krystyna Kersten, *Miedzy wyzwoleniem a zniewoleniem: Polska 1944–1956* (London: Aneks, 1993), pp. 37–42, and Jan Tomasz Gross, *Upiorna Dekada* (Krakow: Universitas, 1998), pp. 93–113.
156. See Ther, *Deutsche und polnische Vertriebene,* p. 45 n. 51.
157. Ther, "A Century of Forced Migration," pp. 35–42; Marek Jasiak, "Ukrainian Resistance in Poland and the Origins of Akcja Specjalna Wisla," in Ther, ed., *Expulsion, Settlement, Integration, Transformation,* pp. 20–22. Timothy Snyder thinks that one to two thousand Ukrainians were killed in the action: see his "'To Resolve the Ukrainian Problem Once and For All': The Ethnic Cleansing of Ukrainians in Poland, 1943–1947," *Journal of Cold War Studies,* 1, no. 2 (Spring 1999): 111–115.
158. HIA, Mikolajczyk, box 40, Protocol of Meeting of PPS and PPR, September 28, 1945, p. 6.
159. HIA, Mikolajczyk, box 38, no. 46. Speech in Opole, April 8, 1946.
160. Archiwum Akt Nowych (AAN), PPS Wydzial Ziem Odzyskanych, collection, 235/XXIII-9, ll. 25–27a.
161. Madajczyk, *Przylaczenie Slaska Opolskiego do Polski,* p. 111.
162. Linek, *"Odniemczenie" wojewodztwa slaskiego w latach 1945–1950* (Opole: Wydawnictwo Instytut Slaski), p. 42.
163. Berlinska, "Narodowo-etniczne stosunki," p. 36.
164. Linek, *"Odniemczenie" wojewodztwa slaskiego,* p. 11.
165. From Z. Zaba, "Wroclaw nasz," in *"Wach auf, mein Herz, und denke" . . . "Przebudz sie, serce moje, i pomysl" . . . ,* p. 433.
166. Linek, *"Odniemczenie" wojewodztwa Slaskiego,* p. 50.
167. Senft, "Weryfikacja Narodowa i repolonizacja na slasku w latach 1945–1949," in *"Wach auf, mein Herz, und Denke" . . . "Przebudz sie, serce moje, i pomysl" . . . ,* p. 449.

168. Linek, *"Odniemczanie" wojewodztwa slaskiego*, p. 23 n. 7.

169. Ibid., p. 14.

170. Chiodo, *Sterben und Vertreibung der Deutschen*, pp. 241–242.

171. Danuta Berlinska, "Narodowo-etniczne stosunki miedzygrupowe na Slasku Opolskim: ciaglosc i zmiana," in Krzysztof Fryszlacki, ed., *Polacy, Slazacy, Niemcy: Studia nad stosunkami spoleczno-kulturowymi na Slasku Opolskim* (Krakow: Universitas, 1998), p. 43.

172. Berlinska, "Narodnowo-etniczne stosunki," p. 43.

173. Gerhard Koselleck, "Deutsche und Polen in Silesia," in Valeria Heuberger, Arnold Suppan, and Elisabeth Vyslonzil, eds., *Das Bild vom Anderen* (Frankfurt an Main: Peter Lang, 1998), pp. 80–81.

174. AAN, PPS, Wydzial Ziem Odzyskanych, Zawadzki memorandum of October 24, 1945, 235/XXIII-11, p. 5.

175. Linek, *"Odniemczanie" wojewodztwa slaskiego*, pp. 72–73.

176. For the first time, Polish schoolbooks are talking frankly about the expulsion of the Germans. Jacek Kowalski, Miroslaw Sielatycki, and Wieslawa E. Kozlowska, *Polacy i Niemcy w nowej Europie: Partnerzy* (Warsaw: Wydawnictwa CODN, 1998).

5. The Wars of Yugoslav Succession

1. Ivo Banac, "The Demise of Yugoslavia," draft ms., April 2000, p. 4.

2. Cited in *Newsweek*, February 19, 1996, p. 30.

3. For a review of the literature and issues, see Gale Stokes, John Lampe, and Dennison Rusinow with Julie Mostov, "Instant History: Understanding the Wars of Yugoslav Succession," *Slavic Review*, 55, no. 1 (Spring 1996): 136–160.

4. Ivo Banac, "Nationalism in Southeastern Europe," in Charles A. Kupchan, ed., *Nationalism and Nationalities in the New Europe* (Ithaca: Cornell University Press, 1995), pp. 109–111.

5. This is a take-off from Miroslav Hroch's schema of the stages of national development in Eastern Europe. Miroslav Hroch, *Die Vorkämpfer der nationalen Bewegungen bei den kleinen Völkern Europas* (Prague: Historia Monographa XXIV, 1968). For an English abridged selection, see Miroslav Hroch, "From National Movement to the Fully-Formed Nation: The National-Building Process in Europe," in Eley and Suny, eds., *Becoming National*, pp. 60–77.

6. *Kossovo: Heroic Song of the Serbs*, tr. Helen Rootham (Boston: Houghton Mifflin, 1920), p. 75.

7. Wayne S. Vucinich and Thomas A. Emmert, eds., *Kosovo: The Legacy of a Medieval Battle* (Minneapolis: University of Minnesota Press, 1991).

8. The powerful effects of the mythology of Kosovo is present even in contemporary scholarly writing. See, for example, Branimir Anzulovic, *Heavenly Serbia: From Myth to Genocide* (New York: New York University Press, 1999), pp. 11–44.

9. For Njegos's extraordinary life, see Milovan Djilas, *Njegos: Poet, Prince, Bishop,* tr. Michael B. Petrovich (New York: Harcourt, Brace & World, 1966).

10. *The Mountain Wreath of P. P. Nyegosh, Prince-Bishop of Montenegro, 1390–1851,* tr. James W. Wiles (London, 1930), p. 209. This fragment is also cited in Tim Judah, *The Serbs: History, Myth and the Destruction of Yugoslavia* (New Haven: Yale University Press, 1997), p. 77.

11. Ivo J. Lederer, "Nationalism and the Yugoslavs," in Peter F. Sugar and Ivo John Lederer, *Nationalism in Eastern Europe* (Seattle: University of Washington Press, 1994), p. 405.

12. See Mirjana Gross, "Social Structures and National Movements among the Yugoslav Peoples on the Eve of the First World War," *Slavic Review,* 36, no. 4 (December 1977): 643. See also David Mackenzie, "Serbia as Piedmont and the Yugoslav Idea," *East European Quarterly,* 28, no. 2 (June 1994): 176; and "Serbian Nationalist and Military Organizations and the Piedmont Idea," *East European Quarterly,* 16, no. 3 (September 1982): 323. On Pasic, see Djordje Dj. Stankovic, *Nikola Pasic i jugoslovensko pitanje,* vol. 2 (Belgrade: Izdavacko-graficki zavod, 1985), pp. 274–275.

13. Nicholas J. Miller, *Between Nation and State: Serbian Politics in Croatia Before the First World War* (Pittsburgh: University of Pittsburgh Press, 1997), p. 179.

14. Wolf Dietrich Behschnitt, *Nationalismus bei Serben und Kroaten 1830–1914: Analyse und Typologie der nationalen Ideologie* (Munich: Oldenbourg Verlag, 1980), p. 233.

15. Cited in Andrew Baruch Wachtel, *Making a Nation, Breaking a Nation: Literature and Cultural Politics in Yugoslavia* (Stanford: Stanford University Press, 1998), p. 27. See also John Lampe, *Yugoslavia as History: Twice There Was a Country* (Cambridge: Cambridge University Press, 1996), pp. 43–46.

16. Ivo Banac, *The National Question in Yugoslavia: Origins, History, Politics* (Ithaca: Cornell University Press, 1984).

17. Gale Stokes, *Nationalism in the Balkans: An Annotated Bibliography* (New York: Garland Publishing, Inc., 1984), p. xv.

18. See the chapter, "Creating a Synthetic Yugoslav Culture," in Wachtel, *Making a Nation, Breaking a Nation,* pp. 67–127.

19. Malcolm claims—with little evidence—that 250,000 people were killed by Tito's partisans in the years 1945–46. Noel Malcolm, *Bosnia: A Short History* (New York: New York University Press, 1994), p. 193.

20. Ivo Banac, "The Fearful Asymmetry of War: The Causes and Consequences of Yugoslavia's Demise," *Daedalus,* no. 121 (Spring 1992): 148.

21. Wachtel, *Making a Nation, Breaking a Nation,* pp. 165–172.

22. For the role of "self-management" in this process, see Jill A. Irvine, *The Croat Question: Partisan Politics in the Formation of the Yugoslav State* (Boulder: Westview Press, 1984), pp. 254–257.

23. See Noel Malcolm, *Bosnia: A Short History*, pp. 200–201, and his *Kosovo: A Short History* (New York: New York University Press, 1998), pp. 327–328.

24. Wachtel, *Making a Nation, Breaking a Nation*, p. 226.

25. Irvine, *The Croat Question*, p. 290.

26. Susan Woodward, *Balkan Tragedy: Chaos and Dissolution after the Cold War* (Washington DC: The Brookings Institute, 1995), p. 73.

27. Malcolm, *Kosovo: A Short History*, pp. 334–346.

28. Woodward, *Balkan Tragedy*, pp. 74–75.

29. Marcus Tanner, *Croatia: A Nation Forged in War* (New Haven: Yale University Press, 1997), pp. 203–206.

30. Malcolm, *Bosnia: A Short History*, p. 208.

31. Ibid., p. 208.

32. Warren Zimmermann, "The Last Ambassador: A Memoir of the Collapse of Yugoslavia," *Foreign Affairs*, 74, no. 2 (March–April 1995): 3.

33. Olivera Milosavljevic, "Zloupotreba autoriteta nauke," in Nebojsa Popov, ed., *Srpska strana rata* (Belgrade: Republika, 1996), pp. 306–307. The article is available in English translation as "The Abuse of the Authority in Science," in Nebojsa Popov, ed., *The Road to War in Serbia: Trauma and Catharsis* (Budapest: Central European University Press, 2000), pp. 274–302.

34. Laura Secor, "Testaments Betrayed: Yugoslavian Intellectuals and the Road to War," *Lingua Franca*, September 1999, pp. 26–42.

35. Kosta Mihailovic and Vasilije Krestic, *Memorandum of the Serbian Academy of Sciences and Arts: Answers to Criticisms* (Belgrade: Serbian Academy of Sciences, 1995), p. 118.

36. *Memorandum of the Serbian Academy of Sciences*, pp. 119, 127.

37. Ibid., p. 138.

38. Ibid., p. 139.

39. Laura Silber and Alan Little, *Yugoslavia: Death of a Nation* (New York: TV Books, 1995), p. 42. Dusko Doder and Louise Branson, *Milosevic: Portrait of a Tyrant* (New York: The Free Press, 1999), pp. 16–17.

40. Silber and Little, *Yugoslavia: Death of a Nation*, p. 37.

41. Ibid., p. 38.

42. Cited in Veljko Vujacic, "Serbian Nationalism, Slobodan Milosevic and the Origins of the Yugoslav War," *Harriman Review*, 8, no. 4 (December 1995), p. 29.

43. Malcolm, *Kosovo: A Short History*, p. 344.

44. Eric D. Gordy, *The Culture of Power in Serbia: Nationalism and the Destruction of Alternatives* (University Park: Pennsylvania University Press, 1999), pp. 23–30.

45. Judah, *The Serbs*, p. 164.

46. "Program Srpske Radikalne Stranke," *Velika Srbja*, 7 (July 1997): 401, special ed., back cover.

47. "Srpska Narodna Obnova," proposed program, p. 50.

48. Xavier Bougarel, "Yugoslav Wars: The 'Revenge of the Countryside,'" *East European Quarterly,* 32, no. 2 (June 1999): 165. Sabrina Ramet, "Nationalism and the 'Idiocy' of the Countryside: The Case of Serbia," *Ethnic and Racial Studies,* 19, no. 1 (January 1996): 71–77.

49. Stokes, *The Walls Came Tumbling Down,* p. 223.

50. Sabrina Petra Ramet, *Balkan Babel: The Disintegration of Yugoslavia from the Death of Tito to the War for Kosovo,* 3rd ed. (Boulder: Westview Press, 1999), p. 51; Mihailo Crnobrnja, *The Yugoslav Drama* (Montreal: McGill-Queens University Press, 1994), pp. 151–152.

51. Silber and Little, *Yugoslavia: Death of a Nation,* pp. 91–92.

52. Kosta Cavoski, *Slobodan protiv slobode* (Belgrade: Dosije, 1991), p. 17.

53. Vujacic, "Serbian Nationalism," pp. 28–30. Ivo Banac, "Historiography of the Countries of Eastern Europe: Yugoslavia," *American Historical Review,* 97, no. 4 (October 1992): 1088.

54. Ramet, "Nationalism and the 'Idiocy' of the Countryside," p. 77.

55. Stokes, Lampe, and Rusinow, "Instant History," p. 145.

56. Silber and Little, *Yugoslavia: Death of a Nation,* p. 171.

57. Zoran Kalicanin, ed., *Republika Srpska Krajina* (Topusko: Srpsko kulturno drustvo "Sava Mrkalj"; Belgrade: Radnicka Stampa, 1996), p. 9.

58. Popov, *The Road to War in Serbia,* p. 88.

59. Tanner, *Croatia: A Nation Forged in War,* p. 267.

60. *New York Times,* March 21, 1996.

61. *Tribunal Update,* February 2–6, 1998.

62. "Memorandum Vlade Jugoslavije o zlocinima genocida u Hrvatskoj i skrnjavanju Spomen-producja Jasenovac, 31.januar 1992," in Radovan Samardzic, ed., *Ratni zlocini i zlocini genocida, 1991–1992* (Belgrade: SANU, 1993), p. 117.

63. Lampe, *Yugoslavia as History,* p. 207. Anzulovic, *Heavenly Serbia,* pp. 103–104.

64. Robert M. Hayden, "Recounting the Dead: The Rediscovery and Redefinition of Wartime Massacres in Late- and Post-Communist Yugoslavia," in Rubie S. Watson, ed., *Memory, History, and Opposition under State Socialism* (Santa Fe: School of American Research Press, 1994), p. 171.

65. Bette Denich, "Dismembering Yugoslavia: Nationalist Ideologies and the Symbolic Revival of Genocide," *American Ethnologist,* 21, no. 2 (1994): 369, 383.

66. Mart Boax, "War in Bosnia," *Ethnologia Europea,* no. 26 (1996): 18. See also his "Civilization and Decivilization in Bosnia: A Case Study from a Mountain Community in Herzegovina," *Ethnologia Europea,* no. 27 (1997): 169.

67. Sabrina P. Ramet, "Liberalism, Morality, and the Social Order: The Case of Croatia's Corrupt Populist Pluralism," *Ohio Northern University Law Review,* 25, no. 3 (1999): 352.

68. Silber and Little, *Yugoslavia: Death of a Nation,* p. 228.
69. United Nations General Assembly, "Report of the Secretary-General pursuant to General Assembly resolution 53/35," in *The Fall of Srebrenica,* November 15, 1999, p. 9.
70. *New York Times,* February 7, 1993.
71. *Tribunal Update,* April 20–25, 1998.
72. Louis Sell, "Slobodan Milosevic: A Political Biography," *Problems of Post-Communism,* 46, no. 6 (November–December 1999): 25.
73. Roy Gutman, *A Witness to Genocide* (New York: Macmillan, 1993), pp. 44–52.
74. *Tribunal Update,* April 6–11, 1998.
75. *Tribunal Update,* 129, July 7–13, 1999.
76. Sell, "Slobodan Milosevic," p. 24; Malcolm, *Kosovo: A Short History,* p. 147; *The Guardian* (London), February 3, 1997.
77. Ivan Colovic, "Football, Hooligans and War," in Popov, ed., *The Road to War in Serbia,* p. 387.
78. *Banja Luka—Ethnic Cleansing Paradigm, or Counterpoint to a Radical Future,* CSCE Briefing (Washington, DC, June 11, 1996), p. 51 n. 16.
79. Sell, "Slobodan Milosevic," p. 25.
80. *Banja Luka: Ethnic Cleansing Paradigm,* p. 53.
81. Ibid., pp. 76, 81.
82. Ibid., p. 56.
83. Ibid., p. 63.
84. David Owen, *Balkan Odyssey* (New York: Harcourt, Brace, & Co., 1995), p. 58.
85. See David Rohde, *Endgame: The Betrayal and Fall of Srebrenica, Europe's Worst Massacre since World War II* (New York: Farrar, Straus and Giroux, 1997); Chuck Sudetic, *Blood and Vengeance: One Family's Story of the War in Bosnia* (New York: W. W. Norton, 1998), pp. 253–325; Jan Willem Honig and Norbert Roth, *Srebrenica: Record of a War Crime* (New York: Penguin, 1996); U.N. General Assembly, *The Fall of Srebrenica,* pp. 59–107.
86. See Rohde, *Endgame,* pp. 274–280.
87. U.N. General Assembly, *The Fall of Srebrenica,* p. 105.
88. Honig and Roth, *Srebrenica,* p. 62; U.N. General Assembly, *The Fall of Srebrenica,* p. 82.
89. Rohde, *Endgame,* p. 169.
90. Ibid., p. 313.
91. Sudetic, *Blood and Vengeance,* p. 317; Honig and Roth, *Srebrenica,* p. 65.
92. U.N. General Assembly, *The Fall of Srebrenica,* p. 111.
93. Ibid., p. 6.
94. Ibid., p. 26.
95. Sreten Vujovic, "An Uneasy View of the City," in Popov, ed., *The Road to War in Serbia,* p. 145 n. 3.
96. *Banja Luka: Ethnic Cleansing Paradigm,* pp. 10, 44.

97. Ibid., p. 11.

98. Ibid., p. 13.

99. *Tribunal Update*, 143, September 13–18, 1999.

100. Ibid., September 6–12, 1999.

101. *New York Times*, December 15, 1999.

102. Helsinki Watch, *War Crimes in Bosnia-Hercegovina*, vol. 2 (New York: Human Rights Watch, 1993), p. 21.

103. *Tribunal Update*, 133, July 5–11, 1999.

104. Ibid., 66, March 2–7, 1998.

105. Mladen Vuksanovic, *Pale—Im Herzen der Finsternis, Tagebuch*, tr. Detlef Olef (Vienna: Folio, 1997), p. 25.

106. Catherine A. MacKinnon, "Turning Rape into Pornography: Turning Rape into Genocide," in Alexandra Stiglmayer, ed., *Mass Rape: The War against Women in Bosnia-Herzegovina*, tr. Marion Faber (Lincoln: University of Nebraska Press, 1992), pp. 73–81.

107. See Klaus Theweleit, *Male Fantasies*, 2 vols., tr. Stephen Conway (Minneapolis: University of Minnesota Press, 1987).

108. Woodward, *Balkan Tragedy*, p. 245.

109. Jasmina Mertus, Jasmina Tesandovic, et al., eds., *The Suitcase: Refugee Voices from Bosnia and Croatia* (Berkeley: University of California Press, 1997), pp. 38, 43.

110. Ibid., p. 13.

111. Cited in Norman Cigar, *Genocide in Bosnia: The Policy of Ethnic Cleansing* (College Station: Texas A&M University Press, 1995), p. 92.

112. *Newsweek*, April 22, 1996, p. 50.

113. Beverly Allen, *Rape Warfare: The Hidden Genocide in Bosnia-Herzegovina and Croatia* (Minneapolis: University of Minnesota Press, 1996), p. 71. See Stiglmayer, ed., *Mass Rape*.

114. Francis A. Boyle, *The Bosnian People Charge Genocide: Proceedings at the International Court of Justic Concerning Bosnia v. Serbia on the Prevention and Punishment of the Crime of Genocide* (Amherst, MA: Aletheia Press, 1996), p. 30.

115. Sabrina Ramet, *Balkan Babel: The Disintegration of Yugoslavia from the Death of Tito to Ethnic War*, 2nd ed. (Boulder: Westview, 1996), pp. 258–259, 284.

116. Stiglmayer, ed., *Mass Rape*, p. 160.

117. Adil Zulfikarpasic, Vlado Gotovac, Miko Tripalo, and Ivo Banac, *Okovana Bosna: Razgovor* (Zurich: Bosnjacki Institut, 1995), p. 53 (Banac). See also Banac, "Nationalism in Southeastern Europe," *Nationalism and Nationalities*, pp. 119–120.

118. "The Demise of Yugoslavia," p. 27.

119. Doder and Branson, *Milosevic*, p. 88.

120. See the testimony of Stipe Mesic, *Tribunal Update*, 68, March 16–21, 1998. Bosnian Serb leader Radovan Karadzic and Bosnian Croat leader Mate Boban met in Graz in March 1992, also, one assumes, to talk about the partition of Bosnia.

121. Zimmermann, "The Last Ambassador," p. 15.
122. Gordana Uzelak, "Franjo Tudjman's Nationalist Ideology," *East European Quarterly*, 31, no. 4 (January 1998): 464.
123. See Tudjman's book, *The National Question in Contemporary Europe*, cited in Banac, "The Demise of Yugoslavia," p. 25.
124. *New York Times:* March 3, 1993; August 8, 1993.
125. *Tribunal Update*, 136, July 26–31, 1999.
126. Ibid., 68, March 16–21, 1998.
127. Jasminka Udovicki and James Ridgeway, eds., *Burn This House: The Making and Unmaking of Yugoslavia* (Durham: Duke University Press, 1997), p. 210 n. 59.
128. David Owen rejects accusations that the Vance-Owen plan contributed to or legitimated ethnic cleansing. Owen, *Balkan Odyssey*, pp. 62, 116.
129. Tanner, *Croatia*, pp. 288–289. See also the testimony of Robert Donia in *Tribunal Update*, 34, June 23–28, 1997.
130. *Tribunal Update*, 146, October 4–9, 1999. See Tanner, *Croatia*, pp. 289–290.
131. The British recovered 96 charred bodies. *Tribunal Update*, 34, June 23–28, 1997.
132. *Tribunal Update*, September 29–October 3, 1997.
133. Ibid., 65, February 13–28, 1998.
134. Ibid., 80, June 8–13, 1998; 57, June 15–20, 1997.
135. *New York Times*, December 15, 1999.
136. Tanner, *Croatia*, p. 290. Veljko Vujacic, "Historical Legacies, Nationalist Mobilization, and Political Outcomes in Russia and Serbia: A Weberian View," *Theory and Society*, 25, no. 28 (1996): 795. *Tribunal Update*, 107, December 20, 1998–January 10, 1999.
137. *New York Times*, March 21, 1999; *Tribunal Update*, 118, March 22–27, 1999.
138. *Tribunal Update*, 76, May 11–16, 1998.
139. See Susan Woodward, *Balkan Tragedy*, pp. 236–237, 242.
140. Wohlstetter, "Creating a Greater Serbia," p. 24.
141. *Tribunal Update*, 129, June 7–13, 1999.
142. Ibid., 105, December 7–12, 1998.
143. Ibid., 48, October 13–17, 1997; 87, July 27–August 1, 1998; 40, August 4–7, 1997.
144. The term "ethnic self-cleansing" is used by Stephen Burg and Paul Shoup to describe the "prudent" choice of Bosnian Muslims to flee potential persecution on hearing rumors of Serbian and Croatian excesses. Burg and Shoup, *The War in Bosnia-Herzegovina*, p. 172.
145. *Okovana Bosna* (Zulfikarpasic), pp. 22, 52–53, 78.
146. See Malcolm, *Kosovo*, pp. 239–313.
147. Stefan Troebst, "The Kosovo War, Round One: 1998," *Europe and the Balkans: Occasional Papers*, no. 15 (Ravenna: Longo Editore, 1998), pp. 5–6.
148. Ramet, "Nationalism and the 'Idiocy' of the Countryside," p. 82.

149. Malcolm, *Kosovo*, p. 325. For a variety of conspiracy theories about the riots, see "The 1981 Student Demonstrations," in Julie A. Mertus, *Kosovo: How Myths and Truths Started a War* (Berkeley: University of California Press, 1999), pp. 17–55.

150. *Spotlight On: Human Rights in Serbia and Montenegro* (Belgrade: Humanitarian Law Center, 1996), pp. 64–65.

151. "Repression and Violence in Kosovo," March 18, 1998, and "Kosovo— The Humanitarian Perspective," June 25, 1998, in *Two Hearings before the Commission On Security and Cooperation in Europe* (Washington, DC: U.S. Government Printing Office, 1998), p. 64.

152. Malcolm, *Kosovo*, p. 353.

153. Sell, "Milosevic," p. 8. Banac, "The Demise of Yugoslavia," p. 33.

154. Doder and Branson, *Milosevic*, p. 241; Troebst, "The Kosovo War," p. 12.

155. Mertus, *Kosovo*, p. 6.

156. See Christopher Layne and Benjamin Schwarz, "For the Record," *The National Interest* (Fall 1999): 10.

157. Tim Judah, "Inside the KLA," *New York Review of Books*, June 10, 1999, p. 19.

158. Human Rights Watch/Helsinki, "Yugoslavia (Serbia and Montenegro)," 8, no. 18 (December 1996): 36.

159. There were already monitors on the ground in July 1998, as a result of the "Kosovo Diplomatic Observer Mission," which grew to some 400 members before being integrated with the OSCE group. Stefan Troebst, "Chronologie einer gescheiterten Prävention: Vom Konflikt zum Krieg im Kosovo, 1989–1999," *Osteuropa*, 49, no. 8 (1999), p. 786. Layne and Schwarz, "For the Record," p. 14.

160. Troebst, "Chronologie einer gescheiterten Prävention," p. 790. Information from Robert Sorenson, a State Department official, who was in the immediate vicinity at the time.

161. Doder and Branson, *Milosevic*, p. 249.

162. Ibid., pp. 250–251. Troebst, "Chronologie einer gescheiterten Prävention," p. 791.

163. Banac, "The Demise of Yugoslavia," p. 19.

164. Judah, "Inside the KLA," p. 22. Timothy Garton Ash, "Kosovo and Beyond," *New York Review of Books*, June 24, 1999, p. 4. Doder and Branson, *Milosevic*, pp. 247–248, 259.

165. Ash, "Kosovo and Beyond," p. 4.

166. U.S. Department of State, *Erasing History: Ethnic Cleansing in Kosovo* (May 1999), p. 12.

167. Ibid., p. 14.

168. Ibid., pp. 12–13.

169. Troebst, "Chronologie einer gescheiterten Prävention," p. 792.

170. "Early Count Hints at Fewer Kosovo Deaths," *New York Times*, November 11, 1999.

171. Veton Surroi, "Victims of Victims," *New York Review of Books,* October 7, 1999.
172. It is very hard to know exactly how many have died in the wars of Yugoslav succession, 1991–1999, or specifically in the ethnic cleansing. According to George Kenney, journalists tend to exaggerate the numbers of killed: "The Bosnia Calculation," *New York Times Magazine,* April 23, 1995, pp. 42–43.
173. Banac, "The Demise of Yugoslavia," p. 23.

Conclusion

1. *New York Times,* December 10, 1999.

Acknowledgments

The making of this book depended on the encouragement, advice, suggestions, and criticisms of numerous friends and colleagues. Conceptually it was a difficult book to write. It was also a major challenge to come to terms with the scholarly literature in the five different sets of cases I examined. At the end, therefore, I want to thank several friends, whose repeated involvement in this work, including the reading of drafts, was crucial to the completion of the manuscript: Ivo Banac, David Holloway, Katherine Jolluck, Jim Sheehan, Tom Simons, and Ron Suny. In particular, I want to mention the contributions of Amir Weiner, whose arguments over lunch and coffee forced me to sharpen my own and whose suggestions for further reading continue to broaden my perspectives on problems of mass violence in the twentieth century.

I am grateful to Timothy Garton Ash, Dusan Djordjevic, and Robert Sorenson for reading and criticizing my chapter on former Yugoslavia and to Aron Rodrigue for his remarks on the chapter on the Armenians and Greeks. I enjoyed the privilege of being able to read and cite draft articles and pre-publication manuscripts written by a number of scholars working on related problems. For their generosity in this regard I thank Ivo Banac, John Dunlop, Benjamin Frommer, Peter Holquist, Terry Martin, Pavel Polian, Ron Suny, Philippe Ther, Veljko Vujacic, Amir Weiner, Eric Weitz, and Robert Zajonc. I am also grateful to John Connelly, Vahakn N. Dadrian, Hannes Heer, David Rohde, and Stefan Troebst for useful insights and for sending me copies of their work.

The comparative dimensions of the project demanded that I talk about it as much as possible while preparing the book for publication. Here, too, I am grateful to those scholars and institutions here and abroad that invited me to speak about this work and provided opportunities for criticism and interchange:

Harley Balzer (Georgetown University), Paul Bushkovitch (Yale University), Arch Getty (University of California, Riverside), Manfred Hildermeier (Göttingen), Konrad Jarausch (University of North Carolina), Tony Judt (New York University), Christoph Klessmann (Institute of Contemporary History, Potsdam), Jürgen Kocka (Institute of Comparative European History, Free University of Berlin), Melvyn Leffler (University of Virginia), Semyon Lyandres (East Carolina University), Terry Martin (Davis Center, Harvard), Edward Mühle (Herder Institute, Marburg), Donald Raleigh (University of North Carolina), Sabrina Ramet (University of Washington), and Gale Stokes (Rice University). At these lectures, talks, and seminars—not to mention several Stanford presentations—I gained a great deal from the comments and criticisms of informed audiences and from the letters and email notes that followed. The East Carolina University lecture was published as "The Lawrence F. Brewster Lecture in History," 16 (1997); the University of Washington lecture in "The Donald M. Treadgold Papers," 19 (October 1998); and the Marburg lecture, in *Zeitschrift für Ostmitteleuropa-Forschung*, 48, no. 3 (1999). I also want to acknowledge Aida Donald's enthusiasm for the project at Harvard University Press. I'm not sure I would have finished the book without her unflagging encouragement.

There are also scores of Stanford students, most of them freshmen at the time, who exchanged ideas with me in a series of undergraduate seminars on ethnic cleansing. Their passion for the subject was a genuine fount of inspiration. I am grateful to present and former Stanford graduate students, among them Bradley Abrams, Holly Case, Dusan Djordjevich, Malgorzata Fidelis, Karin Hall, Mikolaj Kunicki, Jennifer Rice, and Marci Shore, for help at various stages of my research and writing. Most recently, Andrej Milevojevic and Benjamin Alexander-Bloch served as able research assistants.

The overseas research for this project was funded in part by IREX, the office of the Stanford Vice Provost for Research, and Stanford's Center for Russian and East European Studies. I spent a glorious sabbatical year at the Center for Advanced Study in the Behavioral Sciences in 1998–99, funded in part by the Andrew W. Mellon Foundation. There were far too many colleagues in my CASBS "class" who offered help, criticism, and suggestions to thank them all here by name. So I will leave it at expressing my deep gratitude to Neil Smelser, Director, and Robert Scott, Associate Director, both of whom also showed great interest in my research. The Hoover Institution provided a home for this work during the year 1999–2000; for that privilege, I am beholden to the director, John Raisian.

The Stanford and Hoover libraries and archives were particularly important resources for carrying out a project of this breadth. Among the many librarians and archivists who helped me along the way, I would like to acknowledge the special contributions of Zbigniew Stanczyk of the Hoover Archives and Helen Solanum of the Hoover Library. I also received important advice from the archivists at the Russian party archives (RTsKhIDNI, now RGASPI) and state archives (GARF) in Moscow. Thanks in particular to Dina Nikolaevna Nokhotovich of GARF, who guided me through the newly declassified archives on the 1944 deportations of Chechens-Ingush and Crimean Tatars.

In the end, of course, I alone am responsible for the scholarship and arguments in this book. This is especially important to emphasize, given the inherently controversial nature of the project.

I confess that immersion in the materials of ethnic cleansing and genocide in our era sometimes led me into moods of overwhelming sadness. Through it all, my daughters, Anna and Sarah, were a source of life-affirming joy, stability, and perspective. I dedicate this work to them and to all of our children: may they never encounter the vengefulness of history described in this book.

Norman M. Naimark
Stanford, California

Index